That We May All (Finally!) Be One

That We May All *(Finally!)* Be One

Covenant, Hospitality, and
the Expanding Identity of
the United Church of Christ

Mary Susan Gast

THE PILGRIM PRESS
CLEVELAND

The Pilgrim Press, 700 Prospect Avenue, Cleveland, Ohio 44115
thepilgrimpress.com
© 2016 by Mary Susan Gast

Scripture quotations, unless otherwise noted, are from the New Revised Standard Version of the Bible, © 1989 by the Division of Christian Education of the National Council of Churches of Christ in the United States of America, and are used by permission. Changes have been made for inclusivity.

Printed in the United States of America on acid-free paper

19   18   17   16   15   5   4   3   2   1

ISBN: 978-0-8298-2031-7

So Jesus came and proclaimed peace

to you who were far off

and peace to those who were near;

for through him both of us have access

in one Spirit to the Author of Life.

So then you are no longer strangers and

aliens, but you are citizens with the saints

and also members of the household of God,

(Ephesians 2:17–19)

Those who were "them" yesterday

are "us" today,

and "we" are forever changed.

CONTENTS

PART IV · *Ministry*

PART V · *Identity and Unity*

INTRODUCTION

Covenant, Hospitality, and the Expanding Identity of the United Church of Christ

COVENANT AND HOSPITALITY ARE THEMES THAT KEEP TURNING UP IN THE life of the United Church of Christ. Each, it seems, is gift, joy, touchstone, and challenge for us.

Because we came into being as a uniting church, hospitality is in our genetic makeup, and we have cultivated our bent for it. Covenant remains more problematic for us and is frequently outdone by autonomy in tests of strength and inclination. Only when I had settled in to produce this volume on life in the United Church of Christ did I realize that hospitality and covenant may well be calling us back to our identity as a united and uniting church. Hospitality and covenant may also carry us forward to new expressions and applications of unity. One thing is certain. For us, unity will never be unanimity. Instead, we seek a unity that holds all of our independent and disparate voices in a creative tension, "a unity that defies our common understanding of the word."[1]

The United Church of Christ is a composite denomination. That is, we are a conceptual whole made up of complicated and related parts. We are a composite of the descendants of native peoples, immigrants, and those forced to come ashore in the Americas. We are a composition, formed and forming, by westward voyagers as well as those who have traveled east, north, and south to take up with this movement of the Spirit.

The United Church of Christ is not hierarchical. There are no imposed doctrines. Congregations do not worship, undertake mission, or organize themselves according to uniform standards. Local Churches are autonomous—not controlled by regional or national church traditions or governance patterns.

Actually, all four settings of the UCC are autonomous—Local Churches, Associations and Conferences (regional bodies), and General Synod (national). Yet our constitution calls upon each setting of the church to honor and respect the work and ministry of the others in a covenantal relationship.

With our diverse cultures and histories, with our organizational autonomy and individual freedom of belief, our UCC identity is complex. Our unity is not always apparent. Who are we as the United Church of Christ? Sometimes the pronoun "we" seems too puny to handle us. The varied voices of the UCC can put a strain on the power of the first person plural pronoun to adequately represent (all of) "us." Who is "we" in the UCC?

Hospitality is all about expanding the definition of "we" to embrace strangers, enemies, those "we" have not looked for, those "we" have not wanted around, those who are alien and "other," those who are "them" *vis a vis* "us." This is of particular importance to us as a composite denomination where we cannot realistically expect to find total accord with one another in belief or in practice. The ethic of hospitality pushes us all and always to reform, restate, and celebrate the dimensions of "we," and to be gracious and compassionate to one another in our common pursuit of the radical and redemptive call to follow Jesus.

For a decade and a half I served as Conference Minister for Northern California and Nevada. This setting of our church is marked by cultural and theological diversity that verges on the flamboyant. The gifts and backgrounds of new congregations and new members continue to amp up the diversity. It was there that I learned, deep down and by heart, the truth of the declaration so often voiced at Conference gatherings, "Those who were 'them' yesterday are 'us' today, and 'we' are forever changed."

It is revealing to take note of how we use "we," "us," "they," and "them" to talk about our church. When do we speak of the UCC as "we"? When does the UCC become "they"? "them, over there"? When does a gap between "we" and "they" call for a diagnostic review of our covenantal relationship?

UCC scholar of Hebrew scripture Walter Brueggemann describes covenantal relationship as "a way of being committed to each other as God is committed to us, a way of being defined by, accountable to, and responsible for each other."[2] In covenant we are "pledged to solidarity across ideological lines and prepared to live in sustained engagement with one another in ways that impinge on and eventually transform all parties to the transaction."[3]

A newspaper reporter once contacted me for an article about City of Refuge UCC. Early in the interview, the reporter asked, "Isn't their worship style hard for you in the UCC to handle?" To this I could only respond, "City of Refuge is a United Church of Christ congregation whose style of worship is Pentecostal. That means that the United Church of Christ's worship style is Pentecostal—*and* high church, and eclectic, and New England Congregational, and Afro-Christian, and Samoan Congregational, and German Reformed, and . . . . Would you like to rephrase your question?"

When City of Refuge joined the United Church of Christ, when Kalavaria Congregational Christian joined, when Community Congregational joined, when any church joins, the "we" we had been is changed. Not homogenized. Not standardized. Not reduced to lowest terms. Those who were "them" yesterday are "us" today, and "we" are forever changed. All parties are eventually transformed.

Transformation is not a wimpy thing. That Latin prefix "trans" is freighted with a mass of meaning: across, on the other side, beyond. Not just predictable developmental changes but a clearer, deeper, truer rendering of that which we are created to be.

There is more to transformation than "self-improvement and spiritual ecstasies."[4] In transformation we are sent from the familiar to face the appallingly, and the appealingly, different. Transformation of lives, of churches, of communities, demands the courage to traverse vast and intimidating terrain, to skate across the predictable and wind up at "beyond" for the sake of becoming who we are called to be.

Those who were "them" yesterday are "us" today, and "we" are forever changed. We are transformed in our understanding of ourselves, transformed as a community. Forever changed. Forever open to more change. Not haphazardly, but in response to the ancient call to relationship in covenant that changes everything: "I will take you as my people, and I will be your God" (Exod. 6:7). Not swept along in a bandwagon mentality, but imbued with the faithful uncertainty and constant trust of Pastor John Robinson, "There is yet more truth and light to break forth from God's Holy Word."[5]

In the next chapters we will follow the roots and gauge the realities of our UCC engagement with covenant and hospitality. We will talk about our life together as united yet autonomous. We will talk story. We will talk "polity."

We can define polity simply as a group's governance structure, how we are constituted as an organized body. We can also take a long view of polity and look into the sense of community among the people who make up any more-or-less organized body, among the people who gather around the table and find the communion of wholeness and healing.

Many years ago, at a gathering of the network of UCC teachers of history and polity, UCC historian Barbara Brown Zikmund remarked that it is impossible to learn UCC polity in isolation. "There must always be conversation," she said. And most likely—although she was too circumspect to mention it—there will be questions upon questions and a certain level of contentiousness. This book is less theory of polity than it is description, based on lots of experience and conversations. It is intended to prompt conversations that engage us all with the various settings of the United Church of Christ, exchanges of ideas and experience with our companions on the journey, and exploration of sources beyond this text. Please stop along the way to talk with others. Our individual stories are the stories of our church. Our shared stories build up the church. This book will, I hope, move us in the UCC to claim the church, in ever deepening ways, even as the church claims us. And I hope that the stories, questions, and histories recorded here will generate insight for the faith journeys of readers who are not part of the United Church of Christ.

USING THIS BOOK

It perhaps goes without saying that you will feel free to contribute your thoughts, narratives, and examples; to interrupt, rearrange, or skip over any of the materials presented; and to raise or research questions at any point.

We will refer to the UCC Constitution and Bylaws as an organizational map. Unless otherwise designated, we'll use the UCC Constitution and Bylaws of 2015. The themes of hospitality and covenant will recur throughout the book. The first part (chapters 1–3) sets the context, with our founding vision of unity and freedom. The three middle parts (chapters 4–17) deal with the arrangements of structure and accountability within our church: Local Churches, the Wider Church, and Ministry. The last part (chapters 18–21) brings us back to consideration of transformation, identity, and unity with an eye toward our future.

You'll find questions for reflection, comment, and conversation—either face-to-face or electronic—throughout the book.

PART I

Our Church's Founding Vision of Unity and Freedom

~

Part I begins with our motto,
"That they may all be one," and
moves into the founding vision
of our church, which assumes an
array of beliefs, interpretations,
and sources of revelation, and is
not distressed at the prospect.
We will look at the distinctions
between unity and unanimity, the
prospects for a unity of multiple
voices, and the risk and fluidity
of life in covenant.

I

THAT THEY MAY ALL BE ONE

WE AREN'T THE ONLY ONES WHO USE THIS MOTTO. THE CHURCH OF South India and the United Church of Canada employ it, along with the Franciscan Friars of the Atonement, the World Student Christian Federation, the YMCA, and six schools and universities in England, Germany, Ghana, India, and Kenya. All of those groups, at their inceptions, chose these words from the Gospel of John as a fitting encapsulation of their ideals or intentions, "That they may all be one."[1]

The churches and schools may have selected this motto because they were formed by mergers that were significant either because of the natures of the bodies who merged or because of the anticipated results of the mergers. With the YMCA, there was an air of disregarding differences and social barriers for the sake of a great cause. The Friars of the Atonement and the World Student Christian Federation were inspired by the ecumenical movement of the nineteenth and twentieth centuries, as were, of course, the Church of South India, the United Church of Canada, and our United Church of Christ.

For the most part we get it that our motto characterizes us as "a united and uniting church." Some of us lament that we have not united with any other denominations and thus have not lived up to one of the guiding principles behind our motto.[2] Others regard our motto as a souvenir from a bygone era's enthusiasm for institutional mergers in the quest for Christian unity, producing nostalgia but irrelevant to current religious affairs. Many hear in our motto a call to carry on the work of making visible the unity for which Jesus prayed. There are those of us who question whether we will ever be united as a church, and those who find talk of unity vaguely threatening to our autonomy and freedom of conscience.

In her sermon at the installation of Conference Minister Felix Villanueva, UCC pastor Mary Sue Brookshire wondered whether

> we in the UCC need a new motto. "That they may all be one" might be a stretch; we might settle for "that they may all be nice," or, in the event that proves too lofty, "that they all may be quiet." But I don't think so. I believe we can continue to embrace our motto, because I believe that our still-speaking God is calling us to a unity that defies our common understanding of the word.[3]

That common understanding would be heavy on "unanimity" and "sameness." But those characteristics are not emphasized in the record of our denomination's launch as a united and uniting church.

Our constitution—referred to by UCC leader and covenantal polity commentator Reuben Sheares as the covenant within our covenant[4]—gives us insight into the unity that began taking shape in 1957 between the Evangelical and Reformed Church and the General Council of the Congregational Christian Churches of the United States to form the United Church of Christ. The intent of the union was "to express more fully the oneness in Christ of the churches composing it," to "make more effective" the "common witness" of the uniting churches, and to "serve His kingdom in the world."[5] This is a carefully stated and far-sighted rationale for uniting. It is the historic, in-that-moment statement of the purposes for which two denominations—whose cultures, histories, and organizational structures were fundamentally different from one another—united.

The second paragraph of the constitution brings us into engagement with our forebears' firm assertions on, and open-ended aspirations for, unity. The implications of those assertions and aspirations stay with us. They are not stuck in time or limited to the viewpoint of mid-twentieth-century ecumenism. With three pairings of declarations, the United Church of Christ sets itself up—then and now—for a multitude of voices and realities to take up life within one church. The UCC establishes a context for unity that will not easily abide or support a lazy slide into conformity or complacency. We will, the "Preamble" states and encourages,

> Acknowledge Jesus Christ as our sole head *and*
>> all who share in this confession as kindred in Christ.
> Look to the Word of God in Scripture *and*
>> to the presence and power of the Holy Spirit to prosper
>> our creative and redemptive work in the world.
> Claim as our own the faith of the historic Church *and*
>> affirm the responsibility of the Church in each generation
>> to make this faith its own in reality of worship,
>> in honesty of thought and expression, and in purity of
>> heart before God.

The first pair of declarations set the context of our unity: Jesus Christ is head of the church *and* all who share this confession are kindred in Christ.

Those who were present at the Uniting General Synod were unequivocal in their explanation of how this unlikely merger had happened. "This union has been made possible because the two companies of Christians have held and hold the same basic belief, that Christ and Christ alone is the Head of the Church. . . . To be drawn to [Christ] is to be drawn to one another, and to acknowledge [Christ] as Head is to feel pain in dismemberment one from the other. So the union has come."[6] This is the first of the declarations of belief in the Preamble.

Acknowledging that Jesus Christ is the sole head of the church has wide repercussions for our church life. Susan E. Davies, a UCC professor active in ecumenical dialogues, says this claim undercuts the possibility of any individual or group claiming absolute authority within the life of the church. Moreover, the Preamble clearly sets forth the ultimate accountability of individual church members, as well as the church's constituent parts, to Christ alone rather than to any particular body within the church. . . . The United Church of Christ's founding document puts the question of authority at the heart of the church, at the same time leaving immense freedom for individuals and the constituent bodies of the church.[7]

This understanding that the church belongs to Jesus—not the other way around—is foundational to our grasp of covenant. God calls us into covenant, Christ calls us into the church. The initiative comes from beyond us. We do not set the terms of this enterprise. Not us as individuals, nor as any particular body within the church. "Covenant," as UCC professor of Hebrew scripture Walter Brueggemann reminds us, "is the recognition that all members stand in accountability to a will and purpose beyond our own will and purpose."[8]

The Preamble then goes on to make a second acknowledgement, this time recognizing and accepting as kindred in Christ all who share in the confession that Jesus Christ is the sole head of the church. "This was not always so," according to Douglas Horton, a Congregational leader who played key roles in shaping the UCC in the 1950s.

When our fathers of the Reformation read of "Antichrist" in the Epistles of John . . . the only figure that rose in their mind was that of the Roman pope . . . . And now the United Church of Christ calls the Pope its brother—along with all others who believe that God was in Christ reconciling the world . . . . Granted that there are profound divergences between the ways of the Roman Church and those of the United Church, granted that no method of reconciling those ways has as yet been conceived or is at the moment conceivable—nonetheless, because Roman Catholics, too, lift up Christ as the sole head of the church, the United Church of Christ approaches them not as old enemies but as brethren with whom Christ can make all things new. And so the United Church of Christ looks toward the Eastern Orthodox Church and to all other churches which profess and call themselves Christian.[9]

Hospitality is implicit in this acknowledgement. Strangers, enemies, those "we" have not looked for, those "we" have not wanted around, those whose ways are profoundly divergent from "ours"—none of those differences are irreconcilable. All who confess that Jesus Christ is the sole head of the church are kin.

The second and third pairs of declarations in the Preamble set up the expectation that there will be a multitude of voices and realties within our church:

> We look to the Word of God in the Scriptures *and*
> to the presence and power of the Holy Spirit
> We claim the faith of the historic Church expressed in the
> ancient creeds and reclaimed in the basic insights of the
> Protestant Reformers *and*
> affirm the responsibility of each generation to make this
> faith its own. . . .

This is a vision for a united church that assumes an array of beliefs, interpretations, and sources of revelation, and is not distressed at the prospect. Our founders did not let go of connection to the scriptures, doctrines, and creeds of Christian heritage but foresaw that the interpretation, appropriation, and application of the Word of God would come to us anew in every age, in all of our languages and through all of our histories, cultures, and social contexts. The relationship described between the Word of God in the Scriptures and the here-and-now presence and power of the Holy Spirit is dynamic. The dialogue anticipated between the faith of the historic church and the responsibility of each generation to make this faith its own is creative. The unity hoped for is not unanimity or sameness as expressed through a commonly held creed, doctrine, or rubric for the interpretation of scripture.[10]

However, the uniting bodies did agree that as a new church they would prepare a statement of faith. UCC theologian Roger Shinn was prominent in drafting the Statement of Faith.[11] He recounts that the United Church of Christ wanted the Statement of Faith to be a "joyful act of worship, not a legal document for the definition of orthodoxy."[12] He and Daniel Day Williams, another UCC theologian, write

> "Statement of Faith" suggests a less rigid, less authoritarian document than "creed." . . . In any case the Statement of Faith is not a standard of objective authority in the United Church. Whatever authority it has is the authority of an honest testimony with the persuasiveness of its contents.[13]

A Statement of Faith that is a joyful act of worship rather than a standard of orthodoxy attests to the hospitality shown to one another by those who formulated our united church. Within our church there is great diversity among and within congregations regarding biblical interpretation. There are wildly varying degrees to which we as members claim the historic creeds and insights of the Protestant reformers as our own. We experience the power and presence of the Holy Spirit in many ways. We take diverse paths to make the historic faith our own, as the Preamble states, "in reality of worship, in honesty of thought and expression, and in purity of heart before God." Only with hospitality to one another's differences can we recognize and incorporate into one church body the full range of our beliefs, interpretations, sources of revelation, and ways of making the faith our own. With hospitality to one another we open ourselves to the unifying love of God.

God's love is the great gift that ultimately unites all creation. Our motto, "That they may all be one," is an appeal made in hope and in trust, a prayer lifted in expectation. Which is appropriate, since, before it became anyone's motto, "that they may all be one" was part of Jesus' prayer for his followers. Jesus, as recorded in John 17:21, prayed for those present at their final meal together as well as those yet be born. Jesus pointed to the disciples in the room and in the future and prayed for our care and protection, "that they may all be one." Both grammatically and biblically, it is noteworthy that "we" (the church) are "they" in this passage. The actual "we" is the triune God, the God-in-Community. This great Love at the center of the universe is the communion of Creator, Redeemer, and Sustainer—the source of life and justice, the human embodiment of compassion's redemptive power, and the unsettling peace that comforts and animates those who are faithful.

The unity for which Jesus prays is not a foreshadowing of ecumenism—after all, when he spoke there were as yet no denominations, let alone divisions among them. Rather, Jesus' prayer is an expression of yearning for the continuation, beyond time and death, of the community that is one in the love of the Holy. As Cyril of Alexandria stated in the fifth century, "We too then are to be combined and commingled into a unity with God and with one another, in spite of our observable separation as individuals distinct in soul and body."[14]

The love lived out by Jesus produced a community inconceivable on human terms. It was an accord of avowed enemies, an embrace of the outcasts, the despised, the prominent, the impoverished, the disillusioned, and the dreamers. Jesus prays that this union will persevere "so that the love with which you have loved me may be in them, and I in them."

For Reflection

1. Read all of John 17. Where does Jesus' prayer lead you as you consider the call to unity?
2. How do you react, what do you pick up on, as an eavesdropper to Jesus' prayer?

For Conversation

1. Read the several versions of the Statement of Faith.[15] How does the Statement of Faith enunciate the faith of our nondoctrinal church? Or does it?

2. How do you define "faith"? Is faith made up of beliefs, or is faith more about an attitude of trust, an orientation for one's life?

3. Does your reflection on John 17 cast greater light on the desire of our UCC founders to express more fully the oneness in Christ of the churches that united to form the UCC?

2

A UNITY OF MULTIPLE VOICES

WE FIND IN THE UCC CONSTITUTION NO TEST OF FAITH TO GAIN admittance or sustain membership or be considered kindred. There is no exam on beliefs to be held, no creeds to which we must adhere. There is trust that, as Augustine of Hippo wrote, "God knows those who are his. . . . There are many who seem to be outside who are really inside, and many who seem to be inside who are really outside. . . . When we speak of people being 'inside' or 'outside' the Church, we need to think of it as a matter of the heart and not of the body."[1]

The statement "What we believe," found on our national website, confirms: "The UCC has no rigid formulation of doctrine or attachment to creeds or structures." These statements of belief are presented:

1. We believe in the triune God: Creator, resurrected Christ, the sole Head of the church, and the Holy Spirit, who guides and brings about the creative and redemptive work of God in the world.

2. We believe that each person is unique and valuable. It is the will of God that every person belong to a family of faith where they have a strong sense of being valued and loved.

3. We believe that each person is on a spiritual journey and that each of us is at a different stage of that journey.

4. We believe that the persistent search for God produces an authentic relationship with God, engendering love, strengthening faith, dissolving guilt, and giving life purpose and direction.

5. We believe that all of the baptized "belong body and soul to our Lord and Savior Jesus Christ." No matter who—no matter what—no matter where we are on life's journey—notwithstanding race, gender identity or expression, sexual orientation, class, or creed—we all belong to God and to one worldwide community of faith. All persons baptized—past, present and future—are connected to each other and to God through the sacrament of baptism. We baptize during worship when the community is present because baptism includes the community's promise of "love, support and care" for the baptized—and we promise that we won't take it back—no matter where your journey leads you.

6. We believe that all people of faith are invited to join Christ at Christ's table for the sacrament of Communion. Just as many grains of wheat are gathered to make one loaf of bread and many grapes are gathered to make one cup of wine, we, the many people of God, are made one in the body of Christ, the church. The breaking of bread and the pouring of wine reminds us of the costliness of Christ's sacrifice and the discipleship to which we are all called. In the breaking of bread, we remember and celebrate Christ's presence among us along with a "cloud of witnesses"—our ancestors, family, and friends who have gone before us. It is a great mystery; we claim it by faith.

7. We believe the UCC is called to be a united and uniting church. "That they may all be one" (John 17:21). "In essentials—unity, in nonessentials—diversity, in all things—charity." These UCC mottos survive because they touch core values deep within us. The UCC

has no rigid formulation of doctrine or attachment to creeds or structures. Its overarching creed is love. UCC pastors and teachers are known for their commitment to excellence in theological preparation, interpretation of the scripture, and justice advocacy. Even so, love and unity in the midst of our diversity are our greatest assets.

8. We believe that God calls us to be servants in the service of others and to be good stewards of the earth's resources. "To believe is to care; to care is to do."

9. We believe that the UCC is called to be a prophetic church. As in the tradition of the prophets and apostles, God calls the church to speak truth to power, liberate the oppressed, care for the poor, and comfort the afflicted.

10. We believe in the power of peace, and work for nonviolent solutions to local, national, and international problems.

11. We are a people of possibility. In the UCC, members, congregations, and structures have the breathing room to explore and to hear . . . for after all, God is still speaking, . . ."[2]

These beliefs are beautifully articulated and match up well with the theological statements in our constitution and the actions of General Synod. It's quite possible that most of us in the UCC do agree with most of these beliefs. And most likely these statements were put together as an invitational piece, a way of describing who we are and how we are a church to those who don't know us. But still. Not every congregation baptizes during worship, nor does every congregation affirm that all people of faith are invited to join Christ at Christ's table for the sacrament of Communion, nor do all our members believe in the Triune God or work for nonviolent solutions to international problems. Statements of what "we" believe and what "we" practice may convey a false unanimity and can unintentionally serve to set standards for who is or is not really UCC, or for who is more UCC or less UCC.

Oliver Powell, who served as an adviser to the Joint Committee on the Basis of Union, memorably called us "a heady, exasperating mix."[3] "Perhaps no other descriptive phrase in the UCC's . . . history has been used as often, or as accurately, to describe us."[4] So, we're heady and exasperating, and we can probably embrace that. But, are we still a mix? Or, more critically, are we all aware that we are a mix? That "there are many who seem [from our point of view] to be outside who are really inside"?

You may have heard other characterizations of the United Church of Christ. Some take on a humorous tone pitched somewhere between folk-lore-ish and sophisticated: "You know what UCC stands for, don't you? 'Unitarians Considering Christ.'" Then there are the brightly mocking commentaries along the lines of "I'm going to quote from the Bible now— oh, but we don't do that in the UCC, do we?" Many who hear this are amused; many are discomfited. I find myself reacting as if to the sound of acrylic fingernails raking a schoolroom chalkboard. My internalized grammar check mechanism goes bananas as someone, who is doubtless very well-meaning, defines the "we" of the UCC in a cramped and exclusionary manner, granting unconscious credence to the notion that everyone in the UCC is of the same type and culture and theological predisposition. While employing the mode of self-deprecation, the self doing the deprecating posits a UCC norm and standard that denies or unthinkingly dismisses as irrelevant UCC congregations and UCC folk who have never stepped away from their strong scriptural base, who hold Christ as the center of their lives. Who *is* "we" in the UCC? And who gets to decide?

When we have "difficult moments" we may, in Mary Sue Brookshire's words,

> start to hear ourselves say about some churches or some pastors or some hymns or some styles of worship that they "are not very UCC." Not very UCC, as if somewhere in a vault in Cleveland there is a UCC meter that can determine to the hundredth of a percentage point just how "UCC" something is.

The irony, of course, is that welcoming all those different voices IS very UCC. . . .

The unity that God desires includes—or actually, re-quires—multiple voices. Left to our own devices, we as humans tend to surround ourselves with those who speak our language. We seek the security and comfort found in the unity of our likeness.[5]

In contrast to the human inclination toward those who are like us, "God's very life is a dynamic eternal dance of unity-in-difference."[6] T. V. Philip, historian and former professor at United Theological College, Bangalore, elaborates, "The unity and oneness in the Godhead is not be-cause the three persons are of the same or uniform nature. They are dif-ferent, yet there is community and communion. We often think that for the sake of unity we need uniform structures, the same doctrine, the same language and culture, and all should become of one race and color."[7]

We might not think that unity requires uniformity. On many levels we probably give thanks that we are diverse, that those who were "them" yesterday are "us" today we are forever changed. But the "changed" part, the transformation, is more difficult to effect institutionally and procedu-rally than it is spiritually. Which is to say that the transformation of hearts does not immediately or inescapably lead to the reformation of, say, struc-tures, rules, procedures, or what happens at meetings. As one Conference staff member exclaimed, "We have great diversity in our Conference, except that we're all Balkanized. Each ethnic community does wonderful things. So does the LGBT community. But it's all self-contained. The mostly white rural churches feel at odds with the mostly white churches in and near the big cities. And the Conference committees, commissions, and Board of Directors keep on as they have always kept on. How do we become a church, one church, a United Church?"[8]

Mary Sue Brookshire suggests we move toward a "dialogical unity" where there are many voices *and* we unite in conversation, in dialogue.[9]

Hospitality persuades us to take part in dialogue, to hold in a creative tension all of our independent and disparate voices.

Tension, all by itself, is the state of being stretched tight, in mental or emotional strain. "Creative tension," though, refers to a situation where "disagreement or discord gives rise to better ideas or outcomes."[10] Creative tension can also refer to "the gap between where we are now and where we want to be."[11] Dialogue—with its give and take between and among those who are in conversation—happens in creative tension, maybe it happens *as* creative tension.

UCC scholar Rosemary McCombs Maxey decries furrow-browed attempts to find alikeness in our unity.

> If this church can relinquish its defensive power posture and assume a listening posture, then we can sit at the Lord's Table as I believe God intends us to do. Let the United Church of Christ forthrightly say, "We don't see one strand of commonality on which to base our unity, but let's be our unique selves at the Lord's Table. . . ." At the Lord's Table, there is a theology of listening toward mutual hearing. Our various voices, the voices of all creation, and the voice of the Creator can speak and be heard.[12]

This is the hospitality that persuades us to take part in dialogue, to hold in a creative tension all of our independent and disparate voices.

Bill Hulteen, a church leader who has reflected extensively on the development of structure and relationships within the UCC, sees hospitality as a spiritual discipline. "Hospitality . . . has to do with an abiding sense of engaging and welcoming the other, knowing that the other can be a source of insight into the ways and will of God . . . . Instead of 'you can't tell me,' hospitality looks forward to considering and learning from the other."[13] It is in dialogue that we consider and learn from one another.

Sitting in a circle on typically uncomfortable folding chairs at a Church Day gathering in California's Central Valley, twenty or so folks took part in a forum on the theologies of the UCC. Each of us offered synopses of the beliefs we grew up with. We discussed how our theologies have changed. Since few of the participants had grown up in the UCC, we mused on the gifts and turmoil brought into the UCC from members new to the UCC, and on the gifts and turmoil those new to the UCC receive. As the forum concluded, four ordained ministers who had recently come into the UCC faith family through privilege of call were asked a question: "Although we are not a doctrinal church, have you heard some persistent proclamation? What, for us as the UCC, is the heart of the Gospel?" The response—one response, the same response—from Samoan, Filipino, African-American, and Euro-American ethnic heritages and from denominational histories ranging from Roman Catholic to Samoan Congregational to UCC Philippines to Church of God in Christ—was, "Extravagant welcome. And let me tell you why . . ." We went way beyond our scheduled ending time to hear the stories of the shout-out from the ethic of hospitality that had drawn these church leaders into the United Church of Christ.

"What a beautiful, heady, exasperating, hopeful mix!" That was the complete exclamation from Oliver Powell about our church. Somehow we seem to omit the "beautiful" and the "hopeful" in the popular recounting of it. But I wonder whether it's time for us as a church to connect with the "beautiful" and "hopeful" attributed to us. Musicians enrich the tone of chords through the addition of notes in a creative practice called "tension." We are enriched as we unite in dialogue, in creative tension, among all of our independent and disparate voices. We are enriched as we practice the hospitality of "looking forward to considering and learning from the other." That may be our beauty. That may be our hope.

For Conversation

1. Have you ever found yourself or your congregation coming up short on the "UCC meter"?—either your own internal monitor or the one "in a vault in Cleveland"?

2. What gifts and turmoil have you brought to the UCC? ("You" can refer to you as a person, or you as a Local Church.)

3. What gifts and turmoil have you received from others in the UCC? ("Others" can refer to other Local Churches, to other settings of the church, or to other individuals.)

4. Where have you found—or have you found—unity made up of multiple voices in our church?

5. How have you seen in church life "accountability to a will and purpose beyond our own will and purpose"?

3

A COVENANTAL POLITY

"FROM MOVEMENT TO DENOMINATION" IS THE CHAPTER TITLE USED BY UCC historian Louis Gunnemann to describe the Congregational Christian part of our church's heritage.[1] I would like to borrow that title and apply it more broadly to the shaping of the whole United Church of Christ.

We began as a movement in the sense of a series of actions advancing a principle or tending toward a particular end. In this opening movement our two historic church families advanced the principle of unity in Christ by uniting themselves to one another. The new United Church of Christ then proceeded into the second movement of its church-formation sonata. This was the movement of a group to organize in order to achieve certain goals. To express more fully their oneness in Christ, to make their common witness more effective, and to serve the reign of God in the world, the UCC became a denomination: it drafted a constitution that set up a governance structure. Governance is partly about the exercise of authority and partly about the functioning of "the persons (or committees or departments, etc.) who make up a body for the purpose of administering something."[2] Our governance structure is termed covenantal. We don't go so far as to say that our governance structure is a covenant. Instead, we are covenant-*al*. In our governance structure and in our general being together, we're leaning in the direction of covenant.

Arriving at the designation "covenantal" was not easy. There was distress among many in the Congregational Churches about the possible loss of congregational autonomy to "the presbyterial church order of the Evangelical and Reformed Church where synods and the General Synod made authoritative decisions on behalf of the whole church."[3] In an effort to balance these two governance structures the first UCC Constitution affirmed autonomy for Local Churches, while calling upon all settings of the church to respect each other's actions and give them thoughtful and prayerful response. Soon, however, as UCC theologian Clyde Steckel relates, "Congregationalist autonomy won the day. . . . In the midst of this mix of confusion, dashed hopes and the triumph of one polity tradition over the other, an old word emerged, covenant, put to a new use to characterize and explain the polity of the UCC and to distinguish it from congregational, presbyterial or episcopal polities."[4]

Putting the term "covenant" to a new use is an issue addressed by UCC Conference Minister Jane Fisler Hoffman in her guide to covenant in the UCC. She examines the theological and biblical dimensions of covenant and notes that "the scriptural covenantal tradition is 'all about God.'"[5] She then asks,

> So when, how and why did the predominant referent of the word "covenant" become our current one—about covenants among people and, in the United Church of Christ, among the settings of our church?[6] . . . The word "covenant" entered United Church of Christ life in a formal way with the adoption of the 1959 Statement of Faith, which now in the form of a doxology reads: "You bestow upon us your holy Spirit, creating and renewing the church of Jesus Christ, binding in covenant faithful people of all ages, tongues and races. . . ."[7] But the word "covenant" did not

appear in our Constitution until the 2000 revision. . . . Until then, "covenant" was appealed to regularly . . . in conversations about how we should work together, particularly through challenging times when the temptation to go our separate ways flares up among us.[8]

In part III, "The Wider Church," we will look more carefully at Article III, "Covenantal Relations," which brought the word "covenant" into the UCC Constitution in 2000. Perhaps that addition is a gesture of mediation between denomination and movement, between the structural covenant of our constitution and our more improvisational working covenant of relationship with God and one another.

The improvisational nature of covenant was illustrated for me in 1999 when an ecumenical throng came together in Sacramento to celebrate the full communion of four denominations—known as the Formula of Agreement. Worshipers filled the pews. I was among the musicians, choirs, and soon-to-be-speakers who led the procession. In the chancel, facing the congregation, we were in position to view the sweep of color and motion as representatives of the Evangelical Lutheran Church in America, the Presbyterian Church USA, the Reformed Church of America, and the United Church of Christ flowed up the multiple aisles of the sanctuary bearing bright banners. All of our spirits and voices lifted in song. As the various streams of the procession converged upon the communion table, which was lavish with objects of beauty and symbols of promise, an awareness formed among those of us who were observing (and still singing). There quite simply was not enough room around the communion table for all who were coming forward (while singing) to assemble there. Nor, it seemed, was there a plan in place for, uh, what to do next, movement-wise. We all kept singing. Then there came to pass an interlude of what we who are skilled in worship design refer to as "liturgical milling around." The people who were engaged in this enterprise smiled, made eye contact, sometimes stopped to embrace old acquaintances. Banners swayed, shifted, and took off in new directions to allow those behind to come forward. There was a massive and graceful shuffling, and somehow people got where they needed to go. And we all kept singing, kept being the church.

That day in Sacramento people of God entrusted with the mission of Jesus Christ came together from all over the map but without a clearly charted course. Nevertheless, they persevered in joy. As we talk about our polity—our life together as well as our governance—that image stays with me. The massive and graceful shuffling of a collection of people focused on their shared calling to follow Jesus and to embody their oneness in Christ speaks to us about the ways we work out covenant day by day. It might become a behavioral meme for hospitality, the precursor and sustainer of covenant. Even with no detailed plan in place, in confusion, people somehow got where they needed to go. And everyone kept singing from their hearts. That is, being the church.

There is a mobility to our UCC polity. Sometimes we show this mobility by wandering or milling around, sometimes we run in place, sometimes we proceed with a clear sense of God's purpose leading us. Whatever the form of our mobility on any particular day, our history and our polity create a restlessness that stirs us from placidness (á la Jim Manley's hymn "Spirit"). We draw from and are drawn to the spiritual lineages of pilgrims and exiles, those who journey in search of the sacred, those who have become aliens and seek a new home.

Mobility can be a sign of covenant. Covenant "yields a way of life that is always on the move, always summoned beyond our preferred way stations, always sustained when we move out beyond our comfort zones in faithful obedience."9

Clyde Steckel extends a reminder to be "careful and modest" in our talk of covenantal polity.

> While it is entirely proper theologically to cite God as the gracious witness to our humanly devised covenants and as One who holds us accountable for honoring them . . . we should be clear that we

have taken an ancient biblical and theological word and used it to express something more contemporary in our sense of how God is in a living and loving relationship with those called to the divine mission by following Jesus Christ. This is not a God who sets up covenants of obedience that weak humans are bound to break and then to be punished for their disobedience by God's wrath. These are covenants of grace, where our human service to God is divinely cherished and prospered, and where our failings and rebellions are laid bare, forgiven, and where we are restored to new life.[10]

Walter Brueggemann also emphasizes the divine initiation of covenant. Covenant "begins with a dangerous decision taken in heaven. . . . That risk is to sojourn with and keep company with those unworthy and unattractive and certainly not of his own kind. . . . It is God giving herself away that makes a covenant community possible."[11]

As a church, we are not surprised when we disagree. Or when we find that fundamentalists and near-Buddhists, Socialists and Republicans, farm owners and farm workers are all clustered around the same communion table. How can we account for the crazily self-contradictory covenant community we know as church except by recognizing that Jesus has called each of us to be here, to take part in this massive and graceful shuffling movement that so often takes us beyond our comfort zones?

For Conversation

1. "Those who were 'them' yesterday are 'us' today, and 'we' are forever changed" is an expression of one aspect of covenant, along the lines of Walter Brueggemann's description of the "sustained engagement" of covenant that "eventually transform[s] all parties to the transaction." We've also heard him allude to covenant yielding a way of life that takes us beyond our comfort zones. What is intriguing about covenant, thus described?

2. What hesitations do you have about covenant? or covenantal polity?

PART II

Local Churches

⌒

*In part II we will look to our
Local Churches, defined in our
constitution as "the basic unit
of the life and organization of the
United Church of Christ." It is
within our Local Churches that the
welcome table is spread and where
the primary discernment and the
front-line determination is made
of who is "we" in the UCC.
We will look at hospitality,
discernment, vitality, conflict, and
the ways in which members of
Local Churches live in covenant.*

4

ENCOUNTERING GOD IN A
REAL HUMAN COMMUNITY

IT'S HARD FOR ME TO GO TO CHURCH.

No, it's not particularly difficult for me to preach or preside at the communion table or offer public prayers. At those times God steps in decisively, the Holy Spirit engages me, and I ride that whoosh! of exhilarating ministry with and to the Body of Christ. But it's hard for me to *go* to church, to be a worshiper, especially in my home congregation.

I remember a Sunday several years ago, when I entered my home church and slid smoothly into the third row from the back, only a few minutes into the service. As I was fumbling to get settled, my glance brushed against the gaze of a young woman who had begun chemotherapy on Wednesday. The dedicated political activist sitting in front of me was coping, just barely, with the escalating gusto of her two preschoolers. A family came forward with their baby to be baptized; little Julia, dressed in a long white christening gown and a bonnet, waved her bare feet in delight. The congregation prayed for a member in prison, for those fighting forest fires, for a friend skirmishing with drug abuse, for victims of catastrophe in Haiti. A high school graduate, preparing to leave for college, said good-by to the church to which she had brought her parents when she was three years old.

Here were: Hope in the stronghold of fear. Distraction. Joy and un-bounded beauty. Connection beyond time and distance. Farewells and welcomes. These highly charged ions filled our breathing space. I was a wreck. Tears oozing. No Kleenex. Does this ever happen to you?

I guess I need to be better prepared. And not just when it comes to a personal supply of paper products. Slipping into sacred space is risky. Jacob's story warns us about combative spirits and disturbing visions in the wilderness. Moses alerts us to fiery talking shrubs. Mary prepares us for obstreperous angels barging into our lives and disrupting everything. But somehow we've deluded ourselves into thinking we're safe at church. Or maybe I'm the only one who's been so misled. Maybe the rest of you already knew that through the scent of candle wax, on the strains of shouts and hymns, cradled in clumsy gestures, the atmosphere at church crackles with surges of raw pain and need and grief, desire, gladness, and determination. Invisible inaudible lightning bolts fling themselves through the congregation, only to turn liquid as they strike your heart.

So, there I was that Sunday, drenched to the soul. Unable to sing all the way through the third verse of "Leaning on the Everlasting Arms," much as I wanted to. Grabbing the puny stump of a pencil somebody dropped on the floor to make a few notes on the back of the special offering envelope. To maybe make some sense out of this wash of feelings. To maybe wring out some drops of blessing. Saturated with grace.

Now, this qualitatively acute immersion experience of "being church," with all its attendant risks and glories, is not visited upon us every time we show up among the company of those who seek God's presence. Certainly it is not the exclusive property of our particular UCC faith community. But I wanted to begin our consideration of Local Churches by stirring up memories of times when we have gone to church and heard things that we knew we would not hear anywhere else.[1] When we have gone to church and found an oasis where we can reveal our pain and express our failures in a cultural desert of obsession with success. When we have gone to church and stumbled across the transfiguration,[2] permutation, transmogrification of the heavenly into the earthly, of the spirit into flesh, of cosmic love into intimate compassion. I wanted to trip some of your memories of going to church, in ordinary times as well as in extraordinary circumstances, because our life in Local Churches is the bedrock of our UCC identity.

When we say—as we often do—that the "basic unit of the life and organization of the United Church of Christ is the Local Church,"[3] it isn't a solely structural statement. It reflects and supports the reality that we turn, with great frequency, to our Local Church as our frame of reference for the meaning of "church." It was said in the Massachusetts Bay Colony that the "visible church is a particular congregation, never a diocesan or national body. . . . The supreme head of the church is Jesus Christ, from whom the church has immediate and full power to order its entire life without determination or control by any overhead body."[4]

As we have earlier noted, Local Churches in the United Church of Christ are not all alike; we do not worship, undertake mission, or organize ourselves according to uniform standards. We are not a franchise operation. Paragraph 18 of our constitution states that the autonomy of the Local Church is inherent and modifiable only by its own action. It then gives more detail

[Nothing shall] abridge or impair the autonomy of any Local Church in the management of its own affairs, which affairs include, but are not limited to, the right to retain or adopt its own methods of organization, worship and education; to retain or secure its own charter and name; to adopt its own constitution and bylaws; to formulate its own covenants and confessions of faith; to admit members in its own way and to provide for their discipline or dismissal; to call or dismiss its pastor or pastors by such procedure as it shall determine; to acquire, own, manage and dispose of property and funds; to control its own benevolences; and to withdraw by its own decision from the United Church of Christ at any time without forfeiture of ownership or control of any real or personal property owned by it.[5]

We are, in the United Church of Christ, big on Local Church autonomy. For those who have been part of the UCC for a long time, Local Church autonomy is so much a given factor that it is hardly questioned or wondered at, but might bear some review. Those who are newer to the UCC and come from communities of faith where congregations are answerable to overseeing bodies, or where the authority of the church is entrusted to those who are ordained, may want to pause and look again at those details of Local Church self-determination just mentioned.

It is particularly noteworthy that the autonomy of the Local Church is set within the larger scheme of the autonomy of each of the settings of the church. We profess that each setting—local, Association, Conference, national—is a manifestation of the church and has the responsibility, "in consultation with all other settings, to discern God's will and way for its own time and place."[6] We'll get into that larger scheme in the chapters to come.

Local Churches are the starting point for life in the United Church of Christ, and as far back as 1604, in the congregational way, Local Churches were described as "constituted and gathered . . . by a free mutuall consent of Believers joyning and covenanting to live as Members of a holy Society togeather in all religious and vertuous duties as Christ and his Apostles did institute and practice in the Gospell."[7]

Joining and covenanting.[8] Theologian William Ames, writing in 1629, stressed that covenant is what makes a church a church:

> Believers do not make a particular church . . . unless they are joined
> together by a special bond among themselves. . . . This bond is a
> covenant, expressed or implicit, by which believers bind themselves
> individually to perform all those duties toward God and toward
> one another which relate to the purpose . . . of the church.[9]

It is within our Local Church that we first learn and live the covenant that binds us to one another in service to God. In his letters to the churches at Colossae and Ephesus the Apostle Paul refers to the bonds of covenant in terms of ligaments. He describes the whole Body of Christ as "joined and knit together by every ligament with which it is equipped" (Eph. 4:16). He teaches that the Body of Christ is "nourished and held together by its ligaments" and grows "with a growth that is from God" (Col. 2:19). This is covenant gone anatomical. Or, we could say, the Body of Christ is ligamentous. We've got ligaments. We have this "connecting or unifying bond," as the Merriam Webster Online Dictionary defines "ligamentous." Actual physical ligaments are flexible, elastic, tough, and fibrous. They connect bones, form joints, and support our internal organs. Ligaments in our church life allow us to move with grace and ease, to pick up and carry, to go beyond where we now are, and to pull ourselves and each other up and out when we are stuck.

The United Church of Christ is ligamentous. This goes for our church as a whole, between and among all our settings—although the unifying bond may not always be obvious. However, within each Local Church the bond is elemental. All this talk of church-related ligaments calls attention to the root word that "ligament" shares with "religion." Each originates from *ligare*, meaning "to bind." "Re*ligio*"—"*liga*ment."[10]

While driving along Interstate 5 somewhere south of Visalia, California, I happened upon an AM radio show where a pious speaker rattled his take on the linguistic connection between *ligare* and "religion" like a glass jar half full of pennies. He was quite agitated in his presentation, and didn't get into the whole "ligaments" thing. Instead he went straight for "ligature." He did not tarry with the general definition of tying or binding together, but barreled into the extreme usage, "a means for strangulation," as if that were the sole application of the term. He railed on for quite some time, likening the ties of organized religion to bonds of constriction, immobilization, and suffocation. His stated mission was to free people from religion and guide them to the Bible—a mission that he said he would accomplish if we would send him money. I wondered whether he had been proselytized by someone who was "spiritual but not religious."

UCC pastor and author Lillian Daniel has notably recorded her reactions, during bouts of air travel, to the self-disclosing "spiritual but not religious" person seated next to her.

> There is nothing challenging about having deep thoughts all by oneself. What is interesting is doing this work in community, where other people might call you on stuff, or heaven forbid, disagree with you. Where life with God gets rich and provocative is when you dig deeply into a tradition that you did not invent all for yourself. . . . Can I spend my time talking to someone brave enough to encounter God in a real human community? Because when this flight gets choppy, that's who I want by my side, holding my hand, saying a prayer and simply putting up with me, just like we try to do in church.[11]

When we are ready to go beyond an individualized experience of That-Which-Is-Good-And-Holy-And-Of-Knock-Your-Socks-Off-Quality-And-Influence (*comma*) when we come as pilgrims, wanderers, or refugees to a new spiritual home and place of healing (*comma*) when we have hung around and hung with a Local Church long enough to hear the little creaks and jitters within this haven, this sanctuary, and see the fine lines beneath any cosmetically regenerated facial surface of the community (*comma*) and nonetheless decide to grab onto it in a warm, maybe awkward, embrace (*comma*) we "become members" of this rendering of the Body of Christ, "joined and knit together" by every flexible, elastic, tough, and fibrous ligament to promote "the body's growth in building itself up in love" (Eph. 4:16).

When we encounter God in a real human community we get a taste of the unity Jesus prayed for. T. V. Philip elaborates:

> An individual is one who is isolated, self-dependent, self-centred or one who wants to do things in his or her own way [maybe

have deep thoughts all by her- or himself], whereas a person is always a person in relationship with others, one who pre-supposes others, one who recognizes his/her dependence on others. To be in the image of God is to be a person. . . . When the doctrine of the Trinity says that one God exists in three persons, it means that God is a community of three persons . . . in relationship and dependence. . . . We are created to mirror this image of the Trinity in our lives, in our relationship with one another . . . to recognize that my humanity is caught up with others and inextricably bound to them.[12]

Bound by every ligament.

For Conversation

1. Talk about your life in your Local Church. How did you take up with this congregation?

2. Has slipping into sacred space ever been risky for you? Is it ever hard for you to go to church?

3. How do you resonate with Lillian Daniel's esteem for those "brave enough to encounter God in a real human community . . . holding my hand, saying a prayer and simply putting up with me, just like we try to do in church"?

5

WHO IS WELCOME HERE?

EXTENDING WELCOME

"No matter who you are, no matter where you are on life's journey, you are welcome here." Those seventeen words broke into our UCC speech patterns in 2004, greeting newcomers to our church and delivering the simple and practical truth of God's extravagant welcome to people whose connections to any form of religious experience had been devastatingly severed. The statement went liturgical and called us to worship in all settings of the UCC. Congregations joined in as soon as they heard the opening "No matter . . ." When the first Still-Speaking TV spots aired,[1] I watched the reaction to those words from lifelong devoted UCC members, teenagers without a lot of religious awareness, political conservatives, political radicals, and young adults who did not really see the relevance of church life. The raw number of those with tears in their eyes was staggering. Or maybe illuminating, shedding light on the hospitality that has waved us into beloved community, the hospitality that lives in the marrow of our theology.[2]

Through the God Is Still Speaking initiative, many congregations in our church began to experience the seismic effects produced when the tectonic plate of hospitality—extravagant welcome—wedged itself under some well-entrenched attitudes of contentment with serving those who had always been served, in the ways that had always been done. This view was expressed well by the members of the ongoing conversation Confessing Christ.

> We cannot be Christians without extending a sincere welcome to all fellow humans, neighbors and strangers alike, making clear the cost as well as the joy of discipleship. If we fail to offer our embrace to those beyond the doors of our Local Churches, including those whose cultures and habits are different from ours, if we cater only to ourselves and our own social kind, the vitality of our Christian discipleship will be grievously diminished.[3]

"Come and see," said the Samaritan to her compatriots after she met Jesus at the well and concluded that God was still speaking. Contending that God is still speaking, she brought a multitude of new followers to Jesus from a group widely regarded by the religious folk in Jesus' circle as unclean corrupters of the faith, and with whom relationship had been less than affable.

Yvette Flunder, pastor of City of Refuge UCC, says of her congregation's style of welcome:

> We keep pushing ourselves to identify those who are on the farthest margins of church and society . . . those who the church can just barely accept. And then we go to them and ask them in. Church should not be a private social club. If someone isn't making us uncomfortable, we are not being the church.[4]

Come and see.

Patricia De Jong, pastor of the historic First Congregational UCC, Berkeley, California, comments on the way her congregation welcomes new members:

> If we have had success, it is because we have constantly worked at the personal approach to welcoming new persons into our congre-

gation. For example, our last new member class was designed for parents and children specifically. We oriented parents to life at FCCB and at the same time held a workshop/playgroup for the children. We tailored our remarks and our schedule to busy parents who want to participate in church, but often feel pressed on all sides. It worked—all of our inquirers joined, with special thanks for understanding their busy lives and helping them cope with children and commitment. . . . In this busy world, where folks are dealing with institutional ambivalence, we choose to be un-ambivalent about our new members and the process we invite them to participate in![5]

Come and see. And we'll make the trip easy.

The church growth team in Northern California Nevada wanted to identify the first group of Local Churches to be invited to take part in a program of coaching for church growth. To do so the team looked at several factors: Was the congregation free from major conflict? Did they have a sense of who God was calling them to be? Was there a core of people committed to hospitality?

Churches that took part in the program were introduced to a resource designed to "spark fascinating discussions, encourage prayer, and help your congregation reach out to others in a way that fits your personality, theology and faith."[6] True to their personality, theology, faith, identity, and vocation, each congregation felt free to modify the approach and the content. "We were a bit ill at ease with some of the theological language in the resource, so we made some changes," said David Parks-Ramage, pastor of First Congregational UCC, Santa Rosa.[7] Sebastian Ong, pastor of Chinese Congregational UCC, San Francisco, told the Conference Annual Gathering, "You know, we Chinese folk don't always talk so freely in a large group; we're more forthright one-on-one or in a small group. So when we broke up into groups of three or four, things went a lot better."[8]

All of the churches in the program grew in numbers of members. They grew, as do all growing churches, from the spiritual base of their sense of mission, not from their instinct for survival. Local Churches whose membership numbers are in decline will not draw people because they are eager to fill an empty sanctuary, or support a budget, or fill slots on boards and committees. And not all of our Local Churches will grow. As General Minister and President John Dorhauer writes, "Some of our churches are going to die. Some of them will have an opportunity to approach that sacred moment with dignity."[9] But "some are going to thrive. The ones who do will have a clear sense of mission."[10] Each Local Church finds its mission in the mix of abilities, resources, experiences, yearnings, and callings that are present within it. Present within it, yet somehow, in ways consistent with who that church is, pressing to get out.

Each of us, each Local Church, has been entrusted with something incredibly life-giving, a treasure. And, as Cameron Trimble, UCC minister and executive director of the Center for Progressive Renewal, says, "Anytime you receive something precious, you have to make a decision: The gift is so valuable that it can't be risked, or the gift is so valuable that it must be risked."[11] Growing churches risk it. Churches dying courageously risk it. They don't hoard the good news of the gospel. Of strength in weakness, wisdom in foolishness, victory in defeat, life in the barren caverns of death, the triumph of "powerless love over loveless power."[12] Of the full-tilt, *in extremis* impact of the life and death of Jesus: the sick are healed, the needy are made whole, the rejected are loved, people crushed by guilt are not let off the hook for any evil they may do, but guided to restoration of soul (see Luke 7:22). Contending that God is still speaking, we bear witness to all of the above.

FROM WELCOME TO HOSPITALITY

It is within the Local Church that the welcome table is spread. There the primary discernment and the front-line determinations are made of who is "we" in the UCC. The Local Church is the door through which we enter into the expansive sweep of the whole United Church of Christ. Everyone who has been membered into the body of a Local Church is thus joined to the whole of the United Church of Christ.[13]

As we in Local Churches welcome newcomers, we may be jolted by the biblical premise that "the first task before bringing a guest into hospitality is discernment."[14] "You welcome someone at the front door. Hospitality happens when you invite them in."[15]

UCC historian Randi Walker reminded the 2005 Annual Gathering of the Northern California Nevada Conference of the biblical rigor that was applied to that crossing of the threshold from welcome to hospitality.

> The stranger is not automatically someone to whom you would want to offer hospitality. The stranger in the ancient world was always tested first, with questions, or with observation. Only when the stranger was deemed not to be a threat to the community was she or he welcomed. The ceremony of foot washing was the ritual of turning strangers into guests, and therefore into temporary family members. . . . Listening to our guest, really listening, is the first obligation of the radical and prophetic host. [Only then is the determination made on whether you can make the commitment to hospitality, to] wash her feet, feed her, and take on responsibility for the guest's life, even over your own.[16]

Just a couple of months prior to that Annual Gathering I met with College Avenue UCC in Modesto, California. The moderator had contacted me after finding out that a new and frequent visitor was a registered sex offender. At the meeting I attended, the congregation heard from the visitor about his criminal record and about his search to find a worshiping community. Several parents voiced their concerns about the safety and well-being of children in the congregation. And the church as a whole contended with the demands of hospitality.

There is perhaps no more radical—"radical" in the senses of both "extreme" and "deeply rooted"—an example of hospitality than that of welcoming a child into your life. Whether she is born to you or adopted, whether he comes to you as an infant or a ten-year-old, your commitment to that child's safety and well-being claims precedence over all others. With that assertion firmly in place, the congregation in Modesto discussed this registered sex offender as potential guest.

Having already welcomed him, the congregation stepped into the territory of radical hospitality. They listened to him. They asked questions. Then they acted.

What was he seeking? A worshiping community. They listened more deeply to his unspoken wish to not again commit a criminal act. They conferred further as he waited outside the meeting room. They brought him back to the meeting and told him that they would not allow him to be exposed to temptation—or to potential violation of his parole—by being around children. They had already sought the counsel of the Insurance Board's representative regarding their legal liabilities. They barred their visitor from the church grounds whenever children were present and began setting up an adults-only worship service at which he would be welcome. The moderator was to consult with the Kyros Ministry[17] to draft a behavioral and monitoring agreement.

This congregation, which had since its founding lived the message "No matter who you are, no matter where you are on life's journey, you are welcome here," questioned, listened and acted, speaking the truth in love.

We in Local Churches welcome newcomers, listen to our guests, and enter into discernment about who will be invited in. The process of listening and discerning—the "testing" with questions, or with observation—may be formal or informal. But it is within each Local Church that the primary discernment and the front-line determination are made of who is "we" in the UCC. Local Churches determine how the definition of "we" expands, as new members join in the covenant "expressed or implicit, by which believers bind themselves individually to perform all those duties toward God and toward one another which relate to the purpose . . . of the church."[18]

BELIEF AND COMMITMENT

So what commitment do we make when we dedicate ourselves to the life of a particular UCC household of faith, and through that vow of membership to the whole United Church of Christ? In the UCC *Book of Worship*, this question is posed by the pastor to one who is about to become a member:

> Do you promise, by the grace of God, to be Christ's disciple, to follow in the way of our Savior, to resist oppression and evil, to show love and justice, and to witness to the work and word of Jesus Christ as best you are able?[19]

"That is such a great statement of what it means to be a church member," a pastor exclaimed, "but when we really have to hunker into discernment mode is when we have a prospective member who wants to follow Jesus with us, but isn't a believer."

Now, our constitution begins the characterization of a Local Church as "composed of persons who, believing in the triune God, accepting Jesus Christ as Lord and Savior. . . ."[20] This raises questions for many congregations and pastors:

> If someone who does not (yet . . . or ever) believe in the triune God or Jesus as Savior is nonetheless impelled to be in community and communion with this particular band of wayfaring Christians,

> If someone—believer or not—is "brave enough to encounter God in a real human community" and ready to commit to worship and community, mission and ministry as a member of the United Church of Christ,

> If a Christian believer is not quite who you are on life's journey, or if you are part of another religious tradition and wish to retain that identity,

> Can you, can they, join in covenant and "bind themselves individually to perform all those duties toward God and toward one another which relate to the purpose . . . of the church?"[21]

Today in the UCC we are at a moment when the ethic of hospitality is pushing us to reform and restate, celebrate and calibrate who is "we," as pertains to belief. UCC pastor and professor of philosophy Robin Meyers states that, in an age where "belief" has become synonymous with intellectual assent to propositional statements, "We should cease to ask, 'Are you a *believer?*' and ask instead, 'Are you a *follower* of Jesus?' We must not inquire, 'Are you saved?' but instead ask, 'Are you able to drink of this cup?'"[22] UCC theologian Clyde Steckel expounds on the phrase "to follow Jesus," stressing that "to follow Jesus means trusting him and remaining loyal to him. 'Following' is a more relational verb than 'confessing,' 'professing,' or all the others."[23] He goes on to speak of the church as "the followers of Jesus Christ, gathered into faithful local communities of mission and ministry, where at font and pulpit and table, Christ's followers are renewed and empowered to witness in word and deed to the justice and loving compassion of God."[24]

As we take into account the increasing number of individuals who want to follow Jesus, who seek a community of accompaniment on that journey, and who wish to publicly affiliate with the members and mission of a UCC congregation, we have the opportunity to consider and come to working terms with the nature of our church. We can go beyond asking who is welcome here, and question what membership requires.

Most UCC congregations would concur with these statements about themselves and our church as a whole:

We are a Christian church.

We make sense of the world and of our lives and of Divine Presence through the biblical stories, songs, and prayers of faithful communities in struggle and in covenant, seeking and being sought, oppressed, oppressing, liberating and liberated, steeped in wisdom and missing the point.

The substance of our Local Churches consists of "persons who, believing in the triune God, accepting Jesus Christ as Lord and Savior, and depending on the guidance of the Holy Spirit, are organized for

Christian worship, for the furtherance of Christian fellowship, and for the ongoing work of Christian witness."[25]

Holding fast to those qualities, should we consider whether the grammar of covenant might be prompted by hospitality to add a few commas, open up some phrasing, introduce a new gateway, and try on a new depiction of the Local Church and how we enter the UCC community? Our constitution lists the three ways by which, "in accordance with the custom and usage of a Local Church, persons become members."[26] The inclusion of "in accordance with the custom and usage of a Local Church" is a nod in the direction of Local Church autonomy, an allowance for multiple practices, an allusion to each Local Church's ability to "admit members in its own way." However, most Local Churches direct those seeking membership to these routes: (a) baptism and confirmation or baptism and profession of faith; (b) reaffirmation or reprofession of faith; or (c) letter of transfer or certification from other Christian churches.[27]

A modification of our description of members of a Local Church and our means of entry into covenant could look like this (with changes to the wording in the constitution bracketed and in italics):

A Local Church is composed of persons who <*are committed to follow Jesus Christ as members of this community of faith, which includes those who*> believ<*e*> in the triune God, <*those who*> accept Jesus Christ as Lord and Savior, and <*those who are in discernment of belief. D*>epending on the guidance of the Holy Spirit, <*the members of the Local Church*> are organized for Christian worship, for the furtherance of Christian fellowship, and for the ongoing work of Christian witness.

In accordance with the custom and usage of a Local Church, persons <*enter into covenant with the congregation,*> becom<*ing*> members by (a) baptism and confirmation or baptism and profession of faith; (b) reaffirmation or reprofession of faith; <*(c) pledge of commitment to follow Jesus;>* or *<(d)>* letter of transfer or certification from other Christian churches *<or other communities of faith>.*

"Only in the past two hundred years," Robin Meyers tells us, "has faith come to mean believing things that are increasingly easy to disprove. What we have lost in our time are the other three meanings of the word 'faith.' . . . They are faith as *fiducia* (radical trust in God), as *fidelitas* (loyalty in one's relationship to God), and as *visio* (a way of seeing creation as gracious)."[28] "Profession of faith," "community of faith," "Statement of Faith," even "the faith of the historic Church" are nuanced by those latter three meanings.

CLAIMING THE FAITH OF THE HISTORIC CHURCH

Dictionary definitions of "doctrine" and "dogma" usually include the phrase "accepted as authoritative." Many in our church are wary of anything that is tagged as "authoritative." This can result in disregard or shunning of any theological formulation that we have not courted or discovered by ourselves.

Within our church, many of us accept the doctrine and dogma that have been passed along to us through the church of our childhood or from our current Local Church. Sometimes there is shock and discord upon finding that not everyone in our congregation shares the same set of theological beliefs, or that not every UCC congregation hangs out in the same theological neighborhood, or that for some of us "theological assumptions are hidden or taken for granted"[29] and not easily verbalized.

In our church, "the only official or authoritative teaching offices are the individual conscience and the various expressions of the church . . . speaking and acting only for themselves. . . ."[30] This emphasizes a covenantal dilemma raised in chapter 1: How do we, as a church that does not lay out any "test of doctrine" and where each Local Church is free to "formulate its own covenants and confessions of faith," keep faith with our founding intent to "claim as our own the faith of the historic Church"?

The UCC group Confessing Christ seeks "to see how dialogue with one another and with those who believed before we were born can reform the life of the Church."

> Hospitality demands more than acceptance and affirmation of the presence of the guest. To be any kind of host at all, we need to be so at home in our own house that we immediately recognize what distinctive nourishment and refreshment we have to offer our company. In other words, we need to be thoroughly conversant with the priceless treasures of the church, its core beliefs and values, so that we can present them as special blessings to our guests, and even nurture them into the family.[31]

> Do we have a responsibility as a Christian church:
> to raise up the issues and concepts of theology past and present?
> to serve up kernels of dogma and doctrine?
> to keep up with the still-speaking voice of God
> > by attuning our ears to the Dolby surround nature of revelation
> > > through human experience
> > > and holy scripture
> > > and Jesus as living Word?
> so that this and future generations will be conversant with them?
> so that we can lift credible voices within the public arena?
> so that the definition of doctrine and the determination of dogma
> > is not drafted upon a particular popularized set of unquestioned certainties,
> > but provides for an atmosphere of questioning and a fluid "willingness to entertain doubt?"[32]

These are not rhetorical questions.

Local Churches are the basic unit of our church's organization and life. Basic—as in essential, fundamental, indispensable, serving as the starting point, crucial, critical, and prime. For us in the United Church of Christ, those nonrhetorical questions need responses from Local Churches.

Are you willing to address those questions within your Local Church and with other Local Churches, as an act of hospitality, of looking "forward to considering and learning from the other" that enriches us all? (Yes, the last two *were* rhetorical questions. I'm really, really looking for assents.)

INTEGRITY OF WORSHIP AND THE SACRAMENTS

During the years when I taught the course "UCC Faith, Polity, and Practice" at the Pacific School of Religion, I frequently tendered the word "integrity" when discussing the intricate interrelationships between a lay member and his Local Church, between a pastor and the Local Church she serves, and between a particular Local Church and all the other components of the United Church of Christ.

Integrity can be understood as wholeness, undivided and undiminished. Most often the topic came up when the class discussions dealt with the rites of the church, styles of worship, and the meanings of the sacraments. Integrity, within our affinity of covenant and congruent with our freedom of individual conscience, is an exploit of dexterity and mutual respect. How do our own vigorous takes on music or marriage, confirmation or communion reconcile with "the way we've always done it here?" How do they reconcile with whatever is perceived as "the UCC way"? Does "the UCC way" equate with what appears in the *Book of Worship*? How do we uphold the integrity—the unreduced completeness—of the individual, each Local Church, and the wider United Church of Christ?

We "recognize two sacraments: Baptism and the Lord's Supper or Holy Communion."[33] There are many understandings of the sacraments in church tradition, and in our church today. As an example, Randi Walker presents these views from the reformer John Calvin.

Baptism is the initial recognition of our incorporation into the covenant. . . . Calvin was in favor of infant baptism because he viewed incorporation into the covenant of grace as God's gift to us, not something we can ever understand or do for ourselves. . . . This is why for Calvin it was important that each person know of her or his own baptism, not necessarily the literal story, but that each knows what baptism is, because we rely on this memory when we fall away from grace, as we all inevitably do, to find our way back. . . . Communion for Calvin is also a sign, a seal of the covenant of grace, it is a sign of the 'new' covenant, or the covenant written on the heart. . . . Communion signifies the redemption of the person suffering under original sin. Original sin then is the inevitability of our falling away from the covenant. Inevitably we will break the covenant of grace and will not be able to find our way back unaided.[34]

Whatever our own understandings of the bases and meanings of the sacraments, within the UCC each Local Church determines its own practice with regard to the sacraments, including the consecration of the elements for communion. This ranges from churches of German or Samoan heritage putting a very strong emphasis on the need to have an authorized minister consecrate the communion elements, to the New Light Christians' practice of deacons' consecrating and administering the elements, to congregations where anyone may consecrate and administer the elements. So what happens at an Association gathering, or a Conference youth event, when several different congregational traditions are present?

For many congregations, worship is strongly linked to a distinct ethnic or geographic heritage or tradition. How does the regular presence of persons not of that congregation's predominant heritage or tradition affect worship? For example, Filipino spouses of Japanese-Americans in a Japanese-American congregation, Anglo members of culturally Puerto Rican congregations, Native Americans from the Great Plains who are members of historically Congregational churches in New England? How do integrity and hospitality interact?

For Conversation

1. When has your Local Church seemed most alive to you? At what points in your congregation's history has there been the greatest growth in numbers?

2. To whom does your congregation extend the invitation to come and see? How does your invitation reflect your identity and values?

3. Who is welcome at your Local Church? How and to whom do you extend hospitality? What is the custom and usage by which persons are recognized and recognize themselves as connected with, in covenant with, your Local Church?

4. Do members of your Local Church have an approach—or many approaches—to the study of Christian beliefs and doctrine?

5. Is your congregation one where members tend not to state the spiritual? If so, can you identify aspects of the unstated spiritual undergirding of your congregation? How is the spiritual dimension expressed?

6. How does the worship life of your Local Church convey hospitality and covenant?

7. What biblical and theological understandings are expressed, what dialogue with those "who believed before we were born" are evident through words, actions, or physical setting in your congregation's service of baptism? in Holy Communion? Who may be baptized in your congregation? Who may receive communion?

8. What is revealed about God and about humanity in the sacraments as celebrated in your congregation? How are these revelations expressed?

9. What is God calling your congregation to be and do?

For Reflection

1. What does it mean for you to follow Jesus?

2. Have you found in your Local Church a covenant of grace, where "our human service to God is divinely cherished and prospered, and where our failings and rebellions are laid bare, forgiven, and where we are restored to new life?"[35] Have you found a connection between the sacraments and the covenant of grace?

6

CONSTITUTIONS AND COVENANTS

"ALMOST EVERY LOCAL CHURCH HAS A DOCUMENT THAT IT USES TO describe how it is organized and governed. Usually this is a constitution and bylaws."[1]

Constitutions and bylaws state who we are and how we connect with one another within our church community and throughout the denomination. Constitutions and bylaws explain who is a member of this particular body, and what it means to be a member. Constitutions and bylaws record how we've agreed to conduct ourselves and organize our ministry. Constitutions and bylaws provide a safeguard against hasty departures from our charted course. Constitutions and bylaws denote structural covenants—in contrast to and, we would hope, in harmony with, our working covenants of relationship.

A Local Church's articles of incorporation, constitution, and/or bylaws attest to the dilemma and the actuality of being a manifestation of the church of Jesus Christ and a constituting body of the United Church of Christ, as well as a not-for-profit corporation of the state wherein we are physically located. (Please refer to the endnotes for resources and articles on churches as not-for-profit corporations, basics to include in articles of incorporation, legal requirements for church meeting minutes, legal implications for church bylaws, and differentiating between the church as church and the church as nonprofit corporation.[2])

During his service as Conference Minister in Southern California and Nevada, Daniel Romero was revered for many things. Among them was his articulation of a Conference Minister's primary duty to those in his or her care. "Conference Ministers have a lot of experience with churches and ministers. Sometimes the best—and the least—we can do is keep people from doing something stupid." In that genial pastoral spirit, I would like to pass along an array of points in church constitutions and bylaws where I have observed the potential for painful or damaging strain on covenant.

EACH CONGREGATION'S CONTEXT AND VOCATION

The constitutions and bylaws of many of our Local Churches were designed for an era of "churched" culture and cultural devotion to organizations run by Robert's Rules of Order.

That was a time when the label on the social fabric in the United States could have been rendered without much concern for contradiction as, "Content: 90 percent Christian; 5 percent Jewish; 5 percent other." The fabric content label today in Northern California reads more like this: 50 percent on a personal spiritual quest; 40 percent opposed to organized religion; 20 percent aligned with a faith that might be Christian, Jewish, Muslim, Hindu, or other. Warning: fabric overload; components total 110 percent; overlap of categories possible.[3]

Your regional social fabric may be somewhat differently constituted, but overall it seems prudent to assume that standpoints on church and church membership have undergone massive alteration over the past twenty to thirty years. However, many churches' constitutions and bylaws have not made adjustments or gotten the new apps.

"Most constitutions and bylaws are a long list of rules and regulations, conditions and stipulations, policies and procedures that were effective in their day. They were developed during a time when people appreciated extensive structure and were willing to work within that structure." In churches with "complex constitution and bylaws structures . . . significant amounts of time are spent dealing with relatively insignificant issues."[4]

There is, as many UCC members informally report, an impatience with church council meetings where the cost of office supplies and the menu for the next Fellowship Sunday dinner siphon away time that could be used on oversight and visioning for the church's whole mission and ministry. There is frustration with a concept of church membership that channels all members' energies into activities focused on the church's internal life. There is discouragement over the yearly task of "filling slots" on the ballot, and the number of positions that go unfilled—while members go unfulfilled. There may be turf wars between pastor and worship committee, or needless furor over whether the youth minister is part of the pastoral team or is answerable to the education committee, or intermittent sullenness regarding use of the church building.

If such concerns are conditions in which your Local Church finds itself, this might be the time for you to consider who you are now as a church, with all your gifts and quirks, and what God is calling you to do. From that base of understanding and awareness, churches can cultivate ways of conducting themselves and organizing mission that will connect to the Holy One and one another and allow the mobility "to prosper God's work in the world." Our congregational autonomy affords us the freedom to be the congregation God is calling us to be. Forms of organization and administration for each Local Church flow from that covenant community's calling, purpose, and identity.[5]

Being a covenant community has administrative and organizational implications, as Walter Brueggemann points out:

> God has put himself at risk by covenanting with us. . . . It is God giving herself away that makes a covenant community possible. . . . This God . . . [is marked] by faithfulness and vulnerability.

. . . Covenant requires us to think afresh about the organizational, institutional flows of power. . . . Covenanting in the new community under YHWH, [we] will have a sense of what matters and will be able to sort out the things that matter, matter to all, from odd projects to be defended, petty preferences to be guarded and straw ideologies that have had their day.[6]

Thinking afresh about the organizational, institutional flows of power, discerning what matters, and sorting out the things that matter to all from odd projects to be defended or petty preferences to be guarded, we might see that there is not so much a need for a chain of command in church structure as for plainness of accountability based on a shared vision of ministry and mission.

There is, amid the racket of life and the utilitarian quality of so much of human connection, the need for a covenant setting that promotes, demands, teaches, and embodies a genuine and hospitable flow of conversation and dialogue. An incarnational understanding of covenant enables us "to be at the disposal of, dependent upon and prepared to be nourished by the gifts of the others."[7] This embodied wisdom insists we find ways to be together that are worthy of the One who comes to us "in ways that are risky and self-giving."[8]

VOTES, STRUCTURE, AND COVENANT

Majority rule is not a hallmark of covenant. *Vox populi* is not necessarily *vox dei*.[9] Democracy is not discernment.[10]

Back in the 1980s the First Congregational UCC of Ames, Iowa, went through the study process for becoming a Just Peace Church. Then the matter came to the church's Annual Meeting for a vote. The proposal "won" by a vote of 60 percent to 40 percent, after which the Just Peace Committee asked that the vote be declared nonbinding. "It seemed silly to call ourselves a Just Peace Church when there was no consensus," committee chairperson Julianne Pirtle observed. "We agreed at the Annual Meeting that it would be better to let ourselves live into being a Just Peace Church. And we did."[11]

Conference and Association staff regularly counsel churches to consult and follow their congregation's constitution and bylaws when the church is in process of a major decision, like calling a pastor or buying property. Conference or Association staff are occasionally contacted by members of a Local Church who want to utilize the provision in their constitution and bylaws that allows any group of (insert number) members to sign, at any time, a petition that will require a congregational vote at a specially called meeting on whether to retain the current pastor. At such times the counsel given usually goes beyond adhering to the bylaws. The counsel is often along the lines of: In such a vote, everyone loses. No matter the outcome of the vote, the pastor's ministry is compromised and the church is divided.

All of which is to say that the totality of our covenant cannot be penned in our constitution and bylaws, nor is it penned up therein. In covenant we persist in our efforts to match our gait to the pace of the Most High, going beyond what is expected, making commitments that are neither required nor customary, placing relationship to one another higher than individual inclination, and the well-being of the community above all else. Surely we need agreed-upon procedures for making our legal and financial decisions as a Local Church. However, a primacy of parliamentary procedure in our church life can put us disastrously off-stride and impede our walk in covenant. "To put it more bluntly," Clyde Steckel writes, "in the UCC we are not a democracy. We are communities of the followers of Jesus Christ."[12]

The word "parliamentary" suggests a legislative body, with every meeting configured around a list of business items to be disposed of, beset by arguments on every proposal brought forward, with members seated on either side of a very divisive aisle, rallying around "pro" or "con" microphones. Many churches adhere to Robert's Rules of Order, which were created to keep meetings calm and orderly. There is a widespread misperception that churches are required to employ Robert's Rules of Order, that unless an idea is moved, seconded, debated, and voted upon, the church cannot act.[13]

This presumption of a parliamentary context for our church life may indeed maintain order and control, but does this come at the price of haggling with the Holy Spirit over every potential change in the agenda? Does the assumption of adversarial relations preclude the grace of conversation's give-and-receive-and-possibly-all-come-out-in-a-place-of-new-insight-and-concord?

We might want to pause here to consider the words "conversation," "discussion," "dialogue," and "debate." These words are frequently tossed like stones into the same rock tumbler, with the expectation that a matched set of polished gems will emerge. Each, however, is qualitatively unique.

Conversation—an informal exchange of thoughts, views, ideas, or information.

Discussion—an extended conversation that deals with a particular topic; an exchange of views.

Dialogue—a discussion where voices are held in a creative tension and/or a discussion intended to produce an agreement, rather than winners and losers.[14]

Debate—a discussion in which reasons are advanced for and against a proposal, after which a vote is usually taken.

Conversation happens in churches, spontaneously and with conviction. When we get into business sessions and committee meetings, though, we are apt to depart the informal realm, and enter into discussion. And there, like the king of Babylon, we stand "at the fork in the two roads" (Ezek. 21:21), deciding between dialogue or debate as the path to choose. Fortunately we need not turn, as did the king, to the more arcane tools of divination, but to one another and to a Google maps system that allows comparison of various routes to our destination. Is debate the only itinerary to take us to a vote? Is a vote necessarily our destination?

Here again it is important to distinguish between our covenant life as church and our existence as a corporation. When and how do we gather as a covenant community? How and when do we meet as people who are in covenant *and* are transacting business that is governed by state law?

For Conversation

(If your Local Church has a constitution and bylaws, look them over for their content, tone, and effect, then talk over the following questions.)

1. Do the constitution and bylaws provide a true statement and/or vision of your church's identity and purpose?

2. What is said about the worship and spiritual life of your Local Church?

3. What is said about church membership, its costs and joys? Who may join? When and how? Under what circumstances and by what processes can membership be revoked?

4. What is said about the calling or dismissing of a pastor? about the pastor's role, authority, and responsibilities?

5. What is said about the church's relationship with other settings of the United Church of Christ?

7

KEEPING COVENANT IN TIMES OF STRESS

FULFILLING THE VOW OF MEMBERSHIP

A vow of membership reflects a congregation's identity and its expectations of members. The vow of membership (which may appear in the constitution or bylaws) is the basis for assessing whether a member is keeping faith with such values as working for the advancement of the gospel, strengthening and building up the Body of Christ, honoring and respecting fellow members, participating "in the life and mission of this family of God's people, sharing regularly in the worship of God and enlisting in the work of this Local Church as it serves this community and the world"[1] Or whether—by intent or by circumstance—a member is polluting the well of the community's life, hampering the congregation's discipleship, endangering its health.

Almost every congregation faces or has faced a time when relationships were destroyed and mission hobbled by the focus on the needs or demands of one member and a few supporters. This could be a member with a severe personality disorder who increasingly plays out his internal drama amid the congregation. It could be a member who has given much to the church over many years and then becomes disgruntled at a change in policy or pastoral leadership, manifesting her displeasure throughout the church. Or it could be a pastor who suffers a mental collapse and does not recognize her inability to continue to serve. Times like these call for wise discernment of the well-being of the congregation and a firm grasp of the meanings of covenant and hospitality. Such situations are often excruciatingly energy-sapping, and time-ravaging. Few Local Church constitutions and bylaws contain procedures and designated leadership for identifying and addressing ruptures of covenant. But somewhere in the life and practice of each congregation should be an understanding of who is on alert for distress in the congregation's life in covenant and how covenantal distress will be met with clarity and compassion.

CONFLICT

Less grueling than the circumstances just described—but much more frequent—are the church conflicts that snag us in our walk with God and one another.

"How Organizations Function,"[2] a guide for congregations produced by the Office for Church Life and Leadership, delivers an analysis of the strata of the major components of church life. This analysis can be used to assess vitality, deal with conflict, and plan for growth. Beginning with the most easily observable stratum, then digging deeper we uncover:

> Our norms. These are the visible aspects of our life together: programs and actions, structure and relationships, policies, traditions, and practices, use of budget, treatment of members, etc.

> Our beliefs. These lie just below the visible norms and can be brought to the surface. Our beliefs are theological formulations, our stated purpose and goals, and our values—those things we assume are right and important. Our norms, we presume, grow out of and are expressive of our shared beliefs.

Our myth, or mythic identity. This is made up of the very basic assumptions which are at our core, our "life direction," the "largely unconscious values and processes by which we organize and define our experience. Myth is that which exists before belief can be articulated."[3]

At the level of myth we address the question, "Who are we?"

At the belief level the question is, not surprisingly, "What do we believe in?" Remember, this is not limited to beliefs that are explicitly theological, but includes precepts, virtues, and values.

At the observable surface level, the norm question is, "How do we live this out?" This question relies on an internal consistency between and among our beliefs and our myth. In other words, our programs, actions, structure, and relationships only make sense when there is coherence between them and what we believe, when there is coherence between what we believe and who we conceive ourselves to be.

This is who we are. This is what we believe. *Therefore* we structure and order ourselves, distribute our finances, and make public witness in this way at this time. Conflicts within a Local Church usually arise at the level of norms, with questions about program or budget, Christian education curriculum, number and time of worship services, and so forth. Often those conflicts are fairly easily resolved. When misgivings are voiced about a norm—when there is opposition to a visible action or public declaration—the connections between norms, beliefs, and mythic identity must be clarified through dialogue and exploration. Those with misgivings about a norm, a visible action, easily become alienated from the "we" at the heart of the covenant. They may "give up the fight and leave," or they may "attempt to subvert through withholding support or organizing for disruption."[4]

Whatever the source of discord, a church may reach the flash point where a Local Church leader says, "Maybe we should call in someone from the Conference." In those instances I often, as a Conference Minister, turned to the book *Getting to Yes*.[5] I value *Getting to Yes* for its straightforward approach to conflict. It assumes that there can be resolution of at-odds issues in ways acceptable to all. It calls for agreement on ground rules of conduct before dealing with the issues. The ground rules include both the time-honored injunctions to listen to one another; to speak only for oneself; to criticize positions, not individuals; and the ever-disarming regulation that only one person at a time is allowed to lose it. I've used those assumptions and ground rules mostly in one-session or two-session events that were assessments of the climate and situation. In those sessions members of the congregation could cool down the intensity of the conflict long enough to determine how best to address the turbulence for the long term.

Predictably, not every method of dealing with conflict is appropriate to every conflict in every Local Church. Not every consultant on conflict is equipped to work long-term with every congregation's covenantal and cultural realities.

As one church member recalls, "I was present during an attempt at conflict resolution in my small African-American UCC congregation. Our conflict consultant, referred to us from the Conference, applied a basically Euro-American method that seemed geared to a big church. It resulted in failure. The cultural translations were too difficult."

A pastor comments, "Our Filipino church fights are like none other. When conflict directed at me erupted in our congregation, I was grateful for the work of a Filipino consultant from another denomination that the Conference recommended, and for the authoritative presence of the Conference Minister, who is Anglo. The consultant could call us on our destructive patterns, and having the Conference Minister there let us know that our conflict wasn't an isolated event."

A member of a rural German-American Midwestern church reflects, "We've all been here for generations, and we know each other like family. You can't make a comment—whether to criticize or to praise—without calling up tons of experience and memories. But we do want to do the right thing, always. When we had trouble with our pastor, it helped a lot that someone from the Conference came in to listen to us, and to point out how we weren't listening to each other, and how we were letting old grudges interfere with the real issues. After we got through our own difficulties, we were able to make some good decisions about the pastor."

PASTOR AND CONGREGATION

The relationship between pastor and congregation is often delicate as well as strong. The delicacy comes with our polity, where the congregation calls its own pastor, and the pastor, as spiritual leader, is a member of the congregation who calls him or her. It can be difficult for the church and pastor to tread through the ambiguities of multiple unspoken expectations. The sustaining presence of a group of church members who uphold the enduring relationship of pastor and congregation may make things easier.

Whether it's known as the Pastor-Parish Committee, Minister's Aid Society, Pastoral Relations Committee, Pastoral Support Committee, or some variation thereof, this group "supports and maintains an open relationship between the [pastor] and members of the congregation. It helps the pastor and members of the church share ideas, hopes, dreams and interpretations of mission. It lets the pastor know what people in the church are thinking. It gives a framework for dealing with conflict creatively."[6] The UCC Leaders Box resource gives sound guidance as to the qualifications to be sought in members of the committee. These qualities include maturity, trustworthiness, confidentiality, visibility in the congregation, and the abilities to deal with conflict, to see multiple sides of a situation, and "to set clear boundaries with church members so that inappropriate secret-keeping is not an expectation."[7]

The pastoral relations committee is not a personnel committee. The personnel committee and the pastoral relations committee should not be the same committee, for their tasks are different. A personnel committee oversees and evaluates the effectiveness of the pastor's work and determines the pastor's financial compensation. The pastoral relations committee is concerned with supporting the relationship between pastor and congregation.

Drawing from experience with situations where the pastoral relations committee in fact generated conflict between pastors and congregations, I recommend that this committee not include members who are hostile to the pastor or who see their role as "keeping the pastor in line." Pastoral relations committee members must be selected based on their qualifications for the work of the committee. This means that there should not be bylaws that require certain church officers to serve on the committee by virtue of their office. Members of the pastoral relations committee must be known and trusted by both the congregation and the pastor.

How does your Local Church keep covenant in times of stress? What kinds of stress has your Local Church lived through? You can address those questions directly or through these more specific topics:

For Conversation

1. Does your congregation have a vow of membership or other statement of covenantal relationship with God and among the members? How is it worded—or how would you word it?

2. How does your church or would your church deal with conflict among the members?

3. How is the relationship between pastor and congregation maintained?

4. How does your church make decisions?

Ezekiel has this vision (See Ezek. 37). He's plunked down in the middle of a valley, and it's full of bones. In this place of desolation, of carnage, the bones silently sketch a plot line of disaster, of a catastrophe that swept down upon those who once lived in the valley and all who were traveling through the valley. It dropped them were they stood.

Ezekiel has this vision, of bones. Disconnected and strewn in chaos. And in this vision the voice of the Most High asks Ezekiel, "Can these bones live?" Ezekiel's response is frazzled, "Oh God, *you* know." But the Almighty presses on, directing Ezekiel to prophesy to the bones. Prophesy. Speak for God, *to the bones*!

Ezekiel was probably more than a little bewildered by the instructions. Nevertheless, he prophesies to the scattered bones, tells them that they shall live. He hears noise, rattling, and general commotion as the bones come together. The process of decomposition reverses. The bones reassemble; they reconnect to one another with sinews and ligaments. Muscles and flesh surround them and give them form and contour and mobility. "Now," God coaxes Ezekiel, "prophesy to the breath." Ezekiel does. The bones live. And Ezekiel makes his report to the people of Israel, "whose hope had perished."

On the Wednesday before Pentecost 2006, at the conclusion of a church meeting in Fresno, California, I read aloud this story from Ezekiel. Months before, an off-hand remark had passed between friends about College Community Congregational Church maybe "stealing" Zion's music director. That remark led into conversations about a union between these two UCC congregations. Weeks of visitation, discussion, and prayer ensued.

Zion was established in 1900 by Volga Germans,[8] whose ancestors had been brought to Russia by Catherine the Great to teach farming skills to Russian peasants. In 2006, Zion UCC's membership count was in serious decline. College Community Congregational UCC was fifty years old in 2006. From its beginning, College reached out to the wider community as a progressive expression of the gospel. Zion members initially had some hesitancy about joining an open and affirming congregation. But when they came to College Community for worship and fellowship the hospitality was so gracious that they realized "College Community is open and affirming of us, too!" Ultimately the two congregations discovered that their unity in Christ was more fundamental than any interpretations of Christian practice. The report from College Community was that there were more new people showing up at church than could be accounted for by the number of visitors from Zion. "We guess our new attitude of hospitality is a draw."

With words like "transformation" and "union" rightfully supplanting the more corporate-sounding word, "merger," a plan was finalized that late evening in late May. The plan had two parts. Zion would dissolve as a church and sell their building, retaining their historic baptismal font and their verdant contemporary stained glass windows depicting the creation. Then the one-time members of the former Zion UCC would join College Community UCC, bringing their cherished baptismal font and windows. Zion's history, tradition, and identity would bloom anew, and College Community would become a different church. (Another example of how those who were "them" yesterday are "us" today and "we" are forever changed.)

After the meeting ended, one solicitous member of Zion asked me, "Won't this be kind of hard on you, personally?"

"What do you mean?" I responded.

"Well, you're going to have to explain the loss of a church."

"Oh," I said, "I think we're going to have to come up with a new vocabulary and a new inventory system, because this will definitely be a new church."

When we turned to Ezekiel that night, those present reflected with honesty and clarity on how they had prophesied to one another, to the bones and to the breath. The prayer we eventually raised drew on the "who knows?" aspect of grace. Who knows? Who can imagine what lies ahead? "Can these bones live?" God asks. "Only you know," Ezekiel answers. "Only you."

So many—maybe all?—congregations face or will face jogs and detours along the course that they assume is the route provided by the Divine MapQuest. (Yes, yes, I know that MapQuest is antiquated technology; the reference is included intentionally.) This was true in 2006 for Zion and College Community. Yet the two churches were sustained as they moved out beyond their comfort zones in faithful obedience. The union of Zion and College Community came about through hospitality. Each had an abiding sense of engaging and welcoming the other, knowing that the other can be a source of insight into the ways and will of God. The union of College Community and Zion celebrates an incarnational understanding of covenant that insists we find ways to be together that are worthy of the One who comes to us in ways that are risky and self-giving. Grace was with them every step of the way.

PART III

The Wider Church

⁓

*We now proceed to part III, where we
will widen our exploration of covenant to
include the relationships between and
among Local Churches, Associations,
Conferences, and General Synod and its
affiliated and associated ministries.
We will study and question the ways in
which each setting of the United Church
of Christ acknowledges and engages the
"integrity and existence of the other units
of church life and their own legitimacy."[1]
We will reflect on the lapses of hospitality
that can occur within our church when we
come into contact those we perceive as
alien to us. We will face into the difficulty
posed when we find it awkward or
distasteful to use the pronoun "we"
to speak of our church in its entirety.*

8

LOVE ONE ANOTHER

"This is my commandment," Jesus said to his followers, "that you love one another as I have loved you" (John 15: 12).

It is comforting to note that the people who followed Jesus then, like the people who follow Jesus now, had not been handpicked with an eye toward making it easy for them to love one another. Those early disciples included men who were generations deep into the family fishing business and upwardly mobile types with Greek names; a revolutionary intent on freeing Israel from Roman oppression and a collaborator with Rome; a woman who gravitated toward theological matters and a woman who thrived on traditional household tasks. There were two pairs of brothers and one pair of sisters, whose presence doubtless complicated group life with their little in-jokes and sibling rivalries. These were the folks who were told to love one another. They hadn't even chosen to be part of a group. All they had signed up to do was follow Jesus. As individuals. And there they were, stuck with one another.

There is a scene at the end of the film *Places in the Heart* that baffled many movie reviewers. You might remember this saga set in Texas in 1935, starring Sally Field as the undauntable farm woman who survives poverty, natural disasters, and social scorn while helping and being helped by drifters, neighbors, and family. As the story line seems about to conclude, the action shifts to the interior of a rural church building. People are sitting in pews and singing hymns. A communion service is going on. It seems peaceful and predictable until, with a start, we notice that some of the congregation are people who died early in the movie. Avowed enemies are sitting next to one another, serving one another. Poor people and rich; black, brown, and white people; power brokers and outcasts—all are gathered together. "The film is great, but what is that ending all about?" one critic wrote in bewilderment.

"I'm an insurance agent and I know what it means," sputtered Bill Gregor, who was reading the review in the *Grand Rapids Press* before a church breakfast commenced at Smith Memorial UCC. "Well, sure," said fourteen-year-old Nolan Moore, "but you go to church."

You go to church. You know what it means to be part of an improbable community, connected in life and beyond death. You know about the welcome table, and the unlikely group that gathers there.

"You did not choose me, but I chose you," Jesus says. And you, and you, and you. The people who think and act just like you, *and* the people whose ideas are all out of kilter. The polished and the jangling. The courteous and the crude. And because of the One who chose us, we might just be able to move from being stuck with one another to sticking with each other, to, some fine day beyond the horizon of our most fervent eschatological imagining, being stuck on each other. Right now, though, it's enough to contend with the costs and joys of our covenantal relationship with God and one another within the familiar, if not always cozy, precinct of our Local Church. But, oh, wait—that might not, in fact, be enough for us in the United Church of Christ.

The basic unit of the life and organization of the United Church of Christ is, of course, the Local Church.[1] "Basic unit," however, is not the same as "only unit." Local Churches are themselves in covenant with God and with the other ecclesiastical bodies that make up the composite that is the United Church of Christ. In theory, each Local Church, Association, Conference, and national office or agency acknowledges and engages the "integrity and existence of the other units of church life and their own legitimacy"[2] in a relationship that is to be "highly interactive . . . a system of cross-initiatives and cross-influencings."[3]

And here is where Jesus' words function as an irritating pop-up reminder about hospitality. "You did not choose me, but I chose you," says our God, who is Love in Community, who "executes justice for the orphan and the widow, and who loves the strangers, providing them food and clothing" (Deut. 10:17–18). "And," it would not be untoward for the Holy One to point out, "even before I chose you for this covenant, I welcomed you, with all of creation, to the feast of life." This is radical hospitality. Radical, not just with the connotation of "extreme," but with the full vocabulary wallop of "rootage"—down to the roots of the cosmos, and at the root of the Almighty's identity.

Allegedly we are not strangers to one another among the settings of our church. But often, it seems, there is obliviousness,[4] wariness, or hostility between and among the bodies in our wider church covenantal relationship. That's where and when the pop-up intrudes, reminding us that not only prior to covenant, but also in the midst of covenant, hospitality is our ethic. Hospitality is all about expanding the definition of "we." Hospitality's code is openness to and care for those with whom we sojourn. The ethic of hospitality pushes us all and always to reform, restate, and celebrate the "we" that we are as the United Church of Christ, and to be gracious and compassionate in our common pursuit of the radical and redemptive call to follow Jesus.

Perhaps we wouldn't all enunciate the word "we" in tones as stark as those delivered at an interfaith service in San Francisco in 2008. It was the Saturday before Californians voted on marriage equality. Leaders of various religious traditions voiced prayers and read sacred texts at the vigil. The Buddhist monk who came to the lectern was tall and lean, austere in dress, plain and radiant of face, with close-cropped hair. She spoke clearly and pleasantly, without frills. "I will share a Buddhist teaching appropriate to the current situation," she said. "It is a very ancient teaching. This would be the contemporary translation: We're queer. We're here. Get used to it."

She then went on to elaborate on the Zen of it. We're queer. We're straight. We're warmongers. We're agents of peace. We're babies. We're centenarians. We're adolescents. We are all what we all are. And we need to get used to it. Own it, with the complete set of allusions from Acts 4: 32 where "everything they owned was held in common." Pitchforks, cookware, plumbing tools, books, clothes, and cable access. *And,* our Buddhist sister would press us—ever so gently—to consider, everything *is* owned in common: all the clattering, disparate, cacophonous elements of identity, trait, and spirit. Jealousy, meekness, pride, trust, phobia, diligence, left-handedness, right-handedness, highhandedness. All here, glittering and showering down like simulated snow, contained within the glass dome of our "self." All here in each human community. All here in "us." I heard this as an urging toward an attitude of hospitality to our own internal contradictions—"our own" as individuals and "our own" as a community of faith.

That attitude of hospitality lay beneath the process by which the Evangelical and Reformed Church and the Congregational Christian Churches reassembled themselves into a denominational unity.[5] They proceeded along an orderly course of votes and plans and constitutional drafts. The unsettledness of the underlying hospitality—the openness to widely divergent elements of faith, history, and practice—does not always break through the smooth surface of the minutes and reports as we read them in the twenty-first century. But the hospitality factor intrinsic to the movement toward becoming a united church was clear in the message to the churches from the Uniting General Synod in 1957. In that message the leaders of the new United Church of Christ were "fully aware that their union was something extraordinary in the history of Protestantism in the United States, a union of two denominations with different national and cultural origins, different church polity and intradenominational structures. . . ."[6] The message to the churches further "affirmed the conviction that they had come together for theological, indeed Christological reasons. . . ."[7] There was a keenness for a covenantal union that would rise above a corporate merger.

We can hear that dedication in the words written by James E. Wagner in 1945 when he was a member of the General Council of the Evangelical and Reformed Church:

> There was a general concern that the merger, if it is to be effected, must not be simply a superficial paper organization, a merger in form, but rather a union of mind and spirit on the part of two religious bodies which will have pushed beyond their divergent historic traditions and their present differences in organization and thought and found a higher level of oneness in devotion to Christ and His Church.[8]

Some years later Truman Douglass, one of the Congregational Christian architects of the union, expressed the conviction that

> Our great hope in this union is not that we and our churches shall be confirmed and established in our ways, but that we shall be shaken and thrust out into new ways, not mainly that our history and traditions shall be preserved and perpetuated but that by God's mercy we and our churches may be made a new creation fit for the service of [God's] will and purpose in our day.[9]

Those who brought about the union in 1957 looked forward to being able to say, "Those who were 'them' yesterday are 'us' today, and 'we' are forever changed." They were looking forward to a "sustained engagement" that would "eventually transform all parties to the transaction" while yielding a way of life that would take them and us "beyond our comfort zones."[10] They foresaw the spiritual/ecclesiastical equivalent of a chemical reaction, that is, the transformation of one set of substances to another, where the reactants are converted to something substantially different. Our founders' anticipation came through the awareness of a covenant that began with the

Most High calling an unlikely community into relationship, inciting us as a people to seek and to follow that Voice—and none other—over uncharted regions. Then, with our respective guards down, we are to extend to one another—to those now gathered and to those we encounter along the way—the welcome and hospitality that the Holy One extends to us.

Our constitution—our structural covenant—expects "each place of the United Church of Christ to covenant under the Spirit and it trusts the Spirit to act in each locus of the church, whether a local church, association or conference. Each part is accountable to the Head which is Christ and to the Spirit and thus we have the very creative tension of autonomous parts and mutual responsibility."[11] That synopsis of how our covenantal structure should function could have been the foundation for Article III of our constitution, "Covenantal Relations," when it was added in the revision of 2000. Positioned just after such constituting constitutional basics as "Name" and "Structure," and before any of the settings of the church are named, Article III is made up of these six statements:

- Within the United Church of Christ, the various expressions of the church relate to each other in a covenantal manner.

- Each expression of the church has responsibilities and rights in relation to the others, to the end that the whole church will seek God's will and be faithful to God's mission.

- Decisions are made in consultation and collaboration among the various parts of the structure.

- As members of the Body of Christ, each expression of the church is called upon to honor and respect the work and ministry of each other part.

- Each expression of the church listens, hears, and carefully considers the advice, counsel, and requests of others.

- In this covenant, the various expressions of the United Church of Christ seek to walk together in all God's ways.

The "expressions of the church" are the four organizational settings of the UCC: Local Churches, Associations, Conferences, and General Synod. The only elements of our life together that are "defined and regulated" by our constitution are those in the national setting: "General Synod, the United Church of Christ Board and those Covenanted Ministries, Affiliated Ministries, and Associated Ministries, as herein set forth, of the United Church of Christ which are related to the General Synod. . . . "[12] Everything else in our constitution is a "recommendation of relationships and procedures."

As we begin our survey of the constitutionally recommended relationships and procedures among the organizational settings of our church, and of our organizational structure itself, I want to advise you that this discussion may generate some frustration. That happened a great deal when students considered these topics in the classes I taught at the Pacific School of Religion.

Teachers can sense when they're being annoying. My moments of being annoying occurred most often when I responded to students' questions on procedures and structure. Whenever a student asked things like "How are Local Churches organized?" or "How does the Search and Call process operate?" I ended each explanation of structure or procedure with one or more of these disclaimers:

Each church does it differently.

It varies from Association to Association.

It differs from Conference to Conference.

And at least once a semester there would be an earnest request for "the UCC organizational chart." (That's "the" not "a".) Something neat and tidy, centered on an 8½-by-11-inch sheet of paper. A diagram where national councils and commissions and Covenanted Ministries, Conferences, Associations, and Local Churches possess internal processes and organization identical to their counterparts, and they're all connected by uniform up-and-down arrows.

The best depiction I was ever able to come up with involved three circular flat baskets of decreasing size. The largest basket, at the base, would hold fifty-five hundred or so multicolored marbles. Each gorgeous and unique marble would represent one Local Church. Struts emanating upward from the largest basket would support the other two. The middle basket would have thirty-eight bigger marbles, representing the thirty-eight Conferences. Most of the thirty-eight marbles would be marked to show three, six, nine, or however many Associations that Conference has; some, of course, would have no demarcations. The smallest basket would be the platform for a kind of molecular model made up maybe of those big chrome-plated shooter marbles to represent General Synod and the Covenanted Ministries and the United Church Board and their links to one another, with some orbiting bodies to represent the Affiliated and Associated Ministries of the United Church of Christ. One student sculpted this vision, which was artistically and schematically pleasing, while confirming the difficulty of a two-dimensional rendering of our system of organization.

9

REGIONAL ORGANIZATIONAL PATTERNS

ASSOCIATIONS AND CONFERENCES

Article VIII of our constitution, rather tellingly, lumps together Associations and Conferences. That is because the division of responsibilities between a Conference and its Associations (if there are Associations in the Conference) is not standardized.[1] It differs from Conference to Conference, and not all Conferences have Associations. And, although our constitution states that Associations and Conferences are "organized on a territorial basis,"[2] this is not always the case. Both the Association of Hawaiian Evangelical Churches and the Calvin Synod (Acting Conference) are nongeographically defined.[3]

Sometimes we hear the term "middle judicatory" applied to Conferences and/or Associations. "Middle judicatory" refers to an administrative structure that operates between local congregations and, for us, the widest setting of our church.[4] (In hierarchical churches the middle is positioned between local churches and the highest level of church structure.) According to our bylaws, Conferences and Associations definitely perform administrative functions. That is, Conferences and Associations handle, manage, and supervise those in their care and the issues that come to them from the other settings of the church. An Association "receives and acts upon business referred to it by its Local Churches, its Conference, the General Synod, and other bodies."[5] Conferences receive and act upon "business, requests, counsel, and references from Local Churches, Associations, the General Synod, and other bodies."[6] In addition, Conferences choose "delegates and alternate delegates to the General Synod,"[7] and collect and pass along churches' financial contributions to the mission of the wider church.[8]

The attributes and duties of Associations and of Conferences, constitutionally speaking, are as follows, with some inherent blurring of the distinctions between Conferences and Associations. Also included are some criticisms and some accolades for the ministries of Associations and Conferences.

ASSOCIATIONS

An Association is made up of the Local Churches within that Association's geographic boundaries (or other parameters) and those authorized ministers[9] whose standing is in that Association. Associations themselves are members of Conferences. Associations are constitutionally charged with the responsibilities of determining and certifying to the standing of Local Churches, authorizing persons for ministry, and terminating ministerial standing.

More generally, Associations are concerned with the welfare of all the churches;[10] seek "ways and means to assist Local Churches when they are undergoing unusual difficulties requiring help beyond their own resources;[11] offer "encouragement, guidance, and assistance" to churches that are newly forming or exploring affiliation with the United Church of Christ;[12] and the Association, "with the counsel of the Conference, receives Local Churches into the United Church of Christ."[13]

CONFERENCES

A Conference is made up of Associations, which are made up of Local Churches and the authorized ministers whose standing is in those Associations. Or, when there are no Associations in a Conference, the Conference is made up of congregations and the authorized ministers whose standing is in that Conference. In some Conferences there are Associations, but ministerial standing is held in the Conference. Which means that in all cases, Conferences are made up of Local Churches and authorized ministers (who are members of Local Churches).

In our organizational structure where every setting of the church is autonomous, "the conference is the body best able to call forth mutual accountability. The conference is situated, by virtue of choosing the delegates to Synod, as a link between the local congregations and the national setting of the church."[14]

Many Conference administrative functions are detailed in UCC Bylaws, paragraphs 170–78. The bylaws then offer examples of what Conferences might undertake "in the interest of the Local Churches" and to "strengthen the witness of the United Church of Christ. " These include "rendering counsel to Local Churches and ministers in situations calling for help beyond their own resources," and "rendering an advisory service to Local Churches and to ministers with reference to pastoral placement." In addition, a "Conference maintains ecumenical and interfaith relations within its boundaries with other Christian fellowships to the end that mutual understanding and cooperation may be advanced."[15]

THE MINISTRIES OF ASSOCIATIONS AND CONFERENCES

There is a UCC folk saying that Congregations congregate, Associations associate, and Conferences confer. The congregations congregating part is obvious—it happens; usually once or more per week. But do Associations associate? To associate is to make connections, to unify, to keep company with. There has been much moaning across our church about "how many weekend afternoons I've squandered in terminally dull Association meetings going over budgets and hearing reports of the business of committees."

"I agreed to be the Association Moderator," said UCC pastor Janice Steele, "but only if we would do a lot less business and a lot more church

in the Sacramento Valley Association." Certainly the constitutionally conferred responsibilities for the authorization and oversight of congregations
and ministers are generally regarded as "doing church," but much of the
work of a Committee on Ministry is carried out in confidence; not every
Association comes together frequently for the authorization of a minister;
and, it has been said, Associations chronically avoid the responsibility to
determine, confer, and certify to the standing of Local Churches.[16] However, there are some examples of Associations associating, as well as overseeing and authorizing Local Churches.

For a time the Eastern Association of the Minnesota Conference conducted Covenantal visits with churches. "To borrow Randi Walker's teach-
ings on episcopé,[17] the visits were to be an intrusion of love into business
as usual,"[18] says David McMahill, who was Eastern Association Minister.

The Illinois South Conference's Church and Ministry team is very active in the oversight of churches. "They meet monthly to discuss
churches in transition and to share their concerns about the congregations in their Region. More than once they have decided to do an
intervention in a church that is clearly having trouble,"[19] Conference
Minister Sheldon Culver states.

The Chicago Metropolitan Association has a ministry team focused on
the oversight and nurture of congregations. Association Minister Vertie
Powers relates that team's first undertakings were "to determine what
churches are still in covenant and affiliated with the Association and how
we can be a pastoral presence as we share in services of celebration and
farewell." Next will be "to address ethical behavior of congregations"
and offer "UCC history and polity designed for local congregations."[20]

Tauo'a Head, chair of the Authorization of Churches section of his Conference's Committee on Ministry, reports that "In Northern California

Nevada we have worked very closely with new churches and the Associations where they are forming. There are churches from many cultures and traditions who explore membership in the United Church of
Christ. We want the Association to get to know and appreciate each
new church's culture, theology, and structure, just as the churches learn
about the UCC. We want to make sure there is an Association Committee of Support for each new church, a member of the Association
who is the new church's primary contact for any question and is there
for them, and, if the new church wishes, a mentor of the same ethnic
group as the new church."[21]

According to the adage cited above, Conferences confer. Conferences
are the sites and the settings to consult, to talk things over, deliberate, put
heads together, and hash out.

It is not the vocation of Conferences to be bureaucracies. That is, the
administrative tasks of a Conference, though they be many, are not meant
to be self-perpetuating and an end in themselves. Conference websites
make known the ways in which Conferences see themselves as expressions
of our church. The Iowa and Northern California Nevada Conferences
have used the phrase, "a congregation of congregations." The Minnesota
Conference has referred to itself as a "Transformational Regional Body."
The Pennsylvania Northwest Conference has used the term "Covenant
Community." The Kansas Oklahoma Conference has said, "We are a communion of historic and emerging congregations sharing the Good News
of the Gospel of Jesus Christ." These self-descriptions emphasize relationships, and being a manifestation of the church.

CONFERENCE MINISTERS

Conference Ministers are not mentioned in our constitution. This omission
doesn't necessarily make conference ministry unconstitutional, just nonconstitutional, or maybe extra-consitutional. This in-between-and-around-

the-edges course of ministry provides its practitioners with much leeway. As Randi Walker states, the Conference Minister is the "one officer who can call both the Local Churches and the national setting of the church into accountability for their covenants with each other, to ask whether the church at all its levels is being faithful, and to provide oversight of the mission activities of the whole UCC."[22] The actual position description of Conference Minister differs from Conference to Conference, of course. Conferences describe their Conference Minister as spiritual leader, pastor to pastors, chief executive officer, administrator, visionary, or any combination of those and other roles. But there has been accord among Conference Ministers around the notion that the Conference Minister sets the tone for the Conference.

Clyde Steckel suggests a rewording of what is now paragraph 171 of the UCC Bylaws, under Article II. The paragraph states, "A Conference employs such salaried personnel as its program may require." He proposes this revision:

> A Conference calls a Conference Minister to exercise pastoral oversight of its programs and the local communities of ministry within its boundaries. A Conference employs such other salaried personnel as its programs may require.[23]

The authority of Conference Ministers, which plainly does not derive from our organizational chart, is well-illustrated by retired Conference Minister Steve Gray. He recalls,

> When I attended the "Judicatory Executives and Bishops" week-long training event sponsored by Alban Institute prior to beginning my call as a Conference Minister, two new Episcopal Bishops were complaining that while they were given constitutional authority, they rarely could use it, or—if they did—it was largely ignored. Gil Rendle, the event's leader, said to them, "See that UCC Conference Minister and Disciples Regional Minister

sitting over there? (pointing to me and a Disciples colleague). Their authority is not constitutional. It is earned authority. And once it is earned, they can and do use it in ways you Episcopalians can only imagine!"[24]

The nonconstitutional Conference Ministers, by the way, gather regularly as the Council of Conference Ministers, which is, by inference, an extraconstitutional body, although it appears in paragraph 291 of our bylaws.[25]

For Conversation
(Seek your Conference Minister's comments or ask your Conference Minister, or other Association or Conference staff, to join in this conversation.)

1. Would we be strengthened and enlivened as Associations or Conferences if we became more relational, more visitational, more churchy? If our Association (or Conference) councils and executive committees conceived of themselves more as guides or elders for their geographic clustering of churches and ministers than as officers of an organization?

2. Or is this already happening in your Conference/Association?

3. Has your Association/Conference had the opportunity to work with congregations seeking to affiliate with the United Church of Christ or with newly forming congregations?

4. Does your Conference/Association take an active role in the oversight of congregations?

5. How does your Conference define or describe itself?

6. How does Clyde Steckel's articulation of what a Conference calls a Conference Minister to do resonate with you? What tone does your Conference Minister set?

IO

NATIONAL ORGANIZATIONAL PATTERNS

GENERAL SYNOD—THE MEETING

"Synod" is a word that is commonly covered with etymological dust-bunnies. It does not often insert itself into casual conversation. Most denominations that employ the term use it in the sense of a council convened to discuss and decide issues of doctrine or administration. For some denominations the synod is the governing body.[1] Our UCC configuration includes General Synod among the autonomous parts with mutual responsibilities. This usage is atypical in the religious world. It compounds the obscurity of "synod," the word, and General Synod, the reality.

In pre-2013 editions of our constitution, the definition of General Synod opened with a functional description: The General Synod is the representative body of the United Church of Christ and is composed of voting delegates, as described in the Bylaws of the United Church of Christ. . . .[2] It went on to cover the quorum for doing business. Use of a term like "representative body" in the same breath with "voting delegates," followed close behind by references to "quorum" and "national headquarters" kind of solidifies some erroneous impressions about General Synod. It is easy to infer that General Synod is a legislative body with policy-setting powers for the whole church, and that our national offices are our command post, functioning as mission control for Local Churches, Associations, and Conferences.

In the 2013 version of the constitution two new sentences took the leadoff position for Article IX, paragraph 53. First, "The General Synod is the gathering of a faith community representative of the wider church to listen for and discern the call of God to the United Church of Christ."[3] To which I can only say, "Hallelujah! God be praised!" Here is overt acknowledgement that General Synod is a faith community, and that Synod is called together not as a legislative body, nor solely as a corporation, but as church.

That new first sentence sharpens the identity of General Synod and announces why we gather as Synod. The new second sentence went on to make a covenantally based declaration of what we do as Synod: "The General Synod deliberates, discerns, and identifies the mission of the wider church of the United Church of Christ in God's world and receives and offers suggestions, invitations, challenges, and assistance in covenant with Local Churches, Conferences, and other settings as they engage in mission together."

Notwithstanding the straightforward wording of our constitution on the "free and voluntary" nature of the "relationships which the Local Churches, Associations, Conferences and ministers sustain with the General Synod,"[4] the connection of Local Churches, Associations, Conferences and ministers to General Synod is often the most fraught with discord. One Conference Minister spoke for many when he said,

I think I will scream if I ever again have to say that "General Synod does not speak *for* the Church, it speaks *to* the Church." For the framers of the UCC this concept was key. It allowed a setting to debate the ethical issues of the day and respond without committing Local Churches and their members to positions that, at first, they might not be likely to support. It maintained the autonomy of Local Churches and sought to lead them by persuasion rather than an authoritative national vote. This allowed the UCC to address issues that most other Christian bodies would avoid due to the conflict their discussion would engender. It was a great idea. But the people don't seem to get it. Numbers of clergy get it, but it scares them to death. The press don't get it and the culture doesn't get it. Actions of national church bodies are understood only one way: as top down exercises. . . . At its best, General Synod is interpreted by even our most loyal churches as something "they" do "over there" that has little relationship to their congregation.[5]

Susan E. Davies, who co-chaired the Faith and Order Commission of the National Council of Churches from 2000 to 2007, contributed this United Church of Christ perspective on General Synod to the ecumenical conversation on denominational authority (note that she uses the word "pronouncement" in its general sense of an authoritative declaration, rather than in UCC-specific terminology that would imply another set of observations regarding "resolutions"):

Pronouncements, to which we seem addicted in both the Conference and General Synod settings, are generated by local congregations, Associations, and Conferences. Boards of the national ministries (which are elective bodies) may generate pronouncements, but employees at any level may not generate them. These statements must have a prescribed number of signatures or supporting bodies, as well as accompanying theological and biblical rationales, in order to be considered by their respective bodies. Much energy, often too much energy, has been spent on the writing, supporting, debating, and passing or defeating of such pronouncements. Their generation and approval is one of the major ways in which the United Church of Christ carries on its internal political and theological battles.

The pronouncements, at whatever level, have no binding authority on local churches. When adopted by a regional body of the church, pronouncements have status as policy which that body then follows within its own life. Similarly, the biennial meetings of the General Synod produce many pronouncements which serve as policy for the national setting of the church but do not have binding authority on the life of conferences, associations or local congregations. Such General Synod pronouncements do affect the life of the other settings indirectly by changing the types of resources (human, financial and material) which are available to those parts of the body. The reverse is also true: General Synod Pronouncements often affect the financial resources forwarded from congregations to the regional and national settings.[6]

Before beginning conversation on the nature of General Synod, the meeting, you might want to read through the opening paragraph of Article IX of our constitution and the section on the Meetings of the General Synod. You might then venture out into the bylaws, Article III, reading from the Meetings of the General Synod through the Committees of the General Synod. Then you could go to the home page for the upcoming or most recent Synod (http://www.ucc.org/synod/), noting the welcome, the theme, pre-events, presenters and preachers, calendar, business, activities, general tone.

Then you could go to http://www.ucc.org/synod/, noting the welcome, the theme, pre-events, presenters, preachers, calendar, business, activities, and general tone for the next or most recent General Synod. Click "Materials" to find the standing rules and review or get acquainted with the various types of formal motions and the particulars on pronouncements and resolutions.

You might want to look back at past General Synods. Click the "Archive" button on the General Synod page (or use the search function at http://ucc.org/) for General Synod standing rules to find those from other Synods and to check out the resolutions and pronouncements for a particular Synod. There are separate links on the "Archive" page to alphabetical, chronological, and subject indexes of the resolutions, pronouncements, and proposals for action at http://www.ucc.org/synod/resolutions/ABCINDEX.pdf.

Browse through General Synod minutes at http://rescarta.ucc.org/jsp/RcWebBrowse.jsp.

For Conversation
(Expand your study group, if necessary, so that it includes at least one person who has attended General Synod(s), whether as a delegate or in another capacity.)

1. Was there, at the Synod(s) you attended, a shared understanding that you had "gathered as a faith community to listen for and discern the call of God to the United Church of Christ"? How and when did you pick this up?

2. How widely understood or accepted is it that General Synod does not speak *for* our church, but speaks *to* our church, and that the pronouncements and resolutions passed by General Synod have no binding authority on Local Churches, Associations, or Conferences?

3. What—from the website, your experience, or the UCC Constitution and Bylaws—attracts you to Synod? What is off-putting? Where do you find hospitality and covenant embodied?

Susan E. Davies observed that General Synod Pronouncements and Resolutions sometimes affect the other settings of the church, either by changing the types of resources that are available to the other settings or by prompting Local Churches to decrease the financial contributions sent to the national setting, and to Conferences/Associations. There is another financial element in pronouncements and resolutions that also bears consideration. Historically, a statement on funding has appeared at the end of every proposed pronouncement or resolution. In former times it was the catchphrase "subject to availability of funds." In more recent years the wording has been made more descriptive: "Funding for the implementation of this resolution will be made in accordance with the overall mandates of the affected agencies and the funds available." Some refer to it as an escape clause. It saves us from the need to raise money as General Synod in order to make sure that what we have resolved in that setting is seen through to conclusion. But General Synod actions requiring human, material, or financial resources are thus obliged to rely upon the goodwill, commitment, largesse, capacity of budget or designated funds, and overall mandates of the "affected agencies."

For Conversation

1. Go over a General Synod pronouncement or resolution observing which units of the church are called upon to carry out the actions for implementation. How do you imagine—or know—that funding issues affected this resolution/pronouncement?

2. What actions of General Synod have prompted Local Churches to decrease—or increase—their giving to the national setting of our church?

Finally, I would like to pick up on Susan Davies' assertion that the generation and approval of resolutions and pronouncements is one of the major ways in we carry on our internal political and theological battles. Pronouncements and resolutions sometimes generate or reflect clashes over issues of authority and power—the politics—within our church. Pronouncements and resolutions sometimes generate or reflect clashes over theological issues within our church. Let's look at a specific instance, the General Synod resolutions surrounding the publication of *The New Century Hymnal*. There we will find conflict around theological questions and internal politics.

The hymnal was published in 1995, in time for General Synod 20. It had been a long time coming. It was launched by a resolution in 1977 when General Synod 11, by vote of affirmation, "directed the Executive Council to create a new official hymnal using language that is inclusive. . . ."[7] The theological concern was inclusive language.[8] Procedurally, the United Church Board for Homeland Ministries took on the responsibility for staffing, funding, and publishing because it—not the Executive Council—had the resources to do so, and because the production of a hymnal "that expresses the faith of the church in the unchanging Jesus Christ in words and images of our time"[9] was consistent with its mission.

At that point in our church life—pre-dating Covenanted Ministries and the United Church of Christ Board—there were, in the national setting, two kinds of instrumentalities. There were the instrumentalities that had been established by the General Synod of the United Church of Christ (Established Instrumentalities). And there were the instrumentalities that had existed as autonomous (underline autonomous) mission boards before the United Church of Christ came into being. The latter—the United Church Board for Homeland Ministries and the United Church Board for World Ministries—were called Recognized Instrumentalities because they had been recognized by our church at its inception. An Established Instrumentality was to act "in accordance with . . . instructions given it from time to time by General Synod,"[10] with its ministries and programs funded through the General Synod budgeting process. The Board for Homeland Ministries, however, as a Recognized Instrumentality, administered its own program and financial affairs.[11] Having its own substantial sources of income from endowments and investments, it received minimal funding through the General Synod budgeting process.

In October 1989 the Board of Directors of the Board for Homeland Ministries appointed an advisory Hymnal Committee. The advisory committee held meetings for three years in churches across the country and at the national offices. As recounted by UCC pastor James Crawford, chair of the committee,

> At its meetings and at thirty-five public forums the committee, in conversation with United Church of Christ Local Church members, considered hymns celebrating a diversity of thematic

emphases. . . . As a corollary to the hymnal forums, a churchwide research project that ran from the summer of 1990 through the summer of 1991 sought information from every Local Church in the denomination: "What do you sing? What do you want to sing? In a new hymnal, what might be a help or a hindrance?"[12]

After the advisory Hymnal Committee completed its work, the Board for Homeland Ministries Board of Directors appointed an editorial panel to carry out the next stage of the hymnal development.

When General Synod 19 convened in 1993 a sampler of the hymns was already in circulation throughout the church. Reactions to the sampler—and to the hymnal it presaged—were spirited. For many in our church this new hymnal was awaited as "the contribution of the United Church of Christ to the larger quest of the universal church to praise God faithfully in each generation."[13] For others the collection of hymns was taken as an affront and a desecration. These were theological controversies.

On July 19, 1993, General Synod 19 adopted a resolution "recommending that the Editorial Committee restore the word 'Lord' (with balancing metaphors where possible) to those hymns originally using it in reference to Jesus." This resolution had theological and polity components. Initially the proposed resolution "directed" the Editorial Committee to restore the word "Lord" with reference to Jesus. However, Thomas Dipko, then Executive Vice-President of the United Church Board for Homeland Ministries, reminded the General Synod that General Synod could not appropriately "direct" a Recognized Instrumentality to take an action. Some who were present booed at this reminder,[14] in apparent dissatisfaction with the relationship between the Recognized Instrumentalities and General Synod.

After the vote on the resolution was taken, Thomas Dipko was granted a moment of personal privilege during which he said,

> We certainly will do all we can to take to heart what counsel you have offered. At the same time, theologically and out of the integrity of . . . those . . . responsible for this assignment, we must

respect the gifts and consciences of the corporate members and the Board of Directors of the United Church Board for Homeland Ministries. . . .[15]

The next day at Synod, after Bible study and announcements of election results and offering totals, Paul Sherry, President of the church, spoke of the "difficult issues Synod dealt with and the pain that some people felt" after the discussions on the hymnal, and offered a prayer for healing.[16] Next came speak-outs on many topics, followed by a demonstration intended to express concern "regarding the vote taken on the hymnal."[17] Then, after a few more items of business, Donald Freeman, a member of the Executive Council, offered an apology to the General Synod delegates and to Thomas Dipko, stating that the Executive Council, which served as the Business Committee for General Synod,

> had inadvertently placed Rev. Dipko in an extremely awkward situation regarding the relationship of the United Church Board for Homeland Ministries to General Synod and the appropriate language to be used in covenant polity [and] should have alerted delegates to the Issue.[18]

The apology served to underscore the reality that at that time General Synod could only give directives to the Established Instrumentalities—the instrumentalities that the General Synod had established—not to the two Recognized Instrumentalities. Many present at the Synod, though, heard Thomas Dipko's reminder about appropriate wording for the resolution and his statement about respecting "the gifts and consciences of the corporate members and the Board of Directors of the United Church Board for Homeland Ministries" as an indication of a political battle in the making, that is, a controversy regarding authority and power. Some heard in Thomas Dipko's stated openness to "do all we can to take to heart what counsel you have offered" an example of autonomy in a covenantal relationship, what Donald Freeman later wrote about as the "non-transferable responsibility" of each setting of the church to discern and respond to the call of God to it—God's will and way for it—in its time and place."[19]

The pain to which President Paul Sherry referred affected those who demonstrated against the vote seeking restoration of the word "Lord" to familiar hymns and those who opposed inclusive language for God. Both were theological concerns. As it worked out, the Editorial Panel decided to retain the use of "Lord" with reference to Jesus, in what came to be known as "first verse memory bank lines" of hymns. The theological controversy at General Synod, though, brought *The New Century Hymnal* to the attention of the public media in sometimes distorted ways. Interviewed on a radio talk show after the hymnal's publication, one Conference Minister faced a rash of negative comments from the host, whose information on the hymnal seemed not to have come from primary sources.

"You even took the word 'Lord' totally out of the hymnal! How can you justify that?" the host demanded.

"Perhaps," the Conference Minister responded, "you might want to open the copy of *The New Century Hymnal* that you have in front of you and turn to hymn #472. You and I could sing from it together, 'Precious Lord, Take My Hand.'"

After the publication of *The New Century Hymnal* many Local Churches, Associations, and Conferences made decisions to use it as their primary hymnal. Some added it to their collection of worship resources, "not getting rid of the other hymnals on the shelf, but starting a whole new shelf."[20] Some decided against using it. For others, the topic never came up.

One of the recurring statements of adverse reaction to the new hymnal was "They're trying to cram this down our throats." Another reaction was reported by William Imes, a former pastor of First United Church of Christ in Pomeroy, Iowa. He couldn't be present for the congregation's 125th anniversary celebration in 1998. So he stopped by to visit later in the year and was warmly greeted. As it was with most communities in Northwest Iowa, Pomeroy's population had decreased, and the median age had increased. These changes were, predictably, reflected in the composition of the congregation. Meanwhile the church's solid brick architecture and high central pulpit still stood proudly, like the congregation, rooted in the Evangelical and Reformed tradition. At worship that Sunday morning, William Imes admittedly had one minor jab of surprise as the congregation stood for the opening hymn and he found *The New Century Hymnal* in the pew rack. The surprise passed quickly. He thought he knew why it was there. His interpretation was confirmed by members of the congregation during the coffee hour. "Of course we use *The New Century Hymnal*. It's the new one from the denomination."[21]

For Conversation

1. How did issues of authority, autonomy, covenant, and hospitality intertwine with or cross over with theological issues in the development of *The New Century Hymnal*? Have you seen this happen with other resolutions or pronouncements? Did the Board for Homeland Ministries carry out its nontransferable responsibility in covenantal consultation with other settings of the church? Was there honor and respect shown for the work and ministry of each expression of our church?

2. Do you think that the phrase "they're cramming it down our throats" was more a rejection of inclusive language or a perception of the relationship among the settings of our church? Who was "they" and who was "we" in that statement?

3. Do you think the prompt adoption of *The New Century Hymnal* by First UCC, Pomeroy, Iowa, was more demonstrative of the congregation's affirmation for inclusive language or of their understanding of their relationship to the national setting of the United Church of Christ?

4. Who or what was the "you" that the Conference Minister appeared to represent to the talk show host? What issues were raised in that interchange, below the surface of allegation and refutation?

GENERAL SYNOD—THE GOVERNANCE

Here we come upon the elements of, and the relationships in, our church life that are defined and regulated by our constitution and bylaws—not just recommended. Those would be all the aspects of the national setting of our church, starting with General Synod and continuing through those bodies that are related to General Synod: the United Church of Christ Board, Covenanted Ministries, Affiliated Ministries, and Associated Ministries.[22]

Our constitution defines and regulates General Synod—both the meeting and the olio of "other stuff" that make up General Synod's powers and responsibilities.[23] Those powers and responsibilities and the ways in which they are carried out are the governance of the national setting of our church. General Synod as governance derives from General Synod, the meeting. It is important to remember that the word "governance" in this context does not mean that General Synod exercises authority over the other settings of the church. When we speak of General Synod in terms of governance, we're talking only about the ministries and structure of our national setting.

To acquaint—or reacquaint—yourself with the governance of the national setting of our church, you can refer to the section "Powers and Responsibilities of General Synod" in Article IX of our constitution, and the articles "United Church of Christ Board," "Covenanted Ministries," "Officers," and "Affiliated and Associated Ministries."[24] The following questions, suggestions, and observations may help guide and apply your reading and generate conversation on the interrelationships among these Synod-related bodies.

- Get an overview of the breadth of General Synod's powers and responsibilities. Does anything stand out to you? Surprise you? Raise questions?

- The United Church of Christ Board is responsible for policies relating to the mission of the United Church of Christ in its national setting. It shall support the on-going work of the General Synod through its various ministries, planning for and encouraging cooperation among those ministries, with Local Churches, Associations, and Conferences, and with other expressions of the Church which contribute to and embody God's mission in Jesus Christ.[25] The Board was established in 2013, replacing the previous national structure of separate and separately governed boards of directors for each Covenanted Ministry. Commenting on what has been notable about the transition to "unified governance," in the national setting of our church, Executive Minister for Wider Church Ministries James Moos says that it constantly "necessitates further covenantal work . . . we must always ask one another, 'What's your vision?'"[26]

- What do you expect of the Covenanted Ministries and of the United Church of Christ Board? Do these expectations differ significantly from the constitutional descriptions? Look for parallels between the constitutional description of the Covenanted Ministries[27] and the intent expressed in the Preamble to our constitution to make our common witness in Christ more effective.

- How do the Covenanted Ministries relate to General Synod? What implications for our life together do you see in the statement that General Synod may, from time to time, delegate or assign responsibilities to a Covenanted Ministry?[28]

- The Collegium of Officers came into being with the structural changes adopted by General Synod in 1999, as the national setting of our church moved from eleven instrumentalities to four covenanted ministries. Composed of the officers of the church meeting as peers, with the General Minister and President as presiding officer, the Collegium's responsibilities have included leadership for mission programming and the implementation of General Synod actions, along with attending to the quality of relationships among the United Church Board and the Covenanted Ministries and fostering a climate of respect, collaboration, and collegiality among various expressions of the church. In 2015 the United Church Board proposed a constitutional change that would name only the General Minister and President as an officer of the church, with "such other officers as the General Synod may from time to time determine."[29] The vote at General Synod did not carry the proposed change, but conversation throughout the church was to follow before further discussion at General Synod in 2017. What is the current configuration of officers of our church? How do the officers of our church relate to one another, to General Synod, to the Covenanted Ministries, and to the United Church of Christ Board?

■ What makes an Affiliated Ministry an Affiliated Ministry and an Associated Ministry an Associated Ministry? How does each relate to General Synod?[30]

■ General Synod is to "maintain ecumenical and interfaith relations to the end that mutual understanding and cooperation may be advanced"[31] and to "encourage conversations with other communions and when appropriate to authorize and guide negotiations with them, looking toward formal union."[32] Seeking formal union has not been so much our inclination in recent decades. Karen Georgia Thompson, UCC Minister for Ecumenical and Interfaith Relations, affirms the commitment to church unity, while pointing out, "The merging of denominations does not create unity. We must ask, 'What does unity mean?' How does church unity rely upon an understanding that 'Church has a Capital C; Faith has a Capital F'"?[33]

■ Do you have a sense of how the interrelationships and the responsibilities described in the constitution since 2013 are working out? What difficulties do you see or imagine? Have there been new adaptations made since the publication of this book?

To recap, it's General Synod—both the meeting and the governance—that is regulated by our constitution, along with the relationships within the national setting of our church. The relationships of Local Churches, Associations, and Conferences with General Synod are unregulated, free, voluntary, and fairly easy to overlook, until they call out for attention. The call may come from the public sphere or from within the church or both, as in the following instance.

In 1991, at General Synod 18, I was installed as the Executive Director of the Coordinating Center for Women in Church and Society, and thereafter moved into my office at 700 Prospect Avenue, Cleveland. In 1990, the Coordinating Center's Assembly had generated a proposed resolution for General Synod on the negative stereotyping of Native Americans in sports. Synod passed the resolution in 1991. As a consequence my public welcome to Cleveland came in the sports section of the Cleveland newspaper *The Plain Dealer*. With sensitivity to the interests of the local professional baseball team, a local sports columnist dubbed me, as well as several other members of our national staff, a "leg-breaker." At public meetings and church forums there were many subsequent fruitful conversations about the resolution. Long-time Cleveland baseball fans who were devoted to their mascot (Chief Wahoo), church members with varying degrees of fondness for the mascot, and people who appreciated the General Synod resolution joined in. Regrettably, the *Plain Dealer* sports writer had drawn a line of demarcation separating good Clevelanders who cherished Chief Wahoo from those who were set on the path of unprovoked iconoclasm. That division prevailed in the civic consciousness. Cordiality faltered.

Sharon Weiss and Elizabeth Hosbach, lifelong residents of the Cleveland area, joined the staff of the Coordinating Center for Women just after General Synod in 1991. Many of their friends and family were ardent baseball fans. They both received scornful comments regarding the actions and values of their new employer. They handled the tensions with good humor and valuable insights.

Early the following year, not long after the publication of his book *The Once and Future Church*, Loren Mead, founder of the Alban Institute, was the featured presenter at a gathering of UCC Conference Ministers, instrumentality executives, and seminary presidents. The focus of the gathering was the role of the wider church in post-Christian culture. It was probably not Loren Mead's intention, but our national staff left with the impression that their role in the post-Christian era was, in his vision, restricted to serving as providers of resources to Local Churches, as requested by Local Churches. I brought this premise back to our next CCW staff meeting. Sharon Weiss and Elizabeth Hosbach countered immediately with, "No, the national setting of the church has to do more than produce the resources that churches think they want. Look at the whole Chief Wahoo thing" and "Our churches in Ohio would never have requested materials on negative stereotyping of Native Americans. We had to hear that issue through voices raised at General Synod and the responsibilities assigned to instrumentalities."

Their perception of the wider church, living in autonomy and in covenant, was revealed in those comments. They saw clearly that each setting of our church exists for mission and participates in being the church,[34] "to the end that the whole church will seek God's will and be faithful to God's mission."[35] Oh, and that "mission refuses to accept reality as it is . . . its purpose is to transform reality."[36]

II

COVENANTAL RELATIONSHIPS DELINEATED BUT NOT DICTATED BY CONSTITUTION AND BYLAWS

THERE ARE TIMES, I AM SURE, WHEN ANY OR ALL OF US MIGHT PREFER A more structured relationship among our autonomous settings. We might be soothed by something more precise than recommended procedures. We might, like my former students, uphold the notion that each Conference, Association, and Local Church should possess internal processes and organization identical to its counterparts. But that quest is like the attempt to design a clear and uncomplicated nametag for use at an extended family reunion, where a designation like "Cousin Hattie," while accurate, is limited in scope and potentially misleading. There's more to our free and voluntary relationships than what an organizational chart—or a constitution—can get across.

And we might well mention here that our free and voluntary relationships extend beyond the United Church of Christ. As a church we also are in a free and voluntary relationship with the Christian Church (Disciples of Christ).[1] Our constitution includes Article VII, "Recognition and Reconciliation of the Ordained Ministries of the United Church of Christ and the Christian Church (Disciples of Christ)." Our bylaws make reference to Common Global Ministries "in joint venture"[2] and to the members of the Christian Church (Disciples of Christ) who are members of the United Church of Christ Board. But there is nothing more exact about how this ecumenical partnership is to play out with Local Churches, Associations, and Conferences.[3] It's free and voluntary.

So here we are in the wider church. We are all members of Local Churches, and our Local Churches are members of Associations where there are Associations (unless we're authorized ministers who are members of non-UCC churches). Conferences are made up of Local Churches and authorized ministers with standing in that Conference or in one of the Associations that make up the Conference. Conferences send delegates to General Synod (the meeting), so the delegates represent the Conferences, rather than their Associations or Local Churches. Local Church members serve and lead Associations, Conferences, and General Synod—both the meeting and the governance. Members of the Disciples of Christ also serve on the United Church of Christ Board. (Take a breath.) Structurally, things can get messy.[4]

There are, conceivably, jarring intersections or overlaps of our identities and allegiances. These may be mitigated or accentuated by the honor and respect expected of us regarding the work and ministry of each expression of the church.[5] There are, admittedly, shortcomings in the areas of listening for, hearing, and carefully considering the advice, counsel, and requests of all settings of the church, much less making decisions in consultation and collaboration.

Take these situations cited by lay leaders, pastors, Conference/Association and national staff when asked, "What is it about our life together as a church that makes you crazy?"

- Lack of Local Churches' accountability to the wider church coupled with Associations' (or Conferences') indifference to the health and standing of their member churches.

- Associations that "have become little more than regulatory bodies guiding potential ministers through the ordination process or disciplining those who have gone astray."[6]

- Conferences that retain for use in their Conference portions of special offerings intended for wider distribution.

- Covenanted Ministries that launch programs without advance notification to Conferences or consultation regarding possible pitfalls, fallout, or inaccurate assumptions.

- Local Churches that suffer from chronic über-autonomy, where nothing in the history, practice, or life experience of any other congregation or setting of the church is relevant to the present particularity of that one Local Church. Symptoms include defining this Local Church by stating what it is not; only giving to missions it determines on its own to be worthy of support; rejecting call agreements with pastors in favor of employment contracts; calling pastors who don't really care for "all that denominational stuff" and who, when they move on, leave the Local Church foundering as it seeks to discover who it is now that it is no longer the Church of Pastor Mark or the Congregation of Rev. Debbie.

- Authorized ministers who remain in good standing with us while publicly denouncing "the UCC" with seemingly malicious intent and convincing Local Churches that their only lifeline is an escape from the denomination.

- Mistrust of any authority.[7] Mistrust may be revealed when we say that each expression of the church is accountable only to itself and then keep watch to make sure no one crosses the constitutionally granted line. This contributes to the condition where "due process has become increasingly a matter of orthodox belief in the United Church of Christ, but always couched in the language of covenant relations."[8]

- "Even though we talk so much about covenant, when push comes to shove we default to autonomy. . . . We mostly like each other—

but we don't really trust each other—at least not enough to graciously lay aside our own preferences in the interest of the whole."[9]

This might be a good moment, as we contemplate the shortcomings in our free and voluntary relationships, to direct our thoughts toward some of the biblical aspects of covenantal relationships. I'm thinking along the lines of commitment, companionship, and the unexpected. Consider these two biblical narratives. The first features Ruth; the second involves Noah; but the Almighty is definitely in the starring role.

It was a famine that had brought Naomi and her husband and two sons from Israel to Moab. Now, after ten years of living as refugees, Naomi is a widow; her sons have died; and word has reached her that there is again food in Israel; so she prepares to return to her homeland (see Ruth 1:15–18).

Quite remarkably, her two daughters-in-law—women of Moab, both of them—want to accompany her on the dangerous journey to a land foreign to them and a community potentially hostile to them. Naomi urges them to go back to their mothers' houses and find new husbands, have babies. One daughter-in-law acquiesces, but Ruth insists, "Do not press me to leave you or to turn back from following you! Where you will go, I will go." In the face of Ruth's persistence Naomi raises no further objections.

Ruth's dedication to Naomi was love and loyalty totally over the top. In English we translate it "where you go, I will go," because we feel sappy operating without the verbal markers for past, present, and future. But it is the tumbling out of Hebrew words without tenses that discloses the always, for all time, indelible way covenant shapes our lives. The assemblage of words is "where you go, I go," "where you lodge, I lodge," "your people, my people," "your God, my God."

"Don't make me to leave you," Ruth says, with "leave" connoting a change of one's primary allegiance. "You and I are in covenant, Naomi. You weren't just part of a package deal, the bonus miles on my frequent flyer account. Our family bond doesn't dissolve with the death of your son. Where you go, I go. Your God, my God."

In Ruth's story we find commitment that is neither required nor customary, that can verge on the unreasonable, that is not easily shed, but embeds in the heart, placing relationship above personal inclination or comfort and collective well-being above all else.

In Noah's story we have the prequel to the epic of covenant. We all rally around the rainbow scene, of course, stirred by the symbol of peace and hope and reconciliation of differences borne aloft to the heavens. But to locate God's motivation for setting covenant rolling in the first place, we need to bring to mind the glowering menace that preceded the full-spectrum visual display of covenant. We need to recall that the Blessed One might have had some anger management issues. Not that you could really blame the Author of the Universe, the Source of Life, for being more than just a little ticked off at the way this marvel of a planet—resplendent with gorgeousness, replete with luscious foods, abundant with water and sunlight, populated by a dizzying diversity of plant and animal life—had been corrupted.

Before infusing the rainbow with covenantal meaning, the Most High saw that "the wickedness of humankind was great in the earth, and that every inclination of the thoughts of their hearts was only evil continually." And the Holy One said, "I am sorry that I made humankind on the earth, and it grieves me to my heart (Gen. 6:5–6) . . . for the earth is filled with violence because of them" . . . (Gen. 6:13).

Then the grief boiled up and erupted in a lava flow of rage so that God declared, "I am going to bring a flood of waters on the earth, to destroy from under heaven all flesh in which is the breath of life; everything that is on the earth shall die" (Gen. 6:17).

And God, of course, had and has the capacity to do all that. And God did it. Total destruction. Except for Noah and his family and the representation of biodiversity embodied by the animals that obligingly processed onto the ark.

When the storm was over and the flood had receded, God gave Noah and his family a blessing and a responsibility after they got off the boat, saying, "You're in charge now on earth, be fruitful, and I don't want any more violence—no violence to animals, no violence to other human beings" (Gen. 9:1–7). After which God declared, "I am establishing my covenant with you and your descendants after you, and with every living creature that is with you. Never again shall I destroy the earth, never again shall I destroy all living creatures. Never again" (Gen. 9: 8–17). "My bow is in the sky, and whenever I see it I will remember my covenant that is between me and you and every living creature of all flesh" (Gen. 9:15).

Here we see God pointing to the rainbow and saying, "This is my reminder to myself to keep in check my incalculable power." God is out there, risking limitation. Unilaterally and unconditionally the Almighty has pledged to not wipe us out. By any means. This is not a loop-hole ridden contract to be parsed later in some celestial court with the Holy One chiding, "Now, now, I said I wouldn't destroy by flood, I didn't say anything about fire or virus." No. It's all "I am your God and you are my people." "Sure, I've been royally mad—as only I can be. And with good reason. But I can't quite give up on you all. Stick with me, Noah, and you'll be safe" (Gen. 9:9–17).

This is the summons to relationship, to life, to life in relationship with *the* creative, compassionate, and redemptive force field of the universe. Noah's response is the choice of the way of life over the path to death. Every time we go back to that first overture from the Holy One to Noah, we garner more understanding of the full-tilt outlandishness of covenant. Going beyond what is expected, making commitments that are neither required nor customary, placing relationship above personal inclination, and collective well-being above all else.

In seeking the ways in which those free and voluntary relationships among the various expressions of our church meld, mesh, transition, transmute, and transform into covenant, we must not become unduly entangled with articles and paragraphs, definitions, powers, restrictions, recommendations, or due process. Our covenanted relationship of autonomous units of church life must be first of all a relationship, "a relationship delineated but not regulated by a constitution and by-laws."[10] Delineated, but not regulated. Neither required nor customary. Not easily shed. Risky. Non-sensical. For the sake of the whole. Covenantal.

Our constitution and its bylaws are a guide and a safety net, steering us toward covenant and keeping us from precipitous missteps along the way. The totality of our covenantal relationship cannot be penned in our constitution and bylaws, nor is it penned up therein. This certainty was tested and questioned even while the first constitution for our church was being prepared.

The delegates to the Adjourned Meeting of the Second General Synod, in 1960, had already spent nine and a half hours in sessions considering the proposed constitution and bylaws, with another day yet to come, when they broke from deliberations to celebrate communion. Everett Babcock, who was then the Chief Executive Officer of the Ohio Conference of the Congregational Christian Churches, provided the meditation. His testament rested on the communion table like a fine linen cloth, woven from words of faith, insight, and truth about the function of constitutions, the bedrock of formulas of agreement, and the nature of covenant.

> The spirit of the Church, the Christ of the Church, the Church that is not of the world is governed not by a constitution but by the new covenant. The constitution has to do with the affairs of the United Church as it relates to the world of institutions, situations, causes, society. There is nothing in the constitution about love or sacrifice or devotion. There is nothing in the constitution about humility, or meekness, or redemption or forgiveness. The covenant is to be fearless and bold in proclaiming the Gospel, but at the same time to confess our weakness, fear and sin. The covenant includes the promise that those who would be first must be last, that we shall love our enemies, bless them that curse us, do good to them that hate us, pray for them that despitefully use

and persecute us. May the promises of God to us and our commitment to Him become the true agreement among us, and between us, the United Church of Christ, and our Lord.[11]

On the brink of adopting a constitution for the church, that same meeting heard this statement from Co-President Fred Hoskins:

> Just because the word constitution makes some wary and others enthusiastic is sufficient reason for all of us to determine that we shall not go further on the basis of unexamined and uncriticized premises about what a constitution is. Already it is evident that some are evaluating the proposed constitutions of a political unit, say the State of Ohio. It is equally evident that some are judging the proposed constitution by standards that would be acceptable in judging a constitution for a luncheon club. We have to do with a constitution proposed for the United Church of Christ, a part of the body of our risen Lord.
>
> The word constitution derives from two Latin roots which combined mean stand together. The word carries the idea of what it is that gives a body unity. My unabridged dictionary offers "character" as the synonym for constitution. A constitution exposes the character of a body."[12]

For Conversation

1. How does our constitution expose our character?

2. Have we, in our wider church life, turned too easily and too often to the guarantees and restrictions of rights and powers, and shied away from the tumult and transformation of covenant? Have we—or when have we—as a church invoked covenant when we were really appealing for due process?

3. What internal contradictions can you identify within the United Church of Christ? Are there actions, organizations, or opinions

within our church that you just cannot "own"? To what can you point and say, "This is who we are: The United Church of Christ." When do you say of a UCC body, "Why did they go and do *that*?" What happens to shift "we" to "they" or "they" to "we?"

4. As the wider church, how can we differentiate between those times when we are gathered as corporation or as community? Can we, in all settings, be both institution and incarnation?

12

WHEN DEMOCRATIC PROCESS IS NOT ENOUGH

OUR COVENANTAL POLITY POINTS US TOWARD THE PEOPLE-IN-COMMUNITY /interdependence/*ubuntu*[1]-tinged development of the root word *polis*. Yet we know in our linguistic bones that *polis* is also the basis of "politics" and "political." The political course takes us through the byways of debates, the great chasms of pro and con votes, and the treacherous detours around fortified positions. It is often the default itinerary presented by our UCC polity GPS as we drive toward the destination of our calling to seek God's will and be faithful to God's mission. In other words, we go to a lot of meetings if we participate in the life of our wider church. We vote. We follow due process. This is because "In the theory of the United Church of Christ, all authority in the church lies, under Christ, in the church's members. This established it as democratic in polity, though it is not so in the ordinary secular sense, since the authority of the people is secondary to that of the living Christ. . . .[2]" This is our way of seeking the guidance of the Holy Spirit in an environment of two concurrent acknowledgements: Jesus Christ is the head of the church; and decision-making power rests with and blusters forth from all of us who are members. This was seen by our founders as "the best way to translate Christian love into the framework of government."[3]

But, as UCC pastor and author Tony Robinson observes, "denominational meetings often . . . look and operate more like democracy and democratic decision-making than like Christian discernment."[4] Or, as noted in the UCC Leaders Box, "We may have reached a point at which we are effective in governing and politicking as a democratic organization but feel that God did not vote."[5] I certainly find myself more than yearning for a loosening of preoccupation with democratic process. I want us to make a headlong charge into unreasonable covenant, to lace every gathering with hospitality to one another's backgrounds and perspectives, and take part in dialogue throughout our church that welcomes the ideas of the other and risks our transformation. We weren't quite there yet when the proposed resolution "Toward Unified Governance for the National Setting of the United Church of Christ" was brought to General Synod 27 in 2009, after months of discussion in all the expressions of our church.

Pre-Synod presentations of the proposal were marked by references to streamlining and resources, and called forth questions about representation and under-representation of Conferences and of racial/ethnic constituency groups. The presentations met with predictable rejoinders such as, "so what?" or "what structure?" There was also some suspicion regarding the dilution of the strength of the Covenanted Ministries. By the time the unified governance proposal was introduced at General Synod in 2009, positions on the proposal had solidified through debates and e-mail blasts. We were probably way beyond earshot of hospitality's prompting us to look forward to considering and learning from one another. During the most rancorous sessions, both at Synod and before Synod, proponents, critics, and questioners of the structure proposal added ballast to their arguments by drawing upon shared values. Proponents, critics, and questioners all talked of "being one," "honoring diversity," "valuing all members," and "covenantal responsibility."

The resolution adopted at the 2009 General Synod affirmed "the principle of a Unified Governing Board as the basic governance structure of the national setting of the United Church of Christ"[6] and requested that the Executive Council and the Covenanted Ministry Boards bring the actual proposal for restructure to General Synod in 2011. It may be instructive to examine the succession of events at the 2009 Synod related to the vote:

> The resolution that came to the whole voting body began with the acknowledgement that this "dialogue regarding governance has surfaced historical and present tensions regarding issues of race and ethnicity in our denomination . . . we cannot heal relational issues through governance discussions, but we do need to move toward reconciliation. . . ."[7]
>
> After the vote, the Moderator called for the next agenda item. A delegate then reminded the Moderator that there had been an earlier request for prayer for those who were disappointed by the resolution as voted, and that request had not been acknowledged.[8]
>
> The Moderator invited a member of the working group that had drafted the unified governance proposal to offer prayer.[9]
>
> "The Moderator accepted an additional request for two minutes to hear the concerns of those who had been opposed to the Single Governance Resolution."[10]
>
> Another delegate "respectfully requested the house revisit the action related to the Single Governance resolution for the purpose of submitting a minority resolution."[11]
>
> The Moderator "ruled the request out of order in that a minority motion has to be noticed prior to the vote on the resolution.[12]
>
> "There followed a demonstration protesting the adoption of the resolution, 'Toward Unified Governance for the National Setting of the United Church of Christ.'"[13]

When there is urgency compelling structural change, when there is a General Synod agenda to be advanced, when appellations as loaded and as variant as "turf war" and "justice issue" are applied to all positions in a controversy, we can be pretty sure that there are hurts on all sides too raw for salving through the democratic process of move, second, move to amend, vote on amendment, restate, debate, vote. What we lack in our democratic process is human dialogue.

Dialogue is a sign and a strengthener of covenant and hospitality. We seem to know that, and we are led to use the word more frequently than precisely. We often claim to have dialogue, when what we actually have is a one-time forum for expressing opposing views.

As stated toward the end of chapter 6, there is a qualitative difference among these four words that describe verbal interactions:

Conversation—an informal exchange of thoughts, views, ideas, or information.

Discussion—an extended conversation that deals with a particular topic; an exchange of views.

Dialogue—a discussion where voices are held in a creative tension. "Dialogue is collaborative: two or more sides work together toward common understanding."[14]

Debate—a discussion in which reasons are advanced for and against a proposal, after which a vote is usually taken.

Salting the definitions of the three "D" words with inferred intentions and motivations, a secular developer of workplace environments writes:

Debate is combative and seeks to be victorious; it wants to express itself and say it is better than you.

Discussion can be described as debate trying to play nice. Much like debate, it is interested in advocating its viewpoints and challenging those of others.

Dialogue, on the other hand, seeks to find a shared connection. It is not concerned with winning or losing, rather it aspires to listen more deeply, understand more fully, and build a collective point of view. When the diversity of personality and opinion present moments of conflict and tension, dialogue steps in and mediates the conversation back to a renewed sense of connection.[15]

At meetings of the wider church, it seems that we may have unduly restricted ourselves to debate mode, which assumes opposing stands. We thereby constrict the arteries that would allow the flow of dialogue throughout our body. We may have some discussion, but seldom is there the space or the patience at any one meeting for the dialogue that holds voices in a creative tension, that listens and aspires to "build a collective point of view," that "mediates the conversation back to a renewed sense of connection."

"Dialogue," Walter Brueggemann writes, "is not merely a strategy, but it is a practice that is congruent with our deepest nature, made as we are in the image of a dialogic God."[16] Our process, as UCC Philippines theologian Eleazar Fernandez stresses, "is not only a tool, it is a way of walking; the walking itself must reveal the vision."[17]

Maybe we could come up with a new way of walking in our decision-making, a new template for the presentation of matters for consideration by the wider church. Something less alienating and divisive than the current format for Resolutions and Pronouncements. Something more inviting of dialogue than of nitpicking, argument, and defense. Something that would shed the "whereases" and "be it resolveds" in favor of language more consistent with a covenantal body than a legislative session.

Could groups of UCC members come to General Synod, to Conference and Association meetings, with clear statements of the subjects for which they seek the support of, or action by, the wider church? Statements that cite the faith basis that prompts their request and specify what they are asking of whom in the wider church? Could we then take counsel together within reach of hospitality's prompting us to look forward to considering and learning from the other, and dialogue's aspiration to listen more deeply, understand more fully, and build a collective point of view? We could, then, file off the adversarial edges of business sessions by converting "pro" and "con," microphones to something like "affirmations" and "concerns." And so we might, in any gathered manifestation of the church, be more disposed to argue in love than engage in debate over issues. We might be more inclined to walk in hospitality and covenant.

For Conversation

1. Recall and describe a meeting you have attended in the setting of our wider church—Association, Conference, national—where there was a definite sense of Christian discernment, a seeking of consensus of the Spirit.

2. Recall and describe a meeting you have attended in the setting of our wider church—Association, Conference, national—that looked and operated more like democracy and democratic decision-making than like Christian discernment.

3. Were there differences between the two types of meetings in outcome, ethos, or reason for gathering?

4. In a 2004 lecture, then UCC General Minister and President John Thomas expressed regret that "we have inadequate structures for corporate discernment in our life together."[18] What kind of structures for corporate discernment can you envision for—or have you used in—our life together as a church that is "democratic in polity," but not "in the ordinary secular sense"?

5. Where in our wider church life have we cultivated the transformative bonds of covenant? Where have we employed dialogue that supplants indifference and overcomes hurt?

Our enterprise of living in covenant as a wider church only takes wings—only leaves the beaten down pedantic political path—when it is invigorated with a hefty spiking of hospitality. With hospitality we can shake off our wariness as to whether and how covenantal polity and autonomous agency can cohabit. Hospitality alleviates the kind of strain described so often by UCC sage Valerie Russell, who cautioned all seekers after the resolving of troublesome differences, "The lion may lie down with the lamb, but one of them isn't going to get much sleep." With an attitude of hospitality to those with whom we sojourn, we might, even during face-offs, cease to look upon one another as menacing or menaced, but as being of the same fold.

PART IV

Ministry

⌒

*In this fourth part we will examine God's call to
"the whole Church and every member to participate
in and extend the ministry of Jesus Christ."*[1]
*We will consider those ministries in and on behalf
of the church for which authorization is required.*[2]
*We will hear from members of Committees on
Ministry and Conference and Association staff
about the complexities of authorized ministry and
the processes of authorization and oversight of
ministry for the good of Christ's church—which
may be our most visible and most used proving
ground for the workability of covenant and
hospitality. We will also look at how congregations
call ministers and how ministers seek calls.*

*The final chapter in this part, chapter 17,
is a glossary of terms used in the authorization
and oversight of ministry in the UCC.*

13

AUTHORIZATION AND OVERSIGHT OF MINISTRY
Strengthening the Covenant

THE 1986 EDITION OF THE *MANUAL ON MINISTRY* MADE A GREAT IMPACT on our church.[1] Produced by the Office for Church Life and Leadership (OCLL), it set forth things that now seem basic and self-evident. Things like the requirement that an authorized minister[2] be a member of a Local Church. Or the prescription for regular reviews of authorized ministers with their Committees on Ministry.* The publication of these provisions initially brought forth much groaning and some alarm. "What do they think they're doing?" people asked. "They want to jerk our standing!" some ministers cried. In 1986 I was an Associate Conference Minister for the Indiana-Kentucky Conference. I spent two days with other Conference staff and chairs of Committees on Ministry in a training session on the

---

*A Committee on Ministry (COM) may be known in your Association or Conference as Committee on the Ministry, or Church and Ministry Committee, or it may be a team or a board. (See the chapter 17 glossary to help with this and other terms that are used in the authorization and oversight of ministry in the UCC.)

Manual on Ministry (MOM 1986) led by Bill Hulteen of the OCLL staff. Afterward I settled in to field phone calls and contemplate the intensity of the initial and instantaneous resistance to the revised manual. Looking back, I marvel that reactions spread so quickly throughout the church with no assist from e-mail, texts, Facebook posts, or Twitter hashtags like #jerkourstanding.

The mindset of keen caution, watchful prudence, and skepticism that greeted MOM 1986 was, of course, lodged in our polity, the way we are organized. We have an ardor for autonomy. We know that authorization for ministry happens in Associations and Conferences. We are vigilant about the possible imposition of anything that might slow, stifle, enmesh, or limit us in carrying out those responsibilities. This is especially true if the imposition is perceived as "coming down from on high," that is, from the national setting of our church.

After a while people concluded that our church had not morphed into hierarchical mode. Associations and Conferences were still responsible for authorization of ministry. Confidence grew that each Association/Conference could determine how or if it wished to adopt and adapt that which was offered in the *Manual on Ministry.* Reluctance gave way to "let's see how it works." People came to see that the new manual assembled and gave form to practices that aligned with what we value in ministry. Committees on Ministry studied MOM 1986 for its principles and norms, identified familiar elements and practices, adjusted and adopted its recommendations. This was a major step for our church in placing autonomy within the context of covenant. Associations and Conferences used MOM 1986 as an aid to carry out their nontransferable responsibilities for the authorization and oversight of ministers. Because it was developed from knowledge and working procedures gleaned from Associations, Conferences, Local Churches, authorized ministers, and seminaries, MOM 1986 provided a means for each Association and Conference to carry out its responsibilities "in consultation with all other settings to discern God's will and way for its own time and place."[3]

MOM 1986 emphasized accountability, which is a big part of covenant. "Accountability" had always been there in the lexicon of our life together, but it was often passed over as we scanned through the alphabetical listing for "autonomy" farther down the page. With MOM 1986, language about covenant and the accountability of partners in authorization became familiar to us in the UCC.

In 2002 section 8 of the *Manual on Ministry* introduced "oversight" (*episcope*) into our discourse on ministry. This strengthened the concept of accountability. Oversight was present in MOM 1986 in the section "Review and Discipline of Persons Authorized for Ministry,"[4] but "The Oversight of Ministries Authorized by the United Church of Christ" made oversight explicit and theological.

> "Oversight" . . . conveys the commitment of the United Church of Christ to nurture those called to ministerial leadership, while at the same time we hold one another to account for the gospel of Jesus Christ and the ministry of the whole people of God. The word "oversight" is used here because it expresses much . . . that is conveyed by the Greek word *episcopé*. . . . The core meaning of the Greek word *episcopé* implies stepping back to view a situation or circumstance as a whole. It is to see something or someone fully and completely. Such complete understanding of a person or situation enables compassion in pastoral care. It also provides for supervision that is informed as well as merciful and just.[5]

Episcopé "brings the view of the larger church into the local scene; it conveys a sense of the whole to its parts."[6] Allowing that larger view into the work of autonomous Associations and Conferences is an act of hospitality. It benefits all the partners who authorize ministry, the authorized ministers, and our church as a whole. It strengthens our life in covenant.

The oversight and authorization of ministries is our most visible and most effective proving ground for the workability of covenant and hospitality. It is the endeavor that repeatedly brings together all settings of our church. As one Conference Minister said, "The whole dance of discernment, authorization, and oversight that occurs between that committee [on ministry], the authorized ministers, and all settings of the church is a wonder to behold."[7] Our dance performance is sometimes ungainly, but, surprisingly often, we carry it out with dexterity, balance, and grace. Let's look into the steps and the missteps we take in authorization and oversight of ministry with an eye toward covenant and hospitality.

14

AUTHORIZATION OF MINISTRY

MINISTRY STARTS WITH A CALL. CALLS TO MINISTRY COME TO US IN many different ways. Take God's call to Moses and that whole thing with the burning bush.

"Moses, Moses," the voice of the Holy One booms into the pastoral quiet surrounding Mt. Horeb. "Uh, here I am," Moses responds. "OK, says God, "it's *me*, Creator of the Universe, Author of Life, Hope of your ancestors. I'm here. The very ground is holy. Take off your shoes." [Which, as I understand it, is a kind of more dignified way of saying, "I'm gonna knock your socks off."]

Moses covers his eyes. From that humble position, Moses listens. He listens as God says, "I have seen the misery of my people; I have heard their cries from the shackles of their slavery; and I'm here to do something about it. I will deliver them from their captors and give them a good and bountiful land, flowing with milk and honey. So come, I will send you to Pharaoh to bring my people out of captivity."

"Huh? Wait a minute. You're gonna send *me*, to do *what*? Who am I to do this?"

"It's OK. I'm sending you. I'll be with you."

Or we might find ourselves being tugged and shoved over a longer period of time until reluctantly, but ultimately courageously, we pull on our royal robes—or our liturgical gear—as Esther did, for just such a time as this.

For some of us the call is more along the line of Samuel's. It comes in the chill of night, through the fog of dreams, troubling us out of sleep. Groggy, stumbling around, trying to respond, we don't have the slightest clue who is summoning us. But, in due course, after we pester and disturb the people around us for a while, we get the message. God is calling. Security code entered. Password verified.

For others the call is more serene, a growing awareness that comes to light over the course of years.

Jesus told his disciples, "I'm sending you out like lambs in the midst of wolves." Travel light. Move quickly. There's a sense of urgency in his words—and danger. Dispatching the disciples two by two calls up visions of the buddy system in swimming. It hints at deep waters and treacherous undertow, and suggests the wisdom of companionship and accountability in ministry.

We truly don't know what's in store for us when we are called into a particular ministry. Most all of us wrestle with our call to ministry to some degree. There is often an element of "You're gonna send *me*, to do *what?* Who am I to do this?" And we look for the assurance that "It's *ok. I'm* sending you. I'll be with you."

In our church we affirm that "God calls the whole church and every member to participate in and extend the ministry of Jesus Christ."[1] This principle was doubtless the source of a question posed at the gathering of women in authorized ministries right before the 1995 General Synod. The event was kind of a one-day mini-retreat in a ballroom at the Oakland Convention Center. Ordained, commissioned, and licensed women reflected on their vocations, sang, prayed, read scripture, and told stories. As so often happens at church gatherings, there came a moment when the plan or premise for the event was questioned. "Why did you call this a gathering of 'Women in Authorized Ministries'? I mean, really, is there such a thing as an *un*authorized ministry?" The short answer is, yes, there are "unauthorized" ministries. But "unauthorized" should not be confused with "inauthentic." Nor should the weight and consequence of anyone's call ever be underestimated. However, not every call to ministry is a call to authorized ministry. Authorization by an Association or Conference is not necessary for every ministry.

H. Richard Niebuhr, UCC theological ethicist and pastor from our Evangelical and Reformed tradition, identified four facets of the call to ministry. "The call to be a Christian is the beginning of any call to ministry . . ."[2] Some also receive and respond to a "secret call" (sometimes known as the nagging part) where God invites individuals to serve in a church occupation. This can open into a "providential call" where the faith community recognizes and tests the gifts, talents, and traits of personality that reveal the direction of a person's ministry and guides the individual in preparation for service to the church. In the United Church of Christ the providential call happens within a Covenant of Discernment. The Covenant of Discernment involves the member who is in discernment of call, the member's Local Church, and the Committee on Ministry of the Association or Conference. The "ecclesiastical call" occurs when an Association or Conference authorizes a Member in Discernment for ministry. Authorization for ministry in the United Church of Christ does not occur until the person to be authorized accepts a specific call from a congregation or other calling body to take on a particular position as an authorized minister.

Authorized ministers in the United Church of Christ represent the United Church of Christ and maintain ongoing covenant with their Local Church, their calling body, and the wider church. We will go into the covenantal relationships that distinguish authorized ministry as part IV continues. We begin with the Covenant of Discernment.

THE COVENANT OF DISCERNMENT

Discernment of call starts in a Local Church. Whenever someone who is being subjected to the "secret call" thinks they maybe are moving toward authorized ministry and wants to check out what they have to do in order to be authorized for ministry in our church, we ask a refreshingly clear-cut first question: Are you a member of a local UCC church? No one becomes a Member in Discernment without first being a Local Church member. It is necessary to be a member of that Local Church for a period of time long enough to allow the congregation to get to know the person. Only when they know one another can the congregation eventually join with a member and the Committee on Ministry in a Covenant of Discernment.[3] Many Associations/Conferences set a minimum of one year's membership in one Local Church before a Covenant of Discernment is appropriate. If you, as a Member in Discernment, move from one congregation to another you must start the process over again. This is not about "jumping through hoops," with the implication of forced and senseless performance. It's about establishing a covenantal relationship to discern vocation and gifts for ministry. Authorized ministry "is both communal and individual, and the call to authorized ministry is always discerned with others."[4]

In a Covenant of Discernment the primary task is to discern—that is, to detect, understand, and distinguish this member's call. Questions emerge: "To what ministry is God calling this person at this time?" "Does this particular ministry require authorization?" "If so, what form of authorization?" "What preparation is needed for this ministry?" In a Covenant of Discernment there is "continuing openness to a variety of outcomes, even ones that are unexpected."[5] "No single preparation process or path will be appropriate for every candidate. . . . The formation process may take several years."[6]

The need for discernment in exploration of call was lifted up in the the Ministry Issues pronouncement of 2005.[7] Our previous process of authorization for ministry supported and counseled people ("Students in Care") who were studying theology in preparation for ordained ministry. That earlier process presupposed that the call to ministry had already been settled between God and the Student in Care. The change in phrasing from "Student in Care" to "Member in Discernment" denotes the change in outlook.

Preparation for ordained ministry in the in-care process meant "meeting uniform requirements according to an agreed-upon schedule."[8] If a Committee on Ministry found it necessary to say, "no," or "not yet," or "not ordination," to someone who had met all the requirements, the disappointed student in care might flash the badge of entitlement with questions and claims based on due process. These examples illustrate some of those situations.

CONCERN OF THE COMMITTEE	COMPLAINT OF THE STUDENT IN CARE
We're not sure that the ministry to which this student is called is a ministry of word and sacrament.	What do you mean, I should be commissioned instead of ordained?
The person can't articulate her own theology. We don't know what she believes. We want to hear more.	You just don't like my theology.
We are not sure we can recommend for ordination someone whose only church experience has been with the church in which he grew up and now serves as a licensed minister.	I've been the licensed pastor of my church for nine years. I deserve to be ordained without going to seminary. It's one of the multiple paths to ordination.

Covenant, however, is not so much about due process. There is fluidity and openness in a Covenant of Discernment. The partners are committed to arrive at a mutual understanding of the Member in Discernment's call and the preparation necessary for that call, for the good of the church and in response to the needs of the church.

The move to covenants of discernment was a move to respond more fully to the needs of the church. In that move there is the recognition that a college and seminary degree do not always ensure fitness for ordination and that preparation for ministry "must serve unity and mission in the wider Church, and meet particular needs in local settings."[9] There is also the recognition that "in a multi-cultural and diversified culture in which the tasks of ministry for the accomplishment of God's mission are increasingly complex, we must further define and develop multiple paths that lead to and support ordained ministry."[10]

The transition to a process of discernment of call and formation for ministry has been underway for several years. There have been obstacles and rewards along the way as well as a strengthened sense of the responsibilities of Committees on Ministry and Local Churches as partners in the Covenant of Discernment. These Conference staff speak from distinct settings, and speak for many across the church.

"The assumption that someone entering an MID process will end the process by becoming ordained is fading, slowly." (David Gaewski, Conference Minister, New York Conference)

"The Associations here in the Mass Conference have been shifting into an intentional use of the concepts of formation (is this candidate ready for Ordination based on the criteria in the Marks of Faithful and Effective Ministers)11 and discernment (is Ordained ministry really where this candidate is being called?). . . . This has resulted in a "heightened sense that the Committee on Ministry is the crucial hub that monitors and maintains that work with all candidates." (Don Remick, Associate Conference Minister, Massachusetts Conference)

"In the Southeast Conference, the Ministries Issues Pronouncement allowed us for the first time to determine that non-traditional folk were ordainable and I feel the SE Conference gained some of the most gifted ordained ministers serving in their churches today. The rigor of the assessment of readiness for ministry using the Pronouncement was frankly much greater than in the in-care system, and on the part of all candidates I saw a significant increase in the quality of the reflection in preparation for ministry. . . ." (Timothy Downs, retired Conference Minister, Southeast Conference.)

In a Covenant of Discernment there is the general expectation that "'The Marks of Faithful and Effective Authorized Ministers,' the needs of the church, and the gifts of the individual will provide the framework for the discernment process. The specific expectations will be explored covenantally with the individual and the individual's particular faith community."[12]

We've seen how the Covenant of Discernment takes into account the needs of the church and the good of the church. Let's consider now the function of "The Marks of Faithful and Effective Authorized Ministers of the United Church of Christ" in the Covenant of Discernment.

THE MARKS OF FAITHFUL AND EFFECTIVE AUTHORIZED MINISTERS

As Barbara Brown Zikmund states, in authorization for ministry "the church is lifting up someone who is quite ordinary to serve the community. The church is also recognizing someone who is extraordinary to serve God's purposes."[13] "The Marks of Faithful and Effective Authorized Ministers" provides a means to reflect upon foundations and competencies in ministry and to identify areas for growth with those ordinary/extraordinary persons.

The Marks are grouped into four areas of content: Spiritual Foundation, UCC Identity, Personal and Professional Formation, Knowledge and Skills. When the Ministry Issues Implementation Committee drafted the Marks they added a rhythmic theological phrase to each grouping, repeating four times, "for ministry, for ministry, for ministry, for ministry." The recurrence of "for ministry" poetically emphasizes the purpose of the Marks. The repetition exceeds the functional to remind those using the Marks of the purpose and context of their reflections.

The Marks can be used with Members in Discernment or Authorized Ministers.[14] Members in Discernment, their mentors, and Committees on

Ministry increasingly use the Marks within the Covenant of Discernment to develop ministerial formation of the Member in Discernment.[15] The Marks are "descriptive more than prescriptive, serving to illuminate the categories and to highlight a holistic picture of one's formation for and growth in ministry."[16] The Marks are not deemed to be all-inclusive. They may be expanded or modified to respond to "diverse learning edges and styles, additional talents and aptitudes."[17] And "there are places, like the Dakota Association of the South Dakota Conference, where the call to ministry has been discerned in community for generations, and the 'Marks of Faithful and Effective Ministers' as written are totally irrelevant. The community knows the marks that are necessary."[18]

Review and discuss the Marks, not to apply them to a specific Covenant of Discernment or a particular Member in Discernment, but from a wider perspective. Consider the ways in which the marks reflect and shape our expectations of Members in Discernment and authorized ministers.

Spiritual Foundation for Ministry. The critique has been made that "there are no faith qualifications for ministry in the United Church of Christ."[19]

- Do the five marks constitute a spiritual foundation for ministry?
- How applicable are they to Members in Discernment?

UCC Identity for Ministry. These marks are an assertive expansion of our bylaws' references to a demonstrated "knowledge of, and appreciation for, the history, polity, and practices of the United Church of Christ" as a prerequisite to authorization for ministry.

- How well do these marks encompass "knowledge of, and appreciation for, the history, polity, and practices of the United Church of Christ?" Can the participants in a covenant of discernment gauge the strength of UCC Identity of a Member in Discernment using these marks?

■ How might the ability "to articulate the UCC's commitment to being a united and uniting, multiracial and multicultural, open and affirming, accessible to all and just peace church" be shown, with integrity, by a Member in Discernment whose Local Church or Association has not made that commitment?

Personal and Professional Formation for Ministry. These marks seek out the gyroscopic balance of integrity within the context of covenant and hospitality.

■ How do the characteristics and abilities cited in these marks connect the individual character and personality traits of a Member in Discernment with the life of our whole community of faith?

Knowledge and Skills for Ministry. Here we find a synergy of covenant and hospitality. Not restricted to, or forced into, pre-set academic requirements, Members in Discernment are welcomed into an ambience of exploration of means and styles of preparation that fulfill the expectations and needs of our church for authorized ministers. The welcome mat is out and the door is open to all who are in discernment of their call.

■ What are the differences and similarities between the General Knowledge and Skills and the Knowledge and Skills Specific to Authorized Ministry?

■ How do the abilities situate and orient an authorized minister in her or his community? How can those abilities be discerned in someone who is not yet serving as an authorized minister?

THE FORMS OF AUTHORIZED MINISTRY: Ordained, Licensed, and Commissioned

After discerning the call of a Member in Discernment, the partners in that Covenant of Discernment may come to the decision that an authorized ministry is appropriate to the needs of the church and the gifts and abilities of the Member in Discernment. They then consider the form of authorization. In the United Church of Christ the three forms of authorization are ordained, licensed, and commissioned ministry.

Since ordained ministry is the most well-known form of authorized ministry, it is the form of authorized ministry that has received the most consideration and reflection—in writing, teaching, and discernment. The description in our constitution is thorough: "An Ordained Minister of the United Church of Christ is one of its members who has been called by God and ordained to preach and teach the gospel, to administer the sacraments and rites of the Church, and to exercise pastoral leadership."[20]

Each year that I taught UCC Faith, Polity, and Practice I asked students to write their theology of ministry in their final exam. (Yes, it was a take-home final.) One of the outstanding statements came from not-then-Rev. Linda Jaramillo, before Justice and Witness Ministries called her to be Executive Minister. She said, in part, "Ministry is the responsibility to provide leadership that is influenced and guided by God's constant grace. Ordained ministry is an extraordinary appointment from the community and call from God to serve the church as a pastor, leader, teacher, preacher, counselor, and prophetic voice. . . . "

David McMahill has supplied this thumbnail definition of ordained ministry to his polity students: "The ordained person is called on to represent the faith, traditions, values, and covenants *of* the church *to* the church and to the world beyond the church."

These summaries of licensed ministry and commissioned ministry appear in our constitution:

A Licensed Minister of the United Church of Christ is one of its members whom God has called and who has been recognized and authorized by an Association to perform specified duties in a designated Local Church or within that Association, mainly preaching and conducting services of worship, for a designated time within a covenant of mutual accountability. . . . The license may be renewed.[21]

A Commissioned Minister in the United Church of Christ is one of its members who has been called by God and commissioned for a specific church-related ministry.[22]

There are, of course, variations, from Conference to Conference and from Association to Association, in what kind of leadership is needed for Christ's church. Leadership needs may change over time. Singular processes and situations emerge. Quandaries and realizations arise from the crags, gaps, and overlaps of the needs of the church and the gifts of the Member in Discernment. These questions and insights about forms of authorized ministry were voiced by Conference staff and members of Committees on Ministry. They raise matters for consideration.

In the past, all of the Licensed Ministers in our Association were Members in Discernment needing licensure for their internships while attending seminary. Recently we've had a couple of small churches who want to license a lay member to serve as their pastor. We need to re-think what licensing means.

I am a Commissioned Minister for Christian Education. I had assumed I would need to be ordained in order to live out my calling. I was so relieved when my Conference Minister said to me, "I hope you don't feel you must pursue ordination. If Ordained Ministry is your vocation, fine, but maybe your call is more focused on education than on word and sacrament."

Our Association meets to consider each candidate for authorized ministry that is recommended by our Committee on Ministry. We break into circles for discussion and raise questions for the candidate or about the process. When the candidate was one of our Conference Staff, presented for a Commissioned Ministry of Stewardship and Finance, a question that came up was, "Why aren't all Conference Staff

Commissioned Ministers? Why does a Conference Minister need to be ordained?"[23]

During my time with the Committee on Ministry we've worked with two artists who use their gifts for painting and sculpture in their ministries. One is now ordained. The other is commissioned. Arriving at discernment with each was quite a journey. We had to thoroughly consider the setting for the ministry to which each was called.

We have always ordained hospital chaplains. It's one of the ordainable calls listed in the *Manual on Ministry*, but we have one MID who is preparing for hospital chaplaincy and is adamant about being commissioned rather than ordained.

For Conversation
(If possible, include past or present members of your Committee on Ministry in the conversation.)

1. What call or calls to ministry have you heard? How did the call come to you? How did you answer—at first? Later?

2. What experience has your Association or Conference had with licensed ministry? With commissioned ministry? Are the criteria for licensing adapted to the situation of each congregation seeking licensing for their pastor?

3. What elements would you—or do you—consider, in covenant with a Member in Discernment, as you determine together whether his or her call is leading to an authorized ministry, and, if so, what form of authorized ministry that call will take?[24]

A Covenant of Discernment, as we have stated, is open to any outcome, any form of authorization or no authorization. It is indeed "a commitment to be with and for one another for the good of Christ's Church rather than for the good of any one individual."[25]

HOSPITALITY AND RIGOR IN THE AUTHORIZATION OF MINISTRY

"Discernment is a spiritual discipline, a practice of listening, a practice of developing the ability to perceive the various ways God is at work in individual lives, in communities, and in the world."[26] In a Covenant of Discernment, listening together for God's voice and listening to one another's voices helps ensure that the process of discernment is hospitable. At the same time, this "hospitable process will continue to be rigorous in terms of academic, pastoral, and personal expectations for specific forms of authorization. . . ."[27] We as a church need to be able to trust—throughout the church—the rigor and the hospitality of the processes that lead to the commissioning, licensing, or ordaining of a Member in Discernment, or to transferring ministerial standing,[28] granting Dual Ordained Ministerial Standing,[29] Ordained Ministerial Partner Standing,[30] or Privilege of Call.[31]

Hospitality without rigor, as we found in chapter 5, is decidedly non-biblical. "The stranger in the ancient world was always tested first, with questions, or with observation. Only when the stranger was deemed not to be a threat to the community was he or she welcomed. . . . The first task before bringing a guest into hospitality is discernment."[32] Not all of our hospitable impulses in the realm of authorization for ministry are accompanied by rigor. Most of the nonrigorous applications of hospitality do not lead to regret. But some do. Many past and present Conference staff and Committee on Ministry members recall situations like these.

We used to pretty much license anyone a congregation chose to be their pastor. We were just grateful that someone was available to pastor the church. And when no one on the Committee on Ministry spoke the language of the candidate for licensing and the church members who accompanied him, it was extremely difficult and seemed so inhospitable to seriously question his qualifications.

For a long time in our Conference we just granted Dual Standing to any minister from another denomination that a congregation in our Association called to be their pastor. We saw it as part of the ecumenical spirit.

We've found over the years that we do no one a favor by authorizing or granting standing to someone who is not prepared for ministry, or who endangers the members of the congregation, or who does not have or seek to acquire an "abiding identity and affinity with the United Church of Christ."[33]

A Covenant of Discernment requires rigor in its hospitality. A Covenant of Discernment also requires recognition of hitherto unseen barriers to hospitable welcome. "Committees on Ministry will want to be aware of the ever-present danger that the covenantal assumptions of the dominant culture will unknowingly define and frame the discernment process."[34] This applies to all the processes of transferring or granting ministerial standing.

A predominantly European American Committee on Ministry, for example, may be totally if cordially unaware of the esteem with which an African American congregation with a Pentecostal heritage might hold its pastor. A Committee whose members are African American and European American may not understand the expectations for authorization carried by pastors and laypersons rooted in the Congregational Christian Church of American Samoa, where decisions on ordination or ministerial standing emanate from the national setting of the church. Or the Committee might not be aware that congregations nurtured in the practices of the United Church of Christ Philippines may assume that a Bishop (even if called a

Conference Minister in the USA) can and will authoritatively intervene in the life of the congregation.

Although there are Conferences and Associations where, "ethnicity tends to be a question of which country in Europe your ancestors came from"[35] many Committees on Ministry must and do make efforts to cultivate the ethic of hospitality across cultures. The "Ministry Issues pronouncement" offers guidance in this:

> Conferences and Associations are called upon to adapt their procedures of discernment and decision-making by including members of the candidate's own community in the decision-making processes, taking the time and effort to educate themselves concerning the community's traditions and needs, and acknowledging the validity of the community's discernment when a candidate is a member of a racial/ethnic community which is not represented in significant numbers (50% or more) among the members of the Committee on the Ministry.[36]

All matters relating to discernment of call and decisions on authorization require hospitality. We need hospitality that is rigorous, so as not to put the wider church at risk. We need hospitality that is intent on dismantling barriers, so as not to deprive the church of needed leadership. Faithful discernment is in play when the "directions taken contribute to the well-being, empowerment, and health of those involved as opposed to diminished self-insight, creativity, or functioning [and] also contribute to the overall health and well-being of the church and do not diminish or place the church in jeopardy."[37]

For Conversation
(If possible, include past or present members of your Committee on Ministry in the conversation.)

1. What has been the experience in your Association or Conference of rigor in the process of discernment? Has your Committee on

Ministry been called upon to acknowledge barriers to hospitality in the process of discernment?

2. Has your Association or Conference often granted Dual Ordained Ministerial Standing or Ordained Ministerial Partner Standing to an ordained minister from another denomination who has been called to serve a UCC church? How about privilege of call to an ordained minister of another denomination who desires to enter the ordained ministry of the UCC? How has the process worked?

15

OVERSIGHT OF AUTHORIZED MINISTRY

MAINTAINING MINISTERIAL STANDING

Ministerial standing, our constitution tells us, is a covenant of mutual accountability.[1] This covenant "shapes the ongoing relationship among the partners after authorization. Those partners customarily are the authorized minister, the Local Church—which may also be the calling body—and the Association."[2]

Note the anticipation that there will be an ongoing relationship among the partners after authorization, and the supposition that there will be "ongoing formation and lifelong learning" for the authorized minister which "the COM will eventually assume the responsibility of following."[3] This is part of a covenant of mutual accountability.

"Covenants of mutual accountability . . . characterize authorized ministry in the United Church of Christ."[4] Authorized ministers with standing in an Association or Conference, are in covenant with their Local Church, their Association/Conference, and their calling body if that is not their Local Church.[5] The authorized minister and her or his calling body are mutually accountable to one another through a covenantal relationship described in and backed up by a call agreement. The Association/Conference where the authorized minister has standing is accountable to the covenantal partners for the nurture and oversight of the authorized minister. The authorized minister maintains ministerial standing by remaining accountable to the Association/Conference through the Committee on Ministry, and by being fit for ministry.

There are several basic elements of authorized ministry that are easily reportable for the maintaining of authorization in an Association or Conference. The reportable criteria for continuing authorization begin with membership in a Local Church—usually a congregation of the United Church of Christ, but not always.[6]

Then there is confirmation of the authorized minister's current form of authorization. For an active authorized minister that confirmation is record of a call to a ministry that is recognized as valid[7] by the Association/Conference and is consistent with the form of authorization held. Records of the Committee on Ministry can confirm the good standing of authorized ministers who are retired or on leave of absence.

Oversight of these elements of accountability is commonly carried out through written Information Reviews[8] or face-to-face Periodic Support Consultations.[9] Committees on Ministry may look for and call for additional indications of willingness to live in covenants of mutual accountability. Those indications might be fulfilling requirements for continuing education, doing requisite boundary training,[10] being involved in the life of various settings of our church, or meeting other standards set by the Association/Conference.

Intrinsic to those reportable criteria is the recognition that: (a) there are several forms of authorization for ministry and that (b) each necessitates a covenantal relationship with the wider church. Although that may seem clear-cut, questions do arise about how those precepts are to be applied, what each form of authorization signifies, and how mutual accountability is maintained and covenant nurtured in various circumstances.

Some of those questions are found in these incidents and insights from Committees on Ministry.

Our Committee recently received a letter from one of our ministers who is on leave of absence. He wanted to know whether it was OK for him to officiate at a wedding. We had to convince him that while he's on leave of absence he really has ordained ministerial standing.

This is the second Association where I've served on the Committee on Ministry. In my former Association—in another Conference—we often transferred the ministerial standing of UCC ministers who had moved to our area but did not yet have a call here. We placed them on leave of absence while they sought a call. The Committee on Ministry where I currently serve will not do this, which seems to me a misunderstanding of what it means to be in covenant.

We require boundary training for all authorized ministers, but we keep running into questions. How often do ministers need to take the course? What about retired ministers who are in poor health or live far away from anywhere that they can take the course?

In Periodic Support Consultations we ask our ministers what it means to them to be a minister of the United Church of Christ and how they serve the wider church.

For Conversation
(If possible, include past or present members of your Committee on Ministry in the conversation.)

1. How does your Committee on Ministry take on the responsibilities of nurture and accountability, administratively and spiritually? Does

your Committee on Ministry carry out regular Information Reviews and Periodic Support Consultations? If so, how is this done? What kinds of concerns are raised? How is accountability maintained with Authorized Ministers who are retired or on leave of absence?

2. Does your Association/Conference require continuing education or boundary training authorized ministers?

FITNESS FOR MINISTRY

Fitness for ministry is more comprehensive and less easily determined than the basic reportable elements involved in maintaining authorization. Fitness for ministry is a state of being—of being ready, of being able, of being needed to carry out the ministry of Jesus as a representative of the United Church of Christ. Let me remark here that I have had problems with the expression "Fitness for Ministry." I may even have stated a time or two that if somebody had asked me before deciding on that terminology I might have come up with something better—something that didn't call up images of sweaty workouts in gyms or beguile my imagination to wander off hand in hand with the word "fit" into the realm of adages and maxims, stumbling over "fit to be tied," "fit as a fiddle," and "hissy fit."

But wise members of various Committees on Ministry have pointed out to me with great patience that "fitness" is a fitting term. More importantly, they have pointed this out with deep pastoral caring to authorized ministers whose fitness for ministry has been questioned. Just as physical fitness may come and go to greater and lesser degrees in our lives, there may be times in the living out of our ministerial vocations when we are more, or less, or not at all fit for ministry.

Spiritual distress, psychic trauma, or grave physical illness may render us, for a time, at least, unfit to minister. Depression may eclipse our gifts and talents. A brain injury may utterly upend our personality and dependability. In its oversight of authorized ministry a Committee on Ministry needs to be able to say to the authorized minister who is enmeshed in addiction, or coming to grips with an abusive personal relationship, or reeling with grief over the loss of a child, that, right now, your focus must shift to your own healing. Right now—quite appropriately—you may not be capable of serving, of placing the care and well-being of your congregation or calling body above your personal issues. These states of being—of how authorized ministers "be" in the present—can affect short-term or ongoing fitness for authorized ministry. They may or may not be connected to ethical misconduct. Fitness for ministry includes but is not limited to adherence to ministerial ethics.

In the mid-1980s, when we in the United Church of Christ were beginning widespread conversation on "fitness" for ministry, we most frequently and most visibly focused on "un-fitness," and a specific form of "un-fitness." That was sexual misconduct—a breach of ministerial ethics.

The 1986 *Manual on Ministry* offered procedures for conducting disciplinary reviews in an era when notice of clergy sexual misconduct was just breaking the surface of denial.[11] Committees on Ministry reviewed many instances of clergy sexual misconduct after the *Manual* was published. In 1991 General Synod adopted the pronouncement "Sexual Harassment and Abuse in the Church." In October of that year Anita Hill gave public testimony that raised general awareness about sexual harassment by persons in authority. Many more instances of clergy sexual misconduct—some current, some from decades past—came to the attention of Committees on the Ministry following the pronouncement and Anita Hill's testimony.

A set of assumptions quickly arose regarding ministerial ethics and Disciplinary Reviews:

- Clergy misconduct was most likely to be sexual misconduct (although there was recognition of misconduct such as financial malfeasance).

- Clergy sexual misconduct was perpetrated by a male pastor upon a child or an adult female member of the congregation.

- In most instances the accused clergyman was guilty.

- Women who had been targets of clergy sexual misconduct were extremely reluctant to come forward.

As an Associate Conference Minister who served in the Indiana-Kentucky Conference from 1986 to 1991 and then became the Executive Director of the Coordinating Center for Women in Church and Society, I was in position to hear, see, and assist with the flow of information and the development of compassionate responses and just processes around sexual misconduct. The work done in all settings of our church to inform and educate church members, and to support and give voice to those who had been subjected to sexual abuse by trusted pastors was monumental. There has been enduring commitment by the Insurance Boards, by dedicated individuals[12] knowledgeable in the power imbalances inherent in pastoral relationships, and by the successive work of the Office for Church Life and Leadership (OCLL), Parish Life and Leadership (PLL), and the Ministerial Excellence, Support and Authorization Team (MESA) to provide resources and ongoing training and response. This stable presence and attentiveness has shaped our consciousness and provided solid guidance. From the informal commitment by Conference Ministers in the late 1980s to never again allow ministers with a history of sexual misconduct to pass unremarked upon from one setting of ministry to the next, to the more recent institution of criminal background check requirements for those seeking calls to ministry in our church, there has been a steady dedication to forthrightness and to providing true sanctuary, safe space, in our church for those who are vulnerable.

The oversight of ministerial ethics continues. Awareness of fitness for ministry expands. More and more, we recognize that the failure of authorized ministers to maintain the standards of faithful and effective ministry can take many forms. There can be misconduct; lapses due to stress or lack of knowledge; incompetence; insufficient preparation or formation; or an absence—whether temporary or irrecoverable—of the traits of personality that allow for gracious and trustworthy performance of ministry. Not every instance of unfitness for ministry warrants disciplinary measures.

It is significant that "Disciplinary Reviews" in the *Manual on Ministry* of 1986 (MOM 1986) became "Fitness Reviews" in "The Oversight of Ministries Authorized by the United Church of Christ" in 2002.[13] The word "discipline" can mean a field of study or refer to training and systematic instruction. But the phrase "to discipline" carries a connotation of rebuke and punishment. By changing from "disciplinary" to "fitness" language in our review processes, we are better able to foster accountability for the actions of authorized ministers in a climate of nurture for ministers and the church.

Committees on Ministry exercise oversight and nurture when concerns about fitness for ministry are raised by any of the covenantal partners, or when concerns surface in contact with the authorized minister. Sometimes response to these concerns comes through Situational Support Consultations or Fitness Reviews, sometimes through other channels.

A Situational Support Consultation isn't necessarily prompted by a concern about fitness for ministry, but

> takes place when something has occurred that needs to be looked at in some depth. In most cases, this consultation is precipitated by a situation or concern that has arisen with the authorized minister, the setting for ministry, or the relationship between the authorized minister and the local church or other calling body. In a Situational Support Consultation, the . . . Committee on the Ministry is seeking to clarify the specific issues, find the extent to which there may be an impediment to effective ministry, and identify ways for actions to be taken to resolve an identified problem. The desired outcome is for all covenantal partners involved to agree to a course of action that will be evaluated together at a specified later date.[14]

The agreed-upon course of action may, of course, be one that resolves a concern regarding fitness for ministry.

FITNESS REVIEW

There are times when a concern regarding fitness for ministry must be addressed by a Fitness Review, which is

a very serious proceeding that involves a reassessment of a person's fitness for authorized ministry in and on behalf of the United Church of Christ and may result in discipline, including the loss of authorization. For this reason, it is important that a Fitness Review be thorough, providing opportunity for the . . . Committee on the Ministry to be fully informed before taking disciplinary action[15] or recommending disciplinary action to the Association [or Conference].

A thorough review, which ensures fairness to all involved, is equally important when a person's fitness for ministry is reaffirmed. In this case, the Fitness Review facilitates restoration of confidence in the person's fitness for ministry in the United Church of Christ.

The purpose of a Fitness Review is to ensure that those who are authorized for ministry in the United Church of Christ carry out that ministry according to the highest ethical standards and that persons are held accountable to the Association (or Conference) that holds their authorization. Authorized ministers are entitled to the protection of a process that is fair and just should their fitness for ministry be called into question.[16]

In summary, as Committees on Ministry address concerns of fitness for ministry, procedures and policies must be in place to safeguard the integrity of ministry and the processes of discipline, that is, for the imposition of measures of control or censure. Likewise there needs to be leeway and interpretation in order to allow for the contours and subtleties that must be addressed in questions of fitness for ministry. With all that in mind, Conference/Association staff were asked, "Do you have well-conceived procedures in place for responding to questions of fitness for ministry?" With minor deviations, most responded that they use "the fitness procedures found in MOM and the additional Fitness Review materials. This is policy adopted by the Conference and it has worked well over the years, albeit laborious." But there are variations in how the procedures from MOM are applied and whether specific procedures have been developed. Here are some examples.

Although there are procedures in place for Fitness Reviews in Rhode Island, if one were to take place, "Trained fitness investigators would be obtained from neighboring Conferences because we are too small and entwined to do it ourselves," said Beverley Edwards, while Interim Conference Minister for Rhode Island Conference.

While Conference Minister for the Southwest Conference, John Dorhauer reported, "The Western Region has met with leaders from MESA to organize a regional team for fitness reviews."

"The Illinois Conference has long had a Fitness Review Response Team and all Associations were part of developing a very specific process and procedures for such Reviews," notes Jonathan Knight, Associate Conference Minister Fox Valley Association.

The Northern California Nevada Conference Committee on Ministry has handled many Fitness Reviews. There is a specialized subcommittee, made up of people who are not serving on the Committee on Ministry, that does the initial response and interviews of persons making inquiries or raising concerns and of the minister whose fitness is questioned. The subcommittee makes the preliminary determination whether the concerns raised, if true, would question the minister's fitness for ministry. Only when the determination is made that the concerns would question fitness for ministry does the subcommittee notify the COM. This procedure has proved valuable in allowing the Committee on Ministry to continue its ongoing work.

The question "Are questions of fitness for ministry frequently raised in your Conference or Association/s?" brought forth a fairly consistent "not frequently" from most Conference and Association staff. The more qualitative responses of "all too often" and "not nearly enough" occurred in equal number. "We have held four Fitness Reviews and one Situational Support in the past six years. Every one of them is hard work," one Conference Minister reported. The "hard work" component plus the observation that "Hardly anyone is ever happy with the outcome," have been repeated by many Committee on Ministry members and staff. And, as another Conference Minister put it, "One Fitness Review can derail the other work of the Committee on Ministry for weeks, or even months."

A Committee on the Ministry initiates a Fitness Review when it receives information that questions an authorized minister's fitness for ministry.[17] Committee on Ministry members tell how that plays out in their Associations or Conferences.

For a long time we were of the opinion that we, as a Committee on Ministry, could only respond to questions of fitness for ministry that were raised by someone from the minister's church, or someone the minister served. Now we realize that we can—and should—initiate a Situational Support Consultation or other contact with the minister if we know of anything that sounds kind of "off" about one of our ministers.

Our Committee really struggled with the meaning of fitness for ministry when the judgment of one of our ministers became impaired as a result of head injuries sustained in a car crash. He made some very cruel public comments about members of his congregation. It was clear that he could no longer serve faithfully as a pastor. We conducted a Situational Support Consultation and persuaded him to go on leave of absence, because we did not want to remove his standing through a Fitness Review. While he is on leave of absence he can receive his UCC health benefits, which he really needs. On the other hand, because he still has ministerial standing, he can circulate his profile, which concerns us.

Sometimes we have to repeat the obvious to people who want to make a complaint about unethical behavior: we oversee the conduct of authorized ministers and Members in Discernment, but have no authority over their spouses, ministers of other denominations, or ordinary church members.

We've had a couple of Fitness Reviews for retired ministers who have standing in our Association but haven't lived here for years. I know that retired ministers can choose where they hold standing, but it sure makes accountability a hassle.[18]

What have Committee on Ministry members learned or found helpful in Fitness Reviews?

We still use the definition of confidentiality that Gene Kraus from the OCLL staff gave us: Confidentiality is stewardship of information. In inquiries or statements of concern this means that only those who need to know about a particular situation or specific aspects of that situation should be informed, and that those who do need to know are informed at the appropriate time.

The Ordained Minister's Code[19] sure doesn't cover all the fitness questions we've had to deal with.

An ordained minister is one who is "set apart"[20] by prayer and the laying on of hands. I have been quite surprised by the number of ordained ministers who want to fight that. They don't want to be set apart. They insist they're "just one of the guys." That attitude has produced a lot of trouble.

We must get pastors to understand that when they leave their congregation they need to stay away and out of contact with the members, at least until a new pastor has been called and has had a chance to establish a pastoral relationship with the congregation. This is very hard for ministers who retire in the same town where they have served for many years. We've had difficult conversations with the founding pastor of one of our congregations. Although he moved to a different city when he retired, he blogs and, through his blog, is in weekly contact with the members of his former congregation. They still get his theological and pastoral input. He maintains that we can't tell him not to blog. So far two new pastors have been called to this congregation; neither has stayed more than six months.

For Conversation
(If possible, include past or present members of your Committee on Ministry in the conversation.)

1. How do you view fitness for ministry?

2. Suspension of ministerial standing must be reported on a person's ministerial profile as a disciplinary action resulting from a Fitness Review.[21] How could—or should—this reporting be modified if an authorized minister's standing is suspended due to a condition such as clinical depression rather than because of misconduct?

The diligence and compassion with which so many Committees on Ministry work out the particulars and the applications of their oversight responsibilities, even in the most trying and complicated of situations, is remarkable. Committees plumb their collective wisdom, turn to the experience of those who have served before them, consult with staff of the wider church, and check behind all the seat cushions for any coin of knowledge that might have slipped away unrecognized. This is the United Church of Christ, where each Association does it differently, and it varies from Conference to Conference, and a manual on ministry from the national setting of the church has no juridical authority over the authorization and oversight of ministry by Associations and Conferences. Yet we have a commitment to ministry for the good of the whole church that overrides the default to autonomy. Manuals, pronouncements, consultations, and background papers on ministry are respected, fulfilling the hope that coherence of our understandings and procedures for authorization and oversight of ministries will "contribute to the development of unity within our diversity."[22]

"Ministry is a living thing [and] in every age, seeking to understand it in theological, historical, traditional and contemporary ways will help equip those who have responsibility for ministry."[23] In that spirit, the Habakkuk Project for re-visioning the MOM began in 2014. The name comes from the citation in Habakkuk 2:2 to "write the vision; make it plain on tablets." The Ministerial Excellence, Support & Authorization Team (MESA) has stated that, "As we make this announcement, it is important to distinguish that the goal of this group's work is truly one of re-vision rather than revision. The group will look afresh at and imagine a twenty-first-century vision for authorized and authorizing ministry in the United Church of Christ; we will not merely edit MOM in order to produce MOM 2.0."[24]

For Conversation

1. How can a clearer vision—or a re-vision—for authorized and authorizing ministry strengthen the effectiveness and integrity of our ministries?

2. What caution signs or driving directions would you erect along the route to a re-vision for authorized and authorizing ministry?

16

SEARCH AND CALL
Congregations Finding Ministers and Ministers Finding New Calls

Back in the nonvegetarian pre-cholesterol-conscious farm community where I grew up, "meat and potatoes" signified "the basics." Unadorned but hearty. "I'm a meat and potatoes kind of guy," someone would say, meaning, "My tastes are simple." And "Don't expect anything flashy, but I'm here when you need me. You can rely on me." Meat and potatoes.

Over the decades, helping a congregation find a pastor and helping an authorized minister find a place to serve has been a meat and potatoes ministry of Conferences. Search and Call is the name of the process where Conferences and the Ministerial Excellence, Support, & Authorization Team (MESA)[1] assist Local Churches and other calling bodies in their search for authorized ministers, and assist authorized ministers in their search for new settings for ministry. Despite the meat and potatoes disclaimer regarding flashiness, flashy things do happen in the process of ministerial search. These are flashy things of a "match made in heaven" "let's set off the fireworks" nature.

The services that Conferences provide to Local Churches seeking new ministerial leadership are termed "advisory" in our bylaws.[2] This terminology respects the autonomy of Local Churches, who call their own pastors. However, the relationship between Conference staff and a Local Church in search of pastoral leadership is often much more than that of adviser and advisee. It is covenantal—a way of "being defined by, accountable to, and responsible for each other."[3] When asked about the significance of providing resources, guidance, or consultation to churches seeking pastoral leaders, most Conference/Association staff say that this is a ministry "of utmost importance." They also reveal a covenantal understanding of the process of search and call in statements like these.

We always stress with search committees that the decisions they make will affect not only the future of their congregation and the lives of those who consider their pastoral position, but the whole of the Conference, the United Church of Christ, and the [universal] Church (in capital letters.) We encourage the use of the Bible study materials for Search Committees[4] as a means of putting the search into God's care, and a bigger setting.

One of the most difficult things for some of our very dedicated staff members to accept is that our Local Churches can call whomever they choose, as long as it's in accord with their church bylaws. That's one of the reasons why it's so important to have a trusting relationship between the churches and the wider church. Local Churches really are autonomous. And in their autonomy they are vulnerable to a pastor who might carry off a hostile takeover or lead them to their death through ineptitude. We, as the whole church, are vulnerable by extension.

Our small churches out in the plains states don't draw pastoral candidates through our search and call process. We can't just distribute ministerial profiles to churches that are searching. We comment on the profiles and we actively recruit individuals to submit their profiles to particular settings. Often we need to look outside the UCC for someone who is capable, trustworthy, able to drive to the church, and willing to accept a very part-time, not very well paid, position.

Search and call happens differently in each Conference. Even with those differences in procedure, there are some themes that recur in the ways in which staff members develop preliminary understandings with Local Churches.

When I first meet with a search committee, I talk about the Three C's: communication, confidentiality, and consensus. Communication with candidates is a kindness, letting them know where the Committee is in its process, letting them know their profile has been received, things like that. Communication with candidates also keeps a search committee from getting their hearts set on a certain candidate only to find she's accepted a different call. Confidentiality is part of our covenant, particularly important when a pastor is considering a new call. Things can get awkward between the pastor and the congregation he or she currently serves if word of the pastor's search were to "leak." We also stress confidentiality for churches who host "neutral pulpits"[5] for ministers being considered by nearby church search committees. Consensus requires that everyone speak up when decisions are being made, so that there is agreement on what they're looking for in a pastor and on the ways in which candidates they consider do or do not fulfill expectations.

We have a signed agreement between the Conference and the congregation in search, stating what the Conference will offer to the Search Committee and how the Search Committee will conduct their search.[6] Going over that document with the church governing board and/or the Search Committee and making alterations when needed provides a way to introduce most of the major concerns people have about the search process and to anticipate problems before they occur.

When working with churches in the search process we emphasize the importance of preparing a Church Profile[7] that is accurate and tells the best story possible about the church and its circumstances. We teach the Search Committee how to read a Ministerial Profile[8] to find a good match. And we make sure that the Search Committee understands and accepts consensus as its decision-making tool. No one wants to have a candidate selected by a margin of two votes, or to have committee members mumbling that *they* didn't vote for the candidate.

Conference staff often tell search committees that they are not looking for the best-rated minister ever, on some kind of evaluation scale. Rather they need to look for the minister whose gifts and abilities best match the congregation's current needs and vision for the future. This is a message that ministers seeking a call also need to hear. Sometimes authorized ministers or Members in Discernment are so eager to find a call that they promote themselves as being the best possible candidate for all the churches in search. But even the most gifted pastor is not the best match for every church. Neither is there one best church, among the many in search, for all the ministers seeking a call. The reminder to seek the best match rather than the best minister or the best church is an encouragement both to Local Churches and to ministers who are in search.

The Ministerial Profile, the Local Church Profile, the materials on visioning for the Local Church's future, the emphasis on consensus in a search committee's decision-making all seek to bring into sync a Local Church's particular needs and possibilities at this moment with the particular talents and experience of an authorized minister. One size—or shape or style of ministry—will not fit all, although it may fit several. When the match occurs, and someone who is a good match for this Local Church has been selected and has accepted the invitation to serve, there are details of the call that need to be worked on in covenant. In the experience of Conference and Association leaders, here are some steps to take and missteps to avoid in the completion of a Local Church's call to a minister.

A Local Church can, of course, modify our sample call agreement, but we go over it with the Search Committee—to let them know what is expected and usual in terms of vacation time, study leave, sabbatical etc., and to explain the rationale for the "benefits" that most search committee members don't have in their employment. We try to steer churches away from designing call agreements that specify the pastor's office hours or what civic groups they should join or restrict "paid time" to service to that congregation.[9] When a candidate is selected we walk them through the call agreement that the Local Church wishes to offer. We let the candidate know what is usual in our Conference. Sometimes we advocate for the candidate's needs with the Search Committee. Sometimes we advise candidates that their requests can't realistically be met in this situation.

We talk to churches about why it is better for the church and better for the minister to have a call agreement that describes a covenantal relationship, rather than a contract that can become the vehicle for nitpicking—or lawsuits. The "Sample Call Agreement" online[10] is very good about framing the call in terms of faith and relationship, and it goes into areas that need to be considered. Specifying the number of paid sick days, though, sounds more like a contract. Churches rarely dock a minister's pay if he or she has a lengthy health crisis during their first year as pastor. The relationship between pastor and congregation needs to remain flexible.

We try to make sure that the Search Committee and church governing board have gone over all the details regarding the terms of the call and come to an agreement with the candidate prior to the candidating weekend,[11] when the candidate is presented to the congregation. This involves agreement about compensation, start date, percentage vote of the congregation required by the church bylaws to call a minister, and the percentage vote of the congregation that the candidate expects in order to accept the call.

A couple of churches in our Conference have had the upsetting experience of selecting a candidate who accepted their call, only to announce in his candidating sermon[12] that he wouldn't become their pastor, after all. We now tell each candidate that once she or he has agreed to the terms of a call and has agreed to be the candidate presented to the congregation by the search committee, she or he has made a commitment to that congregation, provided the terms of the agreement are met by the church.

Associations/Conferences need to insist that every called minister is part of a Three-Way Covenant or a Four-Way Covenant,[13] and that the wording of each covenant makes clear the roles and relationships of the partners in the covenant.

For Conversation
(Interview or invite to your conversation a staff person from your Association or Conference who works with pastoral search, and maybe someone who has recently served on a search committee.)

1. How does the process of search and call work in your Conference? What resources are used regularly by search committees?[14] How is consensus[15] employed by search committees?

2. What elements need to be in a call agreement? How have Local Churches modified what might be in a sample call agreement? How have ministers negotiated the terms of their call?

3. What elements of covenant have you experienced in the pastoral search process? What aspects of hospitality do you identify?

Authorized ministry does not exist without covenant. From the Covenant of Discernment to Three-Way or Four-Way Covenants of authorization, throughout the process of search and call, the partners in the covenants and the settings of the church "live in sustained engagement with one another in ways that impinge on and eventually transform all parties to the transaction."[16]

Authorized ministry, as Robin Meyers has declared, is a "wild calling—one that [leads ministers] away from more comfortable lives and into the only profession where radical truth-telling is part of the job description."[17] Reinhold Niebuhr, while an Evangelical and Reformed pastor, stewed about the difficulty the pastor "finds in telling unpleasant truths to people whom one has learned to love. . . ."[18] In ministry we are called not only to provide comfort and the assurance of God's unshakeable love to those in our care, but also to lead them into "lov[ing] the seemingly unlovable and shun[ning] what is tempting but deadly."[19] Ministry is a vocation that is relentless in its demand for transformation.

The demands of faithful ministry—transformative ministry—are not always met through compliance with what the congregation wants from their pastor, or what the calling body asks of the minister. Nor is faithful transformative ministry solely determined by what the minister sees fit to do and promote. Faithful authorized ministry requires a high-res vision of the gospel, along with a perspective on how the elements of this particular call to ministry fit into the scope of the big picture. Such clarity cannot be achieved in isolation. It calls for both a strong spiritual base and the viewpoints and overviews of those outside the minister's current setting for ministry. Concentration on the details pertinent to a particular call can induce nearsightedness in ministry. Dedication to major theological or social movements can induce farsightedness in ministry. A life in covenant provides the spiritual base and outside overview that corrects ministerial myopia and hyperopia. The commitment to "be with and for one another for the good of Christ's church"[20] heartens and sustains authorized ministers.

It is covenant that keeps authorized ministers alive and courageous when sent out like lambs in the midst of wolves. It is covenant that keeps authorized ministers true to their calling when in danger of being satisfied with security, like lambs in the midst of lambs. It is life in covenant that transforms church and minister.

17

GLOSSARY OF TERMS
Related to Ministry

Association An Association is made up of the Local Churches within that Association's boundaries and those authorized ministers whose standing is in that Association. Associations are constitutionally charged with the responsibilities of authorizing persons for ministry.

Authorized Minister An authorized minister is one who is ordained, commissioned, or licensed on behalf of the United Church of Christ.

Call In the United Church of Christ we affirm that "God calls the whole church and every member to participate in and extend the ministry of Jesus Christ." Thus, each of us has a call, that is, a vocation to minister.

Call In the context of a Covenant of Discernment, the determination is made whether a Member in Discernment's call to ministry is a call to authorized ministry.

Call A call, as the term is used in the process of Search and Call, is the official invitation from a Local Church or other calling body—such as a Conference, hospital, seminary, counseling center, etc.—to a particular authorized minister to fulfill a position for which the minister is authorized.

Call Agreement A call agreement is covenantal in nature and sets out the terms, conditions, responsibilities, and benefits agreed to by an authorized minister and the Local Church that calls the authorized minister to serve as an authorized minister. It is witnessed by the Association/Conference.

Calling Body A calling body is an organization or institution—such as a Conference, hospital, seminary, counseling center, etc.—that seeks the services of an authorized minister.

Commissioned Minister A commissioned minister in the United Church of Christ is one of its members who has been called by God and commissioned for a specific church-related ministry that does not require ordination or licensing or include sacramental rites.

Committee on Ministry The Committee on Ministry may be known as Committee on the Ministry, or Church and Ministry Committee, or it may be a team or a board. It is the body of an Association or Conference that is delegated the responsibilities for church and ministry concerns. Included among these concerns are participation in discernment of call of Members in Discernment, and the authorization, review, and ongoing oversight of the ordained, licensed, and commissioned ministers of that Association or Conference.

Conference A Conference is made up of Associations, which are made up of Local Churches and the authorized ministers whose standing is in those Associations. When there are no Associations in a Conference, or if the Associations are not the place where ministerial standing is held, the Conference carries out the responsibilities of authorization and oversight of ministry. Or a Conference Committee on Ministry may assist Associations in the authorization and oversight of ministry.

Covenant of Discernment A Covenant of Discernment is the relationship among a Member in Discernment (MID), her or his Local Church, and the Committee on Ministry to explore the nature of the MID's vocation to ministry.

Covenantal Partners A covenantal partner is one of the three or four parties involved in an authorized ministry. The covenantal partners are: the authorized minister; the Local Church where the authorized minister is a member; the calling body where the authorized minister serves in an authorized ministry, if that is not the Local Church; the Association or Conference where authorization is held.

Dual Ordained Ministerial Standing Dual standing may be granted by an Association/Conference to an ordained minister of another denomination who wishes to retain ordained ministerial standing in that denomination and who has become pastor of a Local Church of the United Church of Christ, or serves in a covenanted, affiliated or associated ministry of the United Church of Christ, or has become pastor of a yoked charge or a federated church, one part of which is affiliated with the United Church of Christ, or has been called to an ecumenical ministry one constituent of which is the United Church of Christ. Dual standing is limited to the duration of that pastorate or that responsibility. (Ordained ministers of the Christian Church [Disciples of Christ] apply for ministerial partner standing rather than dual standing.)

Fitness Review The primary purpose of a Fitness Review is to determine whether an authorized minister continues to be fit for the ministry for which he or she is authorized. The Committee on Ministry initiates this review when an authorized minister's fitness for ministry is called into question. A Fitness Review involves the Committee on Ministry and covenantal partners as well as persons directly affected by the review.

Four-Way Ministry Covenant A Four-Way Ministry Covenant is the relationship among an authorized minister, the Local Church where the authorized minister is a member, the calling body, and the Association/Conference.

Information Review The purpose of an Information Review is to provide a regular means by which an Association/Conference verifies that all authorized ministers continue to meet the basic standards required for authorization, such as Local Church membership, a call to ministry appropriate for the authorization that has been granted, or retired or leave of absence status. All authorized ministers are expected to participate in regularly scheduled Information Reviews in order to maintain their authorization.

Leave of Absence Leave of absence is the provision for an ordained or commissioned minister who is no longer engaged in the ministry for which authorized to withdraw temporarily while still maintaining ministerial standing. Leave of absence is granted through the Committee on Ministry and may be granted while the authorized minister seeks a call, evaluates her or his future directions in ministry, recovers from illness or injury, attends to family issues, etc. Leave of absence is reviewed and can be renewed annually, usually for not more than five years.

Licensed Minister A licensed minister of the United Church of Christ is one of its members whom God has called and who has been recognized and authorized by an Association to perform specified duties under supervision in a designated Local Church or within that Association, mainly preaching and conducting services of worship, for a designated time within a covenant of mutual accountability.

Member in Discernment A Member in Discernment is a member of the United Church of Christ who is in discernment of ministerial vocation and has entered into a Covenant of Discernment with his or her Local Church and the Association/Conference Committee on Ministry.

Ministerial Standing Ministerial standing is an ongoing covenant of mutual accountability that recognizes and continues the authorization to perform the duties and exercise the prerogatives of authorized ministry. Ministerial standing in the United Church of Christ is granted by and held in an Association/Conference in cooperation with a Local Church. The good standing of an authorized minister may be active, leave of absence, or retired.

Ordained Minister An ordained minister of the United Church of Christ is one of its members who has been called by God and ordained to preach and teach the gospel, to administer the sacraments and rites of the church, and to exercise pastoral leadership.

Ordained Ministerial Partner Standing Ordained ministerial partner standing is authorization granted to an ordained minister with ordained ministerial standing in the Christian Church (Disciples of Christ) who has a call to perform the duties and exercise the prerogatives of ordained ministry in the United Church of Christ. Ordained ministerial partner standing extends for the duration of the call to a Local Church or agency of the United Church of Christ, and the minister maintains ministerial standing with the Disciples of Christ Region where the minister serves. Ordained ministerial partner standing reflects the mutual recognition and reconciliation of ordained ministries between the UCC and the DOC.

Oversight A Committee on Ministry exercises four forms of oversight in covenant with authorized ministers: Information Reviews, Periodic Support Consultations, Situational Support Consultations, and Fitness Reviews.

Periodic Support Consultation The purpose of a Periodic Support Consultation is to provide direct contact between the Committee on the Ministry and authorized ministers. The goal is to strengthen and support authorized ministries. This consultation is developmental and growth-oriented and is designed to gain further understanding of the kind of support the authorized minister wants or needs. It aims to strengthen covenantal ties and provides an opportunity for reflection and feedback on the call to and practice of ministry.

Privilege of Call An ordained minister of another denomination who desires to enter the ordained ministry of the United Church of Christ applies for Privilege of Call to the Association within whose bounds she or he resides. If the applicant is found to be qualified, the Association grants Privilege of Call, which allows the minister access to the process of Search and

Call. After accepting a call, the ordained minister applies for ordained ministerial standing in the United Church of Christ to the Conference/Association of which the Local Church extending the call is a part. Privilege of Call is granted for a period of one year and may be renewed.

Retired Minister Ordained or commissioned ministers can maintain their ministerial standing in retirement and remain in covenantal relationship with their Association or Conference without a Three-Way or Four-Way Ministry Covenant. A licensed minister who retires from service as a licensed minister may be recognized by the Association or Conference as a retired licensed minister and be granted voting membership in the Association/Conference.

Search and Call Search and Call is the name of the process where Conferences/Associations, and the Ministerial Excellence, Support, & Authorization Team (MESA) assist Local Churches and other calling bodies in their search for authorized ministers, and assist authorized ministers in their search for new settings for ministry.

Situational Support Consultation The Situational Support Consultation is pastoral and developmental in nature. Its purpose is to address and deal with a situation, concern, or problem that has arisen in relation to an authorized minister or ministry setting. It is convened by the Committee on the Ministry in response to a request from any of the covenantal partners, including the authorized minister, the Local Church where the person is a member, the calling body, or the Association/Conference. Covenantal partners may be asked to take part in the consultation.

Three-Way Ministry Covenant A Three-Way Ministry Covenant is the relationship among an authorized minister, the Local Church that has called the authorized minister, and the Association or Conference.

Transfer of Ministerial Standing An ordained or commissioned minister in good standing who moves from one Association/Conference to another and wishes to maintain ministerial standing requests a transfer of standing.

The Association/Conference to which the authorized minister has moved considers the circumstances of the relocation and determines with the minister the nature of the Three-Way or Four-Way Covenant, leave of absence, or retired status. (Because licensed ministry is specific to a location, a licensed minister's standing cannot be transferred.)

PART V

Identity and Unity

⁓

Part V calls us back to our identity,
asks questions about who we are and the
theological grounding of our identity.
Are we "freedom's church"? Are we a
united and uniting church that holds in
a creative tension all of our independent
and disparate voices? Are we "like an
archipelago . . . part of the same group,
but still islands—separate and alone"?
What stories do we tell that incorporate
us all and tie us together, that function
as our myth, that tell us who we are?
Are we caught in a faceoff between
autonomy and unity? Have we rashly
sidestepped the orientation to hospitality?
Are we in covenant?

18

OUR THEOLOGICAL IDENTITY

Maybe we ought to consider crowdsourcing as the way to do theology in our church.

According to the Merriam-Webster Dictionary, crowdsourcing is "the practice of obtaining needed services, ideas, or content by soliciting contributions from a large group of people, and especially from an online community, rather than from traditional employees or suppliers." Wikipedia adds, "this process combines the efforts of crowds of self-identified volunteers or part-time workers, where each one on their own initiative adds a small portion that combines into a greater result."

Upon first exposure to the concept, crowdsourcing seems an ideal method for theological diligence in our nonhierarchical church, where, "without hesitation, we entangle faith and life."[1] There is no one center in our church that lays down doctrine or theological approach and "all parts of the church are actually encouraged to be critically in dialogue with one another about the faith."[2]

There is a basic definition of theology found on our national website. It's very accessible. It speaks of theology in ways that apply to our life situations:

Theology states what is believed about God and all that is related to God. It is reflection on our experience of who God is and what God is doing. The purpose of theology is to understand who God is, what God is doing and what this implies for our actions. The process by which individuals or groups or churches develop a theology is called "doing theology," or "theologizing" or "theological reflection."[3]

There is a human yearning for theological reflection. Interviewed before she served as a theological reflector at the 2013 General Synod, Disciples of Christ minister and author Rita Nakashima Brock upheld that yearning: "Human beings are meaning-makers. We understand our behavior in a larger framework of meaning." One layperson, dissatisfied with a public statement issued by his Conference's Annual Meeting, called for the use of a larger framework of meaning: "That statement could have been made by any socially progressive organization; we need to say it and hear it in church words. That's where our power is." Theological reflection reveals why what we do matters in a larger frame. Theological reflection gives us the words that disclose the entanglement of faith with life, the presence of God in the world.

In the United Church of Christ we affirm that "theology is the work of the whole Body of Christ—not only of ordained ministers or academic theologians. Everyone who loves Jesus Christ and tries to be faithful to the Gospel is a Christian theologian."[4] All of us, in all of the settings of our church, are called upon to do theology. Whether we are, in crowdsourcing terms, a traditional supplier, or an employee, or an as-yet-untapped source of services, ideas, or content for our theological enterprise—that doesn't matter. "Each part of the United Church of Christ—local church, association, conference, seminary and national body—needs to contribute its best insight and understanding to the dialogue."[5]

Before contributing to the dialogue there are a few questions. Just where is the dialogue taking place? Are there several dialogues taking place? Are the dialogues in one setting of the church in dialogue with the dialogues in other settings? How do we find out and take part? In crowdsourcing terms, who solicits the contributions? And how do we reach the crowd? Consideration of these questions leads to the following reflections.

Impressive and exciting work in theology goes on and has gone on throughout our church. However, it is often unremarked upon or unknown beyond the setting and moment in which it emerged. Multiple theological dialogues take place in our church, but overall our theological work can be "disjointed, fragmented and alienating," according to UCC leader Scott Libbey. He suggests that what we lack is a "theological plumb line against which to judge our theological work and our life and mission in a wholistic way."[6]

A plumb line. That's a line from which a weight is suspended to determine verticality or depth. "Verticality" as in uprightness, or unerringly homing to the heart of the matter. "Depth" as a contrast to shallowness. A plumb line is dropped from a point of reference and establishes a line perpendicular to that point. A plumb line, dropped from our community's call to follow Jesus, would judge the depth and worthiness of our theological work and home to the heart of our life and mission.

The challenge is: Who can set a theological plumb line for the United Church of Christ? Who can ameliorate any disjointedness, fragmentation, and isolation that dampens our theologizing? We resist having church leaders or theological schools or settings of the church define our theology for us, but we need a plumb line. We need ways to look holistically at our denomination's theological work. We need "an advocate, critic, lover, prober, searcher, reviewer, affirmer—relating in a covenantal style … in a partnership with all parts of the church, [so that] everybody could be called at least to look theologically at what they are doing."[7] There have been several efforts to fulfill that role.

THEOLOGICAL COMMISSION

The UCC Theological Commission attempted to cast a plumb line. The Commission came into being at the Third General Synod, in 1961, immediately after the resolution to declare our church's constitution in force and the unanimous vote that accepted the new UCC bylaws. It was created to serve the United Church as an instrument of counsel and study on all theological issues arising in the life of the Church . . . [and was to] concern itself further with the responsibility of the United Church of Christ to provide for its members the means of growth in sound doctrine and knowledge of the Scriptures, that the United Church of Christ may become ever more deeply rooted in the great Christian tradition and ever more sensitive to the need for understanding and proclaiming the faith in terms of contemporary life.[8]

At its first meeting, in 1962, the Theological Commission gauged its task. Douglas Horton, a member of the Commission, who had long been a proponent for the union that produced the UCC, "indicated that he hoped that the Commission might be an instrument for unity in the new church. . . ."[9] The Commission viewed the UCC Statement of Faith (1959) as a theological plumb line. It expected the Statement of Faith to shape the work of the other Commissions of the church. "Thinking of the relevance of our Statement of Faith in the light of our whole work as a church," and feeling "that we should review the ongoing work of the church in the light of the Church's faith," the Theological Commission asked each of the other Commissions to provide "a brief statement of how you understand the work of your particular agency in the light of the total theology of the Statement of Faith."[10]

The Theological Commission also concerned itself with the field of interest referred to in the ecumenical movement as Faith (doctrine) and Order (ministerial structure). However, because as a church we were less mindful of Faith and Order concerns than we were of the swiftly moving waters of social action, the Commission did not survive.[11] Taking action for God's mission in the world may have been the less wearying way to search for common commitments among the members of the new church. UCC historian David Greenhaw comments that although Congregational Christian and Evangelical and Reformed people "differed significantly on matters of theology, worship and polity, they did share an interest in social ministry."[12] For reasons that still remain unclear, a sustained disregard for our theological work accumulated, silt-like, in the angle of our bent toward the transformation of society. [13]

OFFICE FOR CHURCH LIFE AND LEADERSHIP

When the Office for Church Life and Leadership (OCLL) was established in 1973, one of its assignments was to carry on the work of the Theological Commission. In 1977 OCLL called together a group of United Church of Christ teachers, ministers, and wider church leaders around the topic "Toward Sound Teaching in the United Church of Christ." From that convocation came the statement,

> Convinced as we are that our church, along with the American churches generally, is excessively accommodated to cultural values and perceptions, our thinking revolved around the conviction that the ministry of the church must become more intentional and disciplined in teaching the faith of the church, in valuing its theological tradition and in responding to the present place of the church in culture.[14]

PRISM—A SCHOLARLY JOURNAL

In 1984 thirty-nine UCC faculty members teaching in theological education signed and sent a letter to the Executive Council of the UCC.

> The letter stated its concern that theology in the UCC was "utilitarian" and without "sustained, disciplined reflection on the condition of the church." . . . [It urged the national leadership of the church] to constitute a new "body of theological leadership and reflection"—to "express the central faith affirmations" of the church. . . . Faculty who signed the letter had no "preconceived notions" about where the process might lead, but they felt a "dire need" for a better "articulation of faith in the life and witness of the church."[15]

In 1985 the deans of the seven UCC-identified seminaries did not wait for action by the Executive Council. They contributed money from their schools and founded a new theological journal, which they named *Prism: A Theological Forum for the United Church of Christ.* The journal did not seek to "promote a single viewpoint, but to allow a variety of perspectives to interact with one another."[16] *Prism* described itself as "a journal for the whole church" whose "goal is to offer serious theological reflection from a diversity of viewpoints on issues of faith, mission, and ministry."[17] Published twice yearly until 2011, *Prism* presented varieties of perspectives and reflection on a range of subjects from the nature of Conferences, to the national structure, to the climate of theology in our church. In 2016 there were plans for *Prism* to produce a yearly issue on a single theological topic.

THEOLOGICAL FORUM

Concern about theology in the UCC persisted. General Synod 28 passed a prudential resolution in 2011 calling for the formation of a theological forum. The resolution referred back to the call in 1977 inviting our church to become "more intentional and disciplined in teaching the faith." It mentioned that the 1984 letter to the UCC Executive Council from thirty-nine faculty members engaged in theological education had not yet received a full response to "its call for 'sustained rethinking of our theological tradition' . . . [or to its request that Executive Council act to] 'constitute a body of theological leadership and reflection responsible for assisting [all the settings of our church] in developing teaching consensus.'" The resolution noted that "no mechanism currently exists specifically intended to promote a denomination-wide theological conversation."

Therefore, the resolution requested

the formation of a theological forum, structured so as to engage the widest possible diversity of perspectives within the United Church of Christ, to promote theological reflection and dialogue within our church and with partner churches, and to be a resource for local churches, local church members, associations, conferences national leadership, and instrumentalities. This forum would not be a prescriptive council, but a forum for descriptive and diverse theologies across the Church.[18]

The Office for Local Church Ministries and the Office of General Ministries were to implement the resolution. Theological materials have been featured on the national website as well as a theological theme reflection loop with the question, "Where Did I See God Today?"[19] An online Theology Forum was set up, but is not currently active.

GENERAL SYNOD

Our Bylaws recognize the General Minister and President as "the principal leader in interpreting the theological perspectives and values of the United Church of Christ as guided by the General Synod."[20] This recognition acknowledges that a lot of vital and groundbreaking theological work is done at Synod. Sometimes it comes through major addresses and sermons. Sometimes it appears in the texts of resolutions or pronouncements. Sometimes it happens before dramatic moments, to prepare and motivate us; sometimes it occurs during the dramatic moments; sometimes it ensues after these dramatic times as we begin to "discover what the Spirit has done with the church and in spite of the church."[21]

I recall the Tuesday morning of General Synod 17, in 1989, when the delegates and visitors gathered to hear reports from the committees entrusted with bringing resolutions forward for vote. Two proposed resolutions on the use of inclusive language[22] had been assigned to Committee Three. One of the proposed resolutions affirmed the use of inclusive language, the other opposed it. Committee Three was to bring one cogent resolution on the use of inclusive language to the plenary session that Tuesday morning. The chair of Committee Three began her report by calling to the podium Marilyn Breitling of the Coordinating Center for Women and Barbara Weller from the Biblical Witness Fellowship. Representing the two original contradictory proposed resolutions, the two women came to the platform together. Both spoke to the Synod delegates in favor of the resolution as revised and honed by Committee Three.[23]

Reaching that point of resolution of the opposing resolutions, however, had taken hours of caustic discussion and ardent debate. Very late on Monday night, we members and adjutants of Committee Three had tottered out of our windowless meeting room into the dingy hallway under the Fort Worth Convention Center. We were seeking a break in all possible senses of the word. Mary Miller Brueggemann of the Coordinating Center for Women staff appeared to be the only animated person left among the numbed and the incoherent. Summoning my, by then, negligible powers of communication, I raised an inquiring eyebrow to her. She responded to my unspoken questioning of her mental state by declaring, "This is wonderful! We're talking theology." And, of course, we were. In that tedious and volatile session we were doing theological work.

Yet the questions still linger over this and all the other intense theological work done at Synod or in seminaries, or by committees on bylaws revision or mission, or in any setting of our church: Does our work go beyond this moment? Can it be heard and received and linked with other theological work?

For Conversation

1. Have you been part of a theological study or conversation that you've wanted to broadcast throughout the church? Where and when did it take place? What did it cover? Can intense theological work done at Synod or in seminaries, or in any other setting of our church be heard and received by the other settings of our church? How can we overcome the isolation of our theological conversations?

2. Can or could our Statement of Faith serve as a theological plumb line, going to the heart of our life and mission, measuring depth? How?

3. What encouragement or suggestions might you offer to the Theological Forum—now or in future incarnations—about how to be the body that is sought out and counted on throughout our church to "support the theological work that is ongoing" and to call upon us

all to "at least to look theologically at what [we] are doing?" About how to cast a theological plumb line and initiate crowdsourcing?

4. Where do you turn for theological reflection and direction? Bible study groups? UCC daily devotionals,?[24] Podcasts?[25] Music? Interfaith study or action groups? Reflection on the creeds and historic prayers of the church? Theological journals?

"The United Church of Christ has been accused of theological vacuity and doctrinal amnesia,"[26] UCC theologian Lee Barrett writes, without apparent blame or defensiveness. He continues,

> Critics have scoffed that theology in the United Church of Christ is little more than "a series of ad hoc opinions usually added on to some practical concern," with "an occasional invocation of biblical and doctrinal proof texts on a basis of convenience."[27]

We might assume that the appraisal of ad hoc opinions and proof texting pertains largely to documents and resolutions produced by the wider church. But Louis Gunnemann observed doctrinal amnesia on a more widespread basis. He commented on how "the steady mixing of faith affirmations with messages of human improvement and psychological well-being," begun in the early 1970s as "the cult of experience," dominated U.S. society in general and reverberated within the UCC. "The authority of the faith for life was in one's experience of the faith, with little or no attention given to the authority of the tradition of the community of faith, the Bible, or faith statements by which groups were identified."[28]

A milder explanation of our supposed inattention to scripture and faith traditions is that, "inspired partly by the Reformed view that God transcends all human efforts to formulate divine truth, the UCC has exhibited a commitment to the revelatory freedom of the Holy Spirit."[29] This is the revelatory freedom of now and the future, where "God is still speaking," and "There is yet more truth and light to break forth from God's Holy Word." It is the revelatory freedom that is alive in the faith traditions of our European founders and forebears, and, for many in the UCC, through the faith communities and traditions of ancestors native to the Americas, island nations, Asia, and Africa.

Doctrinal amnesia is a horror to some, as is doctrinal uniformity to others. Yet we trust that we needn't be stranded on one or the other of the bleak poles of that continuum. I am one who bolted into the UCC's doctrine-free zone, arriving panting and winded from a realm of (what was to me) stifling doctrinal uniformity and theological rigidity. After four decades, I still cannot breathe deeply enough of the sweet oxygenating permission to freely reflect on our faith, to take note and take notice of the Divine Presence that has hustled each of us along the current of current events to this specific moment. I love the way we entangle faith and life in all settings of our church, even when we're moving so fast that we don't bother to explain what we assume everybody—inside and outside our church—just knows is the connection between faith and life. For many years a quote from Conference Minister Emeritus Mineo Katagiri was tacked to the wall above my desk, "Don't forget that the church has a unique mission. We are called to a relationship with God and to live creatively in a society gone mad."[30] That unique mission keeps at us to not isolate our words from our deeds, or the Word from our lives. It wants us to keep on "understanding and proclaiming the faith in terms of contemporary life"[31] and connecting faith and life in words and actions that are not ignored or dismissed—by ourselves or by others—as irrelevant or theologically vacuous. This is the "theology of listening toward mutual hearing" described by Rosemary McCombs Maxey, where "our various voices, the voices of all creation, and the voice of the Creator can speak and be heard."[32]

Theological work and reflection goes on throughout our church. And not surprisingly, as Lee Barrett finds, "No single theological world, no single construal of the essence of Christianity, has ever characterized the United Church of Christ. Several worlds have always thrived, each one with different vocabularies, different moods, different audiences, and different primal hopes and fears. These worlds have sometimes collided, sometimes co-operated, and sometimes formed alliances with one another."[33]

A multitude of UCC voices is set out in the tables of contents for the *Living Theological Heritage's* sections "Doing Theology" and "Living out the Unity." There are voices of individuals, groups, and individuals speaking as one of, but not necessarily a designated spokesperson for, a group. I invite you to listen to two or three of these voices, through the articles referred to on the chart below. What faith traditions are honored? Contrast the voices. Identify the "different moods, different audiences, and different primal hopes and fears" between and among the voices. What happens if you hear African American voices in dialogue with voices of the Craigville Colloquy? Women with Charismatic Fellowship? Biblical Witness with Confessing Christ? Mix and match among these United Church of Christ voices.

VOICES	ARTICLES
African Americans	"Black Theology: The Unfinished Agenda"[34] and "The Power of the Faith Community"[35]
American Indians	"Servanthood"[36] and "An Indian Perspective on the United Church of Christ"[37]
Asian Americans	"On Being Troublemakers"[38] "Theology: Asian American"[39]
Biblical Witness	"Scriptural Primacy,""The Dubuque Declaration"[40] "Apostasy: The Dayton Declaration"[41]
Calvin Synod	"Holy Communion"[42]
Charismatic Fellowship	"Purpose and Theology"[43]
Confessing Christ	"Renewal"[44]
Craigville Colloquy	"A Declaration" and "A Letter"[45]
Latino/Latina	"Our Response to Christ is Different" and " Theology in Context"[46]

VOICES *(continued)*	ARTICLES *(continued)*
Order of Corpus Christi	"What Does Mercersburg Have to Offer?" and "The Order of Corpus Christi."[47]
Pacific Islanders	"Hawaiian Traditions: Music and Metaphor"[48] and "Assimilation: The Asian American and Pacific Islander Experience"[49]
Women [Caucasian writers]	"Feminist Theology"[50] and "Attentive to the Word"[51]

For Conversation

1. What emphasis do you place on scripture, tradition, experience, reason or other sources when you do your theological work?

2. How do you see theological worlds colliding or harmonizing in the paired voices above? Did you find unexpected similarities or overlaps between the paired voices? Differing perceptions or experiences of who God is, what God does?

3. In the groupings you studied, what questions would you ask of each group in order to set up a dialogue?

4. Were there issues raised or presumptions made by one group that were not included by the other? How might this have emanated from the differences in audiences and the "primal hopes and fears" assumed and borne by each?

5. Did the authors' statements convey awareness of their covenantal relationship with the rest of our church?

6. Where and how does or can an attitude of hospitality—of looking forward to considering and learning from the other—enter into our efforts at doing theology in the multiple settings of our church?

Mining gold from the rocky landscape of our heterogeneous belief pattern, Lee Barrett proposes that

> Perhaps the essence of what is Christian can be found only in the fissures, dialectical tensions, and centrifugal forces among the divergent interpretations of the good news. If this is so, the efforts of any of these theological worlds to invalidate the other options should be resisted, even in the name of a collective prophetic voice.[52]

The promised riches to be discovered in those fissures, dialectical tensions, and centrifugal forces depend upon our cultivation of a polyglot faith community. No one language of belief. No invalidation of other dialects or vernaculars. Not a well-intentioned but pizzazz-lacking Esperanto of faith. Rather we need to speak our own languages of belief even as we seek a "vocabulary of the faith . . . elastic enough to express and re-express the meaning of the essential unifying love of God and the mission that love requires us to undertake as a people of deeply diverse histories, cultures, and social contexts."[53] Each one of us "must avoid the arrogance of believing [we] alone know the truth."[54]

Whether with premeditated guile or oblivious wisdom, the apostle Paul anticipated the complexities of multiple belief systems by declaring, "No one can say, 'Jesus is Lord' except by the Holy Spirit" (1 Cor. 12:3b). There is no test of doctrine, belief, or practice in Paul's statement. If someone says that Jesus—not Caesar, not material goods, but righteous, compassionate Jesus—is sovereign in their life, that's good enough. The commitment is there. We'll work out the details along the way. Paul is not making a plea for unity in the face of an unsettling diversity. Rather, the unity is assumed, and it's not uniformity. Paul's words speak plainly to our situation: "No single theological world, no single construal of the essence of Christianity, has ever characterized the United Church of Christ,"[55] while "our ecclesiology requires that we continually honor our covenant as a diverse people in community together."[56]

19

FISSURES AND TENSIONS IN OUR UNITY

"THE UCC IS NOT OF ONE MIND," BARBARA BROWN ZIKMUND TRUTHFULLY recounts, "yet it remains steadfast in its commitment to the 'oneness' of the church of Jesus Christ."[1] That commitment to oneness is at the core of our identity and is a stress point when we are not of one mind.

ADDRESSING DISAGREEMENTS

At General Synod 25, in 2005, delegates passed the resolution "Equal Marriage Rights for All."[2] Some individuals and some congregations disagreed with the resolution and left the UCC in the months that followed. But others who did not support the resolution did not leave the UCC. Some of those who disagreed with the resolution formed a new internal organization known as "Faithful and Welcoming Churches" (FWC). "Faithful and Welcoming Churches is an association of UCC members who consider themselves 'ECOT' (evangelical, conservative, orthodox, or traditional)."[3] The first two aims of Faithful and Welcoming Churches noted on its website are to "call ourselves and others to the founding vision of the United Church of Christ expressed in the UCC's 1957 Basis of Union and 1961

Preamble to the constitution" and to "promote unity in the UCC based on Jesus Christ as Lord and Savior, the Word of God in Holy Scripture, and the historic and apostolic faith."[4]

In 2006, during this turbulent time, Bob Thompson, president of FWC, wrote in an op-ed piece for the *United Church News*:

> We do not seek to divide or disrupt. We are not a cover for an exit strategy. We are simply asking that our presence be recognized and valued. How? . . .
>
>> Ask Associations and Conferences to help us communicate to churches that we are a positive alternative to separation.
>>
>> Give formal representation to ECOT members at every level of the church's life, as the UCC has done with other underrepresented groups.
>>
>> Help us uncover and address theological discrimination against ECOT clergy and laity.
>>
>> Recognize FWC churches along with Open and Affirming churches on the UCC's website.
>>
>> Refrain from painting a single broad-brush picture of our denomination that belies our true diversity.
>
> FWC will make every effort to be constructive in our criticism and dissent. We will continue to encourage churches and individuals to be active and supportive in the UCC. We will look for areas of agreement and partnership rather than focusing exclusive attention on areas of difference and disagreement.
>
> If it is true that "no matter who you are or where you are on life's journey" you are embraced in the UCC, we just want to be welcome like everyone else.[5]

Nancy S. Taylor, pastor of Old South Church UCC, Boston, responded to Bob Thompson's article and to statements he had made elsewhere:

> Bob Thompson's Faithful and Welcoming website identifies the equal marriage resolution vote of General Synod 25 as the decisive event for Faithful and Welcoming Churches' dissatisfaction with the UCC.
>
> That's fair. There is not a person in the UCC who does not recognize wide theological disagreement over same-gender marriage. It is a contentious, utterly immediate theological question.
>
> It is a question to which the church is responding with Bible study, prayer, reading theology, preparing and hearing sermons, talking to family and friends, holding congregational meetings and, yes, by voting on resolutions for and against equal marriage.
>
> As a non-hierarchical, congregationally-based tradition, this is how we live out our covenant together. As we do not recognize bishops or a pope, we engage in this difficult, sometimes divisive, profoundly important theological work from the ground up. If and when contentious matters are brought to a vote at General Synod—as equal marriage was last summer—we trust our delegates (faithful Christians all) to bring their level-best to the work of discernment.
>
> Thompson's response to all this, however, has been to charge delegates with a "declaration of independence from the Bible, the historic faith, and the teachings of Jesus concerning marriage," an incendiary claim he has made on his website and at regional FWC meetings.
>
> I submit that in making such a charge, Thompson has gone beyond the pale. After all, our delegates did their work. The fact that their discernment led them to a conclusion with which he differs should not be grounds for challenging their faith or integrity. . . .

Thompson's own church, Corinth Reformed Church in Hickory, N.C., has dropped UCC from its name and the FWC website encourages other UCC congregations to drop UCC from their names. . . . A full two years before the equal marriage vote, his church decided to significantly defer gifts from the wider church, including support for Our Church's Wider Mission in the Western North Carolina Association, the Southern Conference and the UCC's national and international settings. . . . Thompson believes the UCC is forcing him out. Nothing could be farther from the truth. There is plenty of room in the UCC for everyone who wants to be here. Rather, it is he who is leaving us, by wishing to remain engaged politically in a denomination with which he will no longer associate by name nor support financially. Further, he charges his brothers and sisters who served as delegates with being unfaithful. Thompson is not a loving critic.[6]

The allegations and appeals made by both authors point out fissures and tensions in our unity and call for accountability. In our church, the fissures and tensions—the not being of one mind—provide a rocky field where it is difficult to sustain deeply rooted commitment to unity. How do we overcome the dangers in this irregular landscape?

Let's look again at the major components of a church's life, growth, vitality, conflict, and decline identified in part II, "Local Churches," and now apply them to the totality of our church-ness.

Beginning with the most easily observable stratum, then digging deeper, we uncover:

Our norms. These are the visible aspects of our life together: programs and actions, structure and relationships, policies, traditions, and practices, use of budget, treatment of members, etc.

Our beliefs. These lie just below the visible norms and can be brought to the surface. Our beliefs are theological formulations, our stated purpose and goals, and our values—those things we assume are right and important. Our norms, we presume, grow out of and are expressive of our shared beliefs.

Our myth, or mythic identity. This is made up of the very basic assumptions which are at our core, our "life direction," the "largely unconscious values and processes by which we organize and define our experience. Myth is that which exists before belief can be articulated."[7]

Our norms—that is, our structures/programs/actions—rely upon an internal consistency, a sturdy coherence, with our beliefs and our myth. We do what we do because of what we believe. We believe what we believe because of who we are.

Working up from the level of myth: This is who we are. This is what we believe in. *Therefore* we structure and order ourselves, distribute our finances, and make public witness in this way at this time. The "therefore" is big.

Therefore. Consequently. As a result. Hence. If there is a fault line running through the foundational tiers of our mythic identity and shared beliefs leading up to our norms, the result is an instability that is sometimes perceived as shiftiness. This instability can come close to toppling our trust in one another.

When misgivings are voiced about a norm—when there is opposition to a visible action or public declaration—the connections between norms, beliefs, and mythic identity must be clarified through dialogue and exploration. Those with misgivings about a norm, a visible action, easily become alienated from the "we" at the heart of the covenant. They may "give up the fight and leave," or they may "attempt to subvert through withholding support or organizing for disruption."[8] The church is weakened when the connections between norm and belief are not clear—when the connecting "therefore" is forgotten and lost.

The General Synod vote of support for the equality in marriage resolution was the norm, the public action, with budget and program implications, that precipitated the launching of Faithful and Welcoming Churches. In the preceding interchange both authors refer to other norms. Bob Thompson asks for recognition and representation, in accord with our norms of structure and practice. Nancy Taylor cites the structural norm of nonhierarchical congregational polity and the constitutional norm of each Local Church's God-given responsibility for the United Church of Christ.[9]

Both move to the level of shared beliefs, just below the action itself, to call for accountability. Each invokes honoring of diversity, maintaining of unity, and valuing of all members. Those are beliefs we hold in common. Frustration at the level of our norms cannot be resolved at the norm level of budgets and structure revisions, programs and actions. Dissatisfaction with the norms, or with others' fidelity to the norms, must be addressed at the level of beliefs and values. It is then possible to install new wiring to connect or reconnect the tiers.

Having dialogue throughout our church on what we believe can highlight our many differences. We can also discover areas of agreement on beliefs, provided we move beyond the attitude of, "If you'll just listen to me you'll agree with me." Agreement on every issue is certainly unlikely and probably not to be sought. Often, in a one-time public situation, we strive for agreement. As Jane Fisler Hoffman counsels, this "may actually hinder us from living towards what may be a more faithful and appropriate hope."[10] The hope that is more faithful and appropriate for us is this: that we learn to accept one another as being equally in Christ, learn to respect one another's faith and life as valid expressions of allegiance to Jesus, and learn to welcome one another's attitude and style as absolutely necessary to the living diversity of the faith.[11]

For Conversation

1. How would you describe the two views presented of Faithful and Welcoming Congregations? Is the dispute about theology? At what points are the two writers not of one mind?

2. FWC asks that their "presence be recognized and valued." Who decides who is recognized and valued in our church? How do we express recognition and valuing?

3. What elements of covenant are cited in the two points of view about FWC?

4. Where do you find reference to hospitality—or lack of hospitality?

5. Reuben Sheares stated that our church is grounded in a willingness to "argue in love."[12] Does arguing in love presuppose a commitment to the oneness of our church? How is covenant present when we argue in love? How is hospitality a factor when we argue in love?

SUPPORTING THE UNITY OF INDEPENDENT VOICES

Diversity is a big part of our experience of unity. United and uniting churches, generally speaking,

> are linked not so much by a uniform structure or ecclesiology as by their commitment to visible—that is, structural as well as spiritual—unity and by the actual experience of union. Their ecclesiological life is shaped by their experience of integrating the diverse (indeed, sometimes apparently opposed) understandings and practices brought into the union.[13]

We, as the UCC, began by integrating the diverse and apparently opposed understandings and practices that our church's founders brought into the union back in 1957. Ever since then more practices and understandings have been added and embraced, and our links have been strengthened through our experience of union. But are we also linked by a commitment to structural and spiritual unity? Although we came into being "to express more fully the oneness in Christ of the churches composing it," is being united and uniting at the core of our mythic identity? Does commitment to unity organize and define our experience?

Unity—being a united and uniting church—definitely endures among us as a belief, and the word "unity" stirs up allegiance. But how does unity shape the "largely unconscious values and processes by which we organize and define our experience?" Is unity at the heart of who we are? Or is unity a motto on our logo that no longer appeals to us or animates us?

We started out with a group of Christians intensely committed to the ideal of unity. Unity, for them, was a witness to the all-including wholeness of the Body of Christ and a balm of healing for a rent and aching world. Might that commitment to unity still be with us "at the feeling level before belief can be articulated?"[14] Do notions, dreams, and visions of unity still pester us—in the best possible way? We're not seeking formal mergers of denominations as was the normative expression of our founders' ecumenical idealism in the twentieth century.[15] But, deep in our marrow, we may be hungering for "integrating the diverse (indeed sometimes apparently opposed) understandings and practices" that were not only brought into the union of 1957 but are daily, weekly, monthly, yearly brought into the United Church of Christ so that those who were "them" yesterday are "us" today. Does the light generated from the initial excited molecular state of pressing toward unity still hang around us, drawing people who are seeking a unity in diversity, maybe theologian Paul Tillich's "reunion of the estranged"? This "mythic, nonverbal sense of being united and uniting may be the reason people are joining the UCC. It's not what we are doing or projecting intentionally, but they sense it still, they come and stay."[16]

While we sift through the layers of meaning and significance that a commitment to unity holds for us as a church, it is important that we keep alert to the temptation to make statements that convey a false unanimity about who "we" are, or what "we" do. Whether it's about the way we baptize, or solemnize marriages, or take stands on legislative issues or government policies, we dare not violate our covenantal commitment to honor the integrity of each setting of our church. We need to remember that what has been affirmed in one setting of the church is not always affirmed by all settings, or what applies to some does not always apply to all. Ignoring or disregarding voices is distinctly problematic for us given our nonhierarchical structure. We are called to support a unity that holds all of our independent and disparate voices in a creative tension.

Today, when people ask who we are as the United Church of Christ, the "most typical short answer," as Randi Walker records, "is that we are a multiracial, multicultural, just peace church, open and affirming, and accessible to all."[17]

What does this mean? Let's look at the origin of one facet of that identity statement. A Pronouncement and Proposal for Action, "Calling the United Church of Christ to be a Multiracial and Multicultural Church," was affirmed by General Synod 19, in 1991. It envisions the United Church of Christ as "a venture of faith to be a community of and for all people."[18]

A Multiracial and Multicultural Church:

- affirms and lives out its faith in God as revealed through Jesus Christ;
- knows we are interconnected with people of all races, ethnicities and cultures;
- embodies and rejoices in these diversities as gifts to the human family;
- welcomes all people into the community of faith without discrimination because of color, race, ethnicity, language or culture;
- formally recognizes and utilizes the racial and cultural varieties of gifts within the context of Christian Unity;
- struggles within church and society to rid itself of the sin of racism which has prevented an authentic embrace of the races, ethnicity and cultures in our denomination;
- makes multiracial and multicultural inclusiveness a key organizing principle for church in society;
- works for justice and peace throughout the global community;

- reflects in its membership the changing demographics;
- declares itself an anti-racist congregation.[19]

A Bible study on the Book of Acts connects belief and norm because, "without a clear understanding of the biblical and theological grounding for the vision of diversity and oneness, of a common identity in the context of the whole family of God, the journey toward becoming multiracial and multicultural will never become a living reality."[20]

Some Conferences, Associations, and Local Churches have been daunted by the ethnic homogeneity of their surroundings even as they aspire to be multiracial and multicultural. In living out the spirit of the pronouncement, they are able to say things like, "Around here, ethnicity tends to be a question of which country in Europe your ancestors came from. We try to treat the Swedes just like we do the Germans, but that really isn't the issue." Or they acknowledge, "I don't really expect Tafatolu UCC to become an ethnically diverse congregation. But we're open to it."

Nevertheless there has been dedication in many settings of the UCC to become more multiracial and multicultural.

There's a lot of diversity in our Conference, but not in each church. We look for ways in which the centers of decision-making in our Conference can become more representative of our diversity. We also want our methods of decision-making and the styles and content of our meetings to be accessible and hospitable to persons of all racial and cultural heritages.

We wanted to get a reading on how ethnically diverse our churches are, beyond the usual identifications. When we looked at the ethnic composition of our churches we used two categories for European Americans: "White," to refer to those who claimed no ethnic heritage and "Ethnically Identified European" for others.

We reviewed all our Conference and Association programming in light of the Pronouncement, asking: Who participates? Who leads or plans? Should this be changed? Should new programming be added and some of the old deleted?

We looked at the cultural variables found in our churches, within polarities such as Open and Affirming/Not Open and Affirming; Female-Male Equality in Leadership/Female-Male Specialized Roles; Economic Hardship/Affluence; Rural-Urban-Suburban.

For Reflection

1. Are you aware of ways in which we as a church have begun to address racism?

2. In settings of the church with which you are familiar, is there consciousness of being part of a multiracial and multicultural church?

In 2005, General Synod 25 adopted the resolution "Another World Is Possible: A Peace with Justice Movement in the United Church of Christ."[21] This resolution drew upon "numerous social justice oriented identity Resolutions and Pronouncements" from Synods past, to come up with the call to Local Churches and Conferences to declare themselves "Just Peace, Open and Affirming, Accessible to All, Whole Earth, and/or Multiracial and Multicultural" and to unite for action. *Shine, God's People*,[22] a study guide published in 2006 for the celebration of our church's fiftieth birthday, contains chapters about our identity. Beginning with "We are a united and uniting church," the "we are" statements progress through multiracial and multicultural, accessible to all, open and affirming, and a peace and justice church. What was initiated in 2005 as a stirring call from General Synod to Local Churches and Conferences had, by 2006, evolved into a "we are" statement. Within our experiential unity, we need to ask what is being said: Are we as the whole United Church of Christ a multiracial, multicultural, just peace church, open and affirming, and accessible to all? Are we committed to becoming so? Who is "we" here? Who is excluded from the "we?" To what extent are United Church of Christ congregations, Associations, and Conferences the expressions of a united and uniting, multiracial and multicultural, accessible to all, open and affirming and just peace church?[23]

Reinhold Niebuhr, theologian, ethicist, and Evangelical and Reformed pastor, asserted rather dourly that

> only a romanticist of the purest water could maintain that a national group ever arrives at a "common mind" or becomes conscious of a "general will" without the use of either force or the threat of force . . . even religious communities, if they are sufficiently large and if they deal with issues regarded as vital to their members.[24]

The use of force or the threat of force may be an overstatement when applied to the settings of our church. But, within our experiential unity, how do we make public witness as General Synod or as bodies related to General Synod or as a Conference or an Association without effectively silencing or invalidating as "not UCC" those whose conscience leads them in a different direction or whose take on how church works is at odds with a particular tactic or plan of action or those for whom "the national church is not a natural, organic extension of their local religious life [but] exists as an autonomous actor with its own separate agenda?"[25]

To do these things we need to find ways to raise a collective prophetic voice or claim a public identity without conveying or prescribing a false unanimity. And we don't want the clunkiness of our covenantal interrelationships to blunt our prophetic edge. We want to avoid being dragged down by the penchant of every secular news source ever reporting on us to cast Synod and Conferences in the role of rule-making bodies. We want to pass along the ways in which our experiential unity of autonomous parts and free consciences is able to thrive, without being plodding or disparaging about it. We want to get it across that we honor our covenant as a diverse people in community together. And that there is joy and discipleship in this way of being church. We've seen and heard it done in ways like these.

The welcome on the home page of the Kansas Oklahoma Conference in 2014 expressed that Conference's practical application of how they were multiracial and multicultural, and open and affirming: "We are a communion of historic and emerging congregations sharing the Good News of the Gospel of Jesus Christ. We invite you to join our inclusive community. We are a multi-racial and multi-ethnic Conference embracing congregations from American Samoa, the Marshall Islands, the Federated States of Micronesia, as well as Pentecostal and European traditions. A number of congregations have identified themselves as Open and Affirming (welcoming persons of all sexual orientations)."

UCC pastor and sometime radio commentator Kurt Katzmar preached about our church, "No, it's not a church for everybody. We're like the cartoon there on page one of the bulletin: two booths at a convention of some kind. The first is labeled 'Questions Answered,' and is manned by an older, gruff-looking man. A teenager sits behind the second booth, labeled 'Answers Questioned.' . . . Questioning answers through spiritual inquiry and intellectual freedom is too much work, even for us, sometimes."[26]

"Following Jesus' lead, the United Church of Christ strives to keep doors open to all," a national stewardship resource announced, along with the testimony that "each UCC congregation prayerfully discerns and expresses how wide their doors and arms are open."[27]

Many of us have made the informal assertion, "You know, we're all over the place on this issue—and that's what we love about this church, we're free to be all that. Now, here's what our (choose one) General Synod or Conference or Association or congregation just came out with."

Or as UCC minister Tyler Connoley says in his blog "United Church . . . of Christ," "When people ask me what the United Church of Christ is, I don't say we're the most-progressive Christian denomination—even though we've certainly led the way, on issues from ordaining women to civil rights. Instead, I tell people we're the most-inclusive Christian denomination."[28]

For Conversation

1. In 1989 Avery Post was completing his service as President of the United Church and contemplating retirement when he addressed General Synod Seventeen. He said, "Biblical faith introduced me to a justice lifestyle at the beginning of my ministry and I expect to stay on the case for God's justice until the end of my days."[29] Where do you find connections between biblical faith and a justice lifestyle? How is that connection expressed by settings of our church endeavoring to be and become a multiracial, multicultural, just peace church, open and affirming, and accessible to all?

2. What happens in a Local Church when shared beliefs produce differing views of the ways to express beliefs through actions, budgets, programs, or structures?

3. Could preliminary dialogue on our beliefs within and among Local Churches pave a smoother path to unity in wider church actions and witness? (This would not be about seeking agreement, but nurturing hospitable dialogue.) How soon can we start?

4. What are your thoughts on how we can raise a collective prophetic voice without conveying a false unanimity?

20

THE MYTH OF UNITY, OR THE UNIFYING MYTH

AVING CONSIDERED THE DYNAMICS AMONG NORMS, BELIEFS, AND myth, let's look a bit more closely at myth. Our myth is made up of very basic assumptions. It is our life direction, the largely unconscious values and processes by which we organize and define our experience. Without going all cosmogonic,[1] we can cull from studies on culture that

> Myths are symbolic tales of the distant past, may be connected to belief systems or rituals, and may serve to direct social action and values. Myths are narratives representative of a particular way of understanding nature and organizing thought. Myths are narratives . . . featuring actors and actions that confound the conventions of routine experience.[2]

Tom Tupper, author/editor of the UCC resource "How Organizations Function," points out that in our church life the word myth signifies "the depth of truth that cannot be fully explained through logical or straightforward language but only grasped within the essence of our being. It is our identity. It is how we know who we are. It is 'caught' in community more than it is 'taught' in the classroom."[3]

Underscoring the narrative nature of myth, he says:

We don't use words, definitions, or ideas to communicate our myth. Rather we tell stories. We love to tell stories about ordaining the first woman or the first gay person. . . . Jesus didn't say much about what he believes. But he told a lot of stories that gave clues to his identity and self-understanding.

So, if you asked me what the UCC myth is for me, I would have to tell you the story of my pilgrimage through life and the church. From those stories you would get a sense of who I am, what I believe, and how I live.

In my local church right now, we are celebrating our 175th anniversary, beginning as an Evangelishe church, then an E&R church, and then a UCC church. However, we now have a hodge-podge of people who carry around very different myths about the church. We have a significant group of people who have come from a variety of different denominations, racial groups, and other societal minorities. They each have different "church stories" that guide how they think things should be done. We don't tell many UCC stories [so] that these stories [can] become their stories.

When we became UCC, many of the stories we told about who we are were still grounded in the E&R church. They know the stories of how our church supported the beginnings of hospitals and children's homes, and homes for the developmentally disabled, etc. They still do these things in a generous manner. But they have never bought into the stories that were the stories of the Congregational Churches who took on slavery and racism, etc. Thus, they don't think there is a place in the church for "political action." So there is an uneasiness that has led some to leave and others to demand that we stop taking "liberal" stances.

Theoretically, I know that this can only be addressed satisfactorily by rehearsing our stories and working on creative ways to incorporate all of us in clearly articulated stories about "who we are." This is a lot easier said than done.[4]

In the introduction to a history and polity course she taught with Paul Bradley, Elizabeth Wheeler relates this "tale with a theory," which may function as a mythic story of our church:

The UCC evolved from a narrow sectarian faith into America's most liberal denomination because of shock at the suffering and sorrow caused by Christian people, shame at the dishonor done to Christianity, the love of country and the fear of God's wrath. Repeated shocks over 250 years repeatedly drove us to change our ways and in penance make right what we had done wrong to The Others whether The Others were dissenting Christians, Native Americans, African Americans, women, immigrants, other faiths, the earth. Again and again the daily string of human sins accumulated into major spiritual crises. To relieve the intolerable dissonances between belief and behavior, the faithful applied a rigorous spiritual discipline: the self-examination of their own sins and the systemic evils in which they were complicit. The crises led to turning points in a narrative of increasing openness, inclusion and a new normal.

The UCC is Freedom's church. For over 250 years the sectarian ideas of freedom dear to the UCC's original antecedents were tested by the American experience of freedom. Freedom is the UCC *charism*. Over and over again early Calvinists and the UCC's later strands have adjusted to paradigm shifts that changed them and us profoundly.[5]

Our identity—as individuals, as communities of faith—changes through the stories that we tell about our lives. Changes in our stories refashion our identity.

When I came to Union City, Michigan, in 1978 to co-pastor the First Congregational UCC, I was presented with the history booklet that had been compiled in 1977 for the church's 140th anniversary. There was a detailed listing of the names of those who had served in leadership positions over the years, descriptions of the buildings where the congregation had met, and mention was made that Josh McDowell, of Campus Crusade for Christ fame, had grown up in the congregation.

When I returned in 2012 for the 175th anniversary of the church, a different history booklet had been produced, one that noted in the fourth paragraph that the Ladies Benevolent Society was organized on May 1, 1838, and their purpose was "aiding the Potawatomi Indians who lived in the community and sewing for those in need." The history recorded the involvement of their pastor L. Smith Hobart in the Underground Railroad.

At a youth group meeting in 1978, I picked up a hymnal inscribed "First Congregational Church UCC" and asked what the "UCC" stood for. The group responded, in chorus and with minimal eye rolling, "Union City Church." By 2012 the church's website disclosed no equivocation on their United Church of Christ identity.

Clearly, different stories of this congregation's origins, history, heroic figures, character, and focus were making the rounds in 2012 than those that were circulating in 1977. The facts in each history booklet were true and verifiable. But the emphases, the information included and excluded in each, more than hinted at a recasting of the congregation's mythic identity.

Conference Minister Charles Buck cautions that mythic stories can become the truth itself for us rather than being revelatory of the truth.[6] That is, we might be swept into complacency by the allure of a mythic story such as being "freedom's church." For that myth to reveal the truth, however, we must tell and hear the stories of the "sins and the systemic evils" in which our forebears were complicit and in which we are complicit.

We must hear and tell the stories of the sins and systematic evils to which our forebears and we have been and are subjected. One far-reaching area for historic exploration would be tracing the impact of the so-called doctrine of discovery's assertion that that the lands of peoples who were not Christian could be seized and occupied, and the people suppressed.[7]

For Conversation

1. What stories does your congregation tell about its origins?

2. What stories does your congregation, your Conference/Association, or other setting of our church tell about becoming part of the UCC? How do the stories told by different congregations, Associations, Conferences, and other settings of the church affect one another?

3. What stories do you tell about your life in the UCC?

4. How do these stories shape our identity as the United Church of Christ? How do we shape our church's identity with our stories?

The United Church of Christ is often described as liberal,[8] even though, "in broad terms, UCC members are more likely to identify as conservative—both politically and theologically."[9] The word "liberal" can be understood in many ways. Liberal can mean openness to a diversity of ideas, beliefs, people, and cultures.[10] Liberal can be understood as pertaining to positions taken to influence civil legislation or public policy, or to movements for social change such as women's reproductive rights, same gender marriage, and racial justice.

UCC historian Elizabeth Nordbeck says,

We have this long history that goes all the way back to our beginnings, that we have understood that God is still speaking, that in the words of Pastor John Robinson in 1620 "that God still hath more truth and light to break forth from God's holy word"—and that is profoundly liberal. It means that we are not bound to the shackles of previous generations, and while we do not set out to change the old, old story, we do intend to make it new for each succeeding generation . . . just as the opening words of the UCC Constitution ask of us."[11]

More Topics for Conversation

1. Are we a liberal church? In what sense?

2. How is being liberal, in whatever sense, part of our mythic identity, part of the stories we tell about who we are, or part of our pre-verbal sense of ourselves?

21

CONCLUDING THOUGHTS
ON HOSPITALITY AND COVENANT,
OUR GENIUS AND OUR CHALLENGE

A T MY LOWEST AND MOST DESPONDENT MOMENTS I fear for our church. I worry that we have missed the boat about living in covenant. Maybe not so much missed the boat as failed to configure our individual boats into a flotilla. Too often we are content in our self-sufficiency and/or our conviction that we—in whatever our setting—know how the church should operate. We overlook the strength and blessings to be reaped from lashing our boats together as we venture over the uncertain seas of life and navigate the disorienting currents of faithfulness in deep waters.

My disquieting thoughts take on nightmare quality with "what if's." What if our founders' passionate run from "movement to denomination" caused us to fatally sidestep the "practice of community in which polity reflects the knowledge that we belong to each other and derive our life from each other?"[1] What if our understanding that covenant is "highly inter-active . . . a system of cross-initiatives and cross-influencings"[2] is only theoretical? What if the disposition that "we're all in this together" is never written on our hearts? What if talk of covenant never rises to our lips as effortlessly as talk of hospitality?[3] What if we increasingly default to "covenant" as a cudgel—taken up in accusation, appealed to as a standard in times of disagreement and aggravation?[4]

We are the *United* Church of Christ, and the relationship of covenant to unity is obvious. Covenant lashes our boats together, keeps us in one flotilla. There are those who say that our mythic identity is more about autonomy than unity, that autonomy overshadows and preempts "united and uniting" as our theme. That autonomy—not unity—is evident and recurring in all that we do and espouse.

We need to remember that hospitality and autonomy are related. Hospitality is a first cousin to autonomy, both with an inherited tendency toward the unruly. Hospitality and autonomy recognize their kinship at the family reunions, although they sometimes engage in mulish standoffs, when autonomy actually *does* say, "You can't tell me what to do or think or believe." And hospitality counters with the suggestion from Bill Hulteen that there is much to be learned from the other. More tellingly, hospitality insists that we all—friends, family, strangers, and enemies—live by the grace of divine hospitality. Hospitality applies tension to autonomy, stretching and pulling at our autonomy, elongating it, and preventing its gravitational collapse into itself in a confusion of "biblical freedom with arbitrary assertion of will."[5]

In the movie *The Descendants*, George Clooney's character says, "My family seems like an archipelago. We are part of the same group, but we are still islands—separate and alone. And we're slowly drifting apart." What if, in our chilly bastions of autonomy, we disconnect from covenant and drift apart, unraveling as a church? What if, as the Leaders Box notes, "We tend to be interdependent today when it suits our particular need. This can be as true for a congregation, church member or national body of the church as it is for a group within a congregation, a conference or an association."[6]

We are troubled by signs of a fraying covenant, such as the anticipated shortfall of 3.2 million dollars from the General Synod budget in 2014. We are heartened by newly woven strands of covenant, as more than three hundred new congregations were received into membership between 2007 and 2015.[7] That prickly road trod by General Synod to embrace unified governance for the national setting of our church has let the national setting be "more covenantal, more 'we,'" according to General Minister and President Geoffrey Black, and the members of the Collegium in 2014.[8] The Covenanted Ministries are now united by one governing board characterized by "diversity not representation . . . built on trust."[9] However, the strengthening of covenant within one setting of our church does not necessarily translate into strengthened covenants throughout our church.

In 2015 the United Church of Christ Board brought to General Synod some proposed revisions of our constitution and bylaws that would lead to changes regarding the General Minister and President and the Collegium:

Since the last General Synod the Unified Board . . . and the Collegium of Officers has needed to figure out how to make significant cuts in the budget and expense of the National Setting caused by the trend of shrinking OCWM support and a significant decrease in the amount of endowment funds available for compensating for budget needs not covered by OCWM dollars. . . .

The Collegium of Officers was created at a time when the UCC was actually restructuring from eleven instrumentalities and agencies to four covenanted ministries. It was an idea (the word "Collegium" actually having been created to describe the concept) of how to reflect collaborative leadership and decision making in the National Setting. . . . While collaborative decision making continues to be a valued process in the National Setting, the "Collegium of Officers" model is not the most effective way for our more nimble National Setting at this point. The shift in our sources of operational support . . . [has] forced the issue, but the recommendation of the Board is that our National Setting will be stronger and more effective in the future under the leadership of a General Minister and President who is called to lead in the National Setting with regard to the whole church, including the work of the Covenanted Ministries.[10]

A majority of the delegates voting at the 2015 General Synod accepted the proposed leadership changes, but not by the two-thirds margin to put the changes into effect. Some of those opposed to the changes were concerned about moving from the collaborative leadership pattern in the Collegium to having one officer of the church. This was expressed sharply in an online quip, "Why not just have a pope for the sake of efficiency?" Insinuations were made that consolidating national leadership into one officer prefigured the end of autonomy for all the settings of our church. Proponents of the changes rightly asserted that changes in the organization of the national setting do not affect the organizational life of Local Churches, Conferences, and Associations. Yet others voiced reluctance to support the proposed changes because the whole church had not been engaged in dialogue prior to the vote. One delegate was not sure she opposed the changes themselves, but expressed her uneasiness:

> This is a huge change! And the notice of the proposed changes to the Constitution and Bylaws just popped up among the General Synod materials after the March meeting of the UCC Board. I don't question the motivations of the Board—they're facing tough issues on our behalf—and their actions were perfectly within their constitutional rights, but I'm very disappointed that they proceeded as if we weren't all part of the same church, and that we don't all care about the whole church.

It is useful to recall here that Donald Freeman defines autonomy "while in covenant" as each setting's "non-transferable responsibility to respond to the call of God to it—God's will and way for it—in its time and place."[11] We are so often, in each expression of our church, admirably valiant and intrepid in taking on our nontransferable responsibilities to discern God's will and way for *our* time and place. Our challenge comes with the "while in covenant" part of the definition. To many it seems that "not only local churches but also wider church bodies act most of the time as though they possess, by right, the freedom and authority to carry out their mission mandates"[12] independently—with the autonomy of self-determination and self-sufficiency rather than an autonomy within covenantal relationships. Local Churches, Associations, Conferences, Covenanted Ministries, the United Church of Christ Board, Associated and Affiliated Ministries all do what they are called to do, at times with such fervent concentration as to miss "their" connection to "us."

At the same time, we have a genius—a natural talent—for hospitality. Hospitality is a genetic gift passed along to us by our spiritual forebears, present at the conception of the United Church of Christ in the chromosomes of the UCC ecumenical vision. The Greek word οἶκος (pronounced "oy'-kos," transliterated *oikos*) is the root word for "ecumenical"—as well as for "ecology" and "economy." *Oikos* means "house" or "household," and widens to include all sorts of relationships and connections. Religiously, *oikos* is the household of faith, the family of God—one family, huge and prototypically united. *Oikos* is the venue for hospitality. Historically, the church began in houses, later moving, as it gained public voice and influence, to the realm of the polis—government. When we in the UCC become preoccupied with the mandates and responsibilities with which we have been entrusted in detachment from the other expressions of our church, we ignore the *oikos* ethic of hospitality to one another within our covenantal household of faith.[13]

Local Churches, Associations, Conferences, or Covenanted Ministries do sometimes stray from the standard of autonomy tempered with consultation and are met with only minor squawks of objection. In contrast, when proposed changes for the national governance structure of our church are presented at General Synod there is almost always grievance, indignation, and insistence that the whole church needs to be engaged in the formulation of the changes. It is crucial, as said earlier, to remember that frustrations at the level of structural revisions must be addressed at the level of the beliefs and values that lie beneath structure. They cannot be resolved with the external norms of constitutionally defined procedure.

Members of past national committees on structure and restructure accurately claim that no effort at consultation ever effectively reaches everyone, and that not everyone *wants* to be reached for consultation. However, those who come to Synod care deeply about the whole church and see that our process for structural change "is not only a tool, it is a way of walking; the walking itself must reveal the vision."[14] A walk of covenant, a vision of unity.

In 1969 the Theological Commission wrote an instructive piece on autonomy. It was intended for Local Churches, but the message is applicable to all the expressions of our church. As adapted for the whole church, it reminds us that:

> Our autonomy is completely misunderstood when it is regarded as a means to isolate one expression of the church from the rest of the church. Only the free know the fullness of love; and each setting has its freedom in the United Church of Christ in order that there may be no shadow of outer coercion, but only the inner compulsion of love, in its relationship to the church of the ages, the whole ministering church of this age, and the needs of humanity ministered to.
>
> Each setting of our church is a school in the life of the Spirit. If it closes its mind to the rest of the church, it is comparable to a university that in an insane moment should shut itself off from the findings of scholars in other universities.[15]

We prize our autonomy in the United Church of Christ. Each of the settings of our church is free. We make our way into covenant with no shadow of outer coercion, only the inner compulsion of love. Our church, with its freedom, can be a marvel. When Paul Sherry, President of the UCC, was on a flight home to Cleveland in the early 1990s he had a memorable conversation with the Roman Catholic priest seated next to him. The priest knew nothing (or maybe just a little) about the United Church of Christ. But after a long talk about the contrasts between their faith communities, the priest said, "I am so grateful to learn about your church. And if the United Church of Christ weren't already here, God would need to invent it now."[16]

We are freedom's church. Freedom is our element. We freely ask questions of theology and scripture. In freedom Local Churches call pastors; form services of worship; organize for mission, outreach, and ministry; gather as Associations and Conferences to authorize ministers on behalf of the whole church; unite in ministries of justice and compassion. Our freedom is glorious. But the miracle—the sign that God's fingerprints are all over this, confounding the conventions of routine experience—is that with all our freedom we call ourselves "united." "United" is more than a random name selection or an experimental handle tried on in a burst of mid-twentieth-century ecumenical naiveté. United is a divine gift, present even when "we don't see one strand of commonality on which to base our unity."[17]

During my years of worshiping with churches in the Northern California Nevada Conference, I would, as many Conference Ministers do, use the opportunity to bring greetings from "all of your sister and brother congregations" and to present a little interpretative piece on who we are as the United Church of Christ. I would tell of our Conference's geographic stretch from the Oregon border in the north, to Porterville in the south, and from the Pacific Ocean on the west to Reno in the east. I would tell how, on any Sunday, you might walk into a UCC church and at first think you'd come upon an Episcopal service or a Unitarian service; how worship might flow in Pentecostal style or follow a Congregational order of service, or proceed in a different manner, unique to that congregation; how you might hear hymns, prayers, and sermons in English or Korean, Spanish, Tagalog, Tongan, Cantonese, Samoan, or Japanese. I would conclude with the declaration that we are united through the transforming love of Jesus Christ, which is greater than our differences and cherishes us in our diversity as the image and likeness of our Creator. Which all speaks to the daring and the wonder that comes through and comes with our calling to be united.

Our founders went "from movement to denomination" by an orderly course of votes and plans and constitutional drafts. In the future we may need to get back into movement mode to achieve the unity to which we are called.[18] This would be a movement away from expecting or fearing that General Synod, or our national offices or officers, or the United Church of Christ Board will provide unity for us or impose unity on us. The UCC doesn't work that way. We need to pay attention to the inter-relationship of all our composite parts in order for the rare bloom of unity to blossom and spread through every setting of our church. After all, "we live by a dialectic between Covenant and Autonomy rather than juridical authority. . . ."[19]

Autonomy and Covenant seem contradictory, yet their interaction brings unity that has depth and magnitude. Our movement toward unity is a movement toward dialogical unity, a unity of creative tension among all of our independent and disparate voices. It takes us along a scenic route where we can savor all our contradictions.

The United Church of Christ movement to dialogical unity will never be easy, even when we want to be pulled from the stagnant pools of ignoring or tolerating one another into the moving waters of accepting, respecting, and welcoming one another in all our disheveled states of being.

But this movement to dialogical unity might be simple. We begin with conversation in all settings of our church. We begin by acting—with more joy and less due process—"on creative ways to incorporate all of us in clearly articulated stories about 'who we are.'"[20]

The National Council of Churches suggests ways to start (or start over with) dialogical relationship. (The NCC intended this for interfaith use, but it works with wider church as well.)

All relationship begins with meeting. The model for our meeting others is always the depth of presence and engagement which marked Jesus' meeting with those around him. . . .

True relationship involves risk. When we approach others with an open heart, it is possible that we may be hurt. When we encounter others with an open mind, we may have to change our positions or give up certainty, but we may gain new insights. . . .

True relationship respects the other's identity. We will meet others as they are, in their particular hopes, ideas, struggles and joys. These are articulated through their own traditions, practices and world-views. We encounter the image of God in the particularity of another person's life.

True relationship is based on integrity. If we meet others as they are, then we must accept their right to determine and define their own identity. We also must remain faithful to who we are. . . .

True relationship is rooted in accountability and respect. We approach others in humility, not arrogance. In our relationships we will call ourselves and our partners to a mutual accountability.[21]

There are stories that will tie us together as the United Church of Christ. We can tell personal stories of our life in the United Church of Christ. Congregations can tell about their origins, about how they became part of the UCC. Each Association, Conference, and aspect of the national setting can articulate the stories of its origin. We can pass along the stories we've heard in our Local Churches, at Association, Conference, and national gatherings, at pastors' retreats, lay retreats, and staff meetings of any staff, in any setting. We can tell and retell the stories of what it means to us—frustration, dynamism, whatever—to be part of the United Church of Christ. We can admit the times we've said, about someone or some body of our church, "Why did they go and do THAT?" We can appreciate the times we've said, "This is who we are: The United Church of Christ." All of these stories carry the "depth of truth that cannot be fully explained through logical or straightforward language but only grasped within the essence of our being."[22] In these stories is our identity. Through these stories we know who we are. And we expand the definition of "we."

Our different stories, heard and told in an atmosphere of hospitality, can strengthen our covenant and unite us "if we pray for the grace and courage to speak the truth in love and to hear one another all the way through."[23]

For more than twenty years now, I have been talking to anyone who displays a glimmer of interest about my three abiding hopes for the United Church of Christ:

- that we make clear and explicit connections between our biblical faith and any public actions we take,

- that we never abandon our commitment to justice and to working out our understanding of Genesis 1:27, that all people are created in the image and likeness of God; and

- that in the process of carrying through on those first two hopes we treat one another with hospitable kindness, that we love one another in the midst of everything.

In the early 1990s I received a letter that brought unflinching evidence that our reach for hopes one and two often falls short of our grasp. I know it was a difficult letter to write. I know it was a painful letter to read. It came from a lifelong member of the United Church of Christ, someone whose views on social issues and political realities were most assuredly at odds with mine, but someone whose faith is indisputably rooted in the same gracious Love as mine.

It was a difficult letter to receive because it slashed at the connections between Christian faith and social justice, which, to me, are inseparable and inescapable, and implored the church to "just help us live our lives." It must have been a painful letter to send because it revisited and captured so well the frustration of those who have felt their views demeaned, concerns disregarded, and faith stance unheeded in General Synod[24] and Conference actions and issues that seemed to them politically motivated or even unbiblical. From the perspective of this loyal member, the United Church of Christ had abandoned Christian practice to the spurious zeitgeist of trending causes.

As I drafted my response, I found myself wishing that I could introduce the letter writer to UCC advocate for justice Yvonne Delk so that they could tell their stories to one another about church as lifeline. Yvonne Delk has compellingly written,

> The year 1940 found my mother and my father bringing me in their arms to Macedonia Congregational Christian Church for a dedication service. I was not quite a year old. This was the moment that I was to receive a name, a people, a history, a community. They understood that we needed a support community if we were able to survive the racism of the nation in which I was born. . . .[25]
>
> The division of the human family because of race challenges the Church of Jesus Christ to renew its foundational commitment to the faith. God's promise to us is that we are one people because we are reconciled to God in one body through the cross. Therefore, we cannot support any pattern of subordination or domination that separates and divides.[26]

These words flow from faith, rather than political analysis. This is a story of trust in the sovereign power of God, who transforms "life through freedom from the inward bonds of sin and the outward barriers of society's injustices and unjust patterns of order."[27] It is a story that would resonate with the member in Northern California. It is an invitation that calls forth the stories of those who hear it.

Our different stories, heard and told in an atmosphere of hospitality, can strengthen our covenant and unite us. Here's one example of how that can work. The account begins with the words of Jim Ross, pastor of First Congregational UCC, Ripon, California:

Sometimes when a family has a tragedy, other members of the family just come over and gather around and help them through a tough time. We wanted to do something personally for these folks who had lost so much this fall in the Butte Fire.

So we just closed our church this past Sunday, and twenty of us, adults and kids, piled into cars and drove an hour and a half to our sister UCC church in Angels Camp, to be with them for church and lunch. . . . My folks don't agree with all my ideas, but this one they seemed to take to, that we would just go up there, listen to their stories, and it might help them regain some hope. . . .

"The community feels like it's suffering PTSD," said Liz Armstrong, pastor of Union Congregational UCC in Angels Camp. "There's high depression, tempers are short, there have been five suicides. . . . The response [from the wider church] has been fantastic. . . . But Jim Ross kept saying, 'We want to come and see you.'" And they did.

So on All Saints Day, they gathered around the communion table and then the potluck table. "It was a tremendous uplift for all of us," Liz said. "It was perfect."[28]

This was a visitation of love that reminded all who were involved— and all who hear of it—of our connection in covenant. Visitations of love are meetings with a depth of presence. They are occasions to meet others as they are while being who we are, with humility and respect. They are "honest, open, caring but challenging, a reminder of things that it is in our nature to forget."[29] Periodic Support Consultations, Conference Board meetings, trainings in Church Growth, meetings of the Council of Conference Ministers can be perfunctory and *pro forma*. But those same kinds of gatherings can be visitations of love by the intent or expectation of the visitors and/or the visited.

I remember, as a young pastor, receiving visits from staff of the Office of Church in Society, Board for Homeland Ministries, Office for Church

Life and Leadership, and Office for Church in Society that were visitations of love. They challenged those gathered at regional, Association, and Conference events to take effective faith-based action for justice and peace; to teach the faith creatively and with integrity; to design worship that listens for God's voice and speaks the language of the people; to address ministerial formation with accountability and discernment. I remember visits that I made as Executive Director of the Coordinating Center for Women, when I danced on the sand hills in western Nebraska; talked story in Hawai'i with people who were "houseless, not homeless"; discussed the nature of forgiveness while monitoring the first free elections in South Africa; and in so many other times and places where I was received with openness, caring, and reminders of things that it is in our nature to neglect, if not forget. "I have found no more powerful thing that church leaders can do to strengthen the churches than visit them with love," says Randi Walker.[30] In that same frame of heart and mind, visiting one another with love throughout the settings of the church, extending and receiving hospitality, is a powerful means of strengthening covenant and uniting the whole church.

All of this takes time. Time spent together. Hearing. Seeing. Listening. Across cultural canyons and racial divides. Beyond comfort zones. Despite fears. Risking offense. Hazarding indifference.

It will take time for hospitality to work its way into the crannies of our structures and procedures and make us brave enough for unity. It will take time for covenant to transform our preoccupation with autonomy into an openness to unity.

It will take time to get to the point where each of us can affirm from our own life story as UCC pastor Arthur Cribbs does,

> There is something deep inside of me, as an African-American man, that says that this is a safe place for me. As an adopted person into the UCC, [whenever] I pass a place that says "UCC" on its marquee, I feel connected. I feel it's safe to go inside. That's

all relationship, and it's understood that we do not have to agree in order to be family. I hope we never, never lose the importance of relationship. If we ever do that, the prayer of Jesus—"That they may all be one"—will never be understood or affirmed, it will just be a slogan."[31]

It will take time for us all to get there. We have been headed this way for such a long time.

It will take time, as we continue to call upon the energies of the Holy One to build up a unity without coercion or rancor. A unity where we are neither homogenized, standardized, or reduced to lowest terms, but transformed to be clearly and truly who we are called to be.

It will take time, while we keep on learning how to bear witness to a unity that is not a "unity of like-mindedness," but a unity that "defies our common understanding of the word.[32] A unity that holds dear the fact that we are made up of complicated yet related parts.

It will take time get to the place where we can fully be the *United Church of Christ*. It will take time, but we'll keep at it. We'll keep at it with the blessed assurance that is inherent in the nature of God, who is One in beloved community, and who creates humankind in the Divine image. This will be time well-spent.

Acknowledgments

T HIS BOOK BEGAN WITH A CONVERSATION. AS I WAS PREPARING to retire from Conference ministry Randi Walker suggested that I might want to write a book about life in the United Church of Christ. She pointed out that the breadth of my experience gave me a unique view of our church and how it operates. This, I had to agree, was true. I have been privileged to serve as a campus minister at Iowa State University, as the pastor of a rural congregation in Union City, Michigan, and an inner city congregation in Grand Rapids, Michigan, as an Associate Conference Minister with the Indiana-Kentucky Conference, and as Executive Director of the UCC Coordinating Center for Women in Church and Society, before coming to Northern California Nevada as Conference Minister. In each of the geographic and administrative settings of the United Church of Christ, I have been received with hospitality. And in each setting I have learned more about how we live in covenant.

So I thank Randi Walker for getting me started on this book, and for the many subsequent conversations where we talked about who we are as the UCC, and she provided theological, historical, and ecumenical context.

Many thanks to Barbara Brown Zikmund for shepherding this book into its final form, and for being so generous with her time and her wisdom. Her attentiveness to logical progression of thought and clarity of language made the book much more readable. Her alertness to what might be missing greatly improved the content.

Jane Fisler Hoffman was stalwart in commenting on the book in its many stages of development. Her suggestions were always apt. Thank you, Jane, and all who read the more unwieldy drafts and offered wise counsel: David Bahr, Carol Barriger, Martha Baumer, Jerry Bolick, Dakota Brown, Sonny Graves, Ashley Hiestand, Eric McCuen, Roy Mosley, Daniel Schlorff, Deborah Streeter, and Ally Vertigan.

The Network of Teachers of UCC History, Polity, and Theology has been immensely supportive of this project, posing insightful questions and engaging in spirited dialogue. Special thanks to those who took portions of the text to their polity classes for reaction and review.

Holly MillerShank and Kathryn Clark made it possible for me to present my work in progress at meetings of the Network. I am very grateful for that and for their assistance with part IV, "Ministry," particularly in refining the glossary of terms related to authorization and oversight of ministries. Any errors there—or anywhere else in the book—are totally mine.

A huge thank-you to publisher Christina Villa at Pilgrim Press. She has offered great encouragement while providing patient explanations of the details of manuscript preparation.

Chief Administrative Officer Lee Foley responded with grace and accuracy to all my questions about the UCC Constitution and Bylaws, and General Synod votes. Archivist Edward Cade provided access to documents that linked our present to our past. Thank you.

My thanks to all who have been in conversation with me about our church over the past forty-five years. I give particular thanks to those who responded in loving detail to questions I sent out with regard to the book, and to those who offered their stories and perspectives on the UCC.

Finally, I want to thank my spouse, Roger Straw, for making this book possible. His domestic skills and computer expertise kept me sane through the push to completion. More fundamentally, he introduced me to the United Church of Christ. We met as students at Chicago Theological Seminary. I was there in response to an aggravatingly persistent call to ordained ministry, but I had left the church of my childhood, which does not ordain women. At CTS I did my research on denominations and concluded that, in theory, the UCC was the place for me. Roger then brought me to his home church, South Congregational UCC in Grand Rapids, Michigan, where I was received with hospitality, and the theory became reality. Thank you, Roger, for that introduction and for all the joy and companionship over the years.

Notes

Introduction

1. Mary Sue Brookshire, "That We May All Be One," sermon, February 20, 2011, quoted with permission.

2. Walter Brueggemann, "The Risk of Heaven/The Possibility of Earth," "Minutes, Twelfth General Synod," June 22, 1979, 124, http://rescarta.ucc.org/jsp/RcWebImageViewer.jsp?doc_id=General+Synod+Minutes%2Fucoc0000%2FUD000001%2F00000013&collection_filter=true.

3. Walter Brueggemann, "Introduction," in Jane Fisler Hoffman, *Covenant* (Cleveland: United Church Press, 2008), 7–8.

4. This was a spoken comment by Jim Wallis of *Sojourners*; it might also be found in his writings.

5. See "John Robinson's Farewell Sermon," July 1620, http://www.pilgrimhall museum.org/pdf/John_Robinson_Farewell_Sermon.pdf.

Chapter One

1. The King James Version's rendering, "that they all may be one," predominates among those using John 17:21 as their motto. Our founders chose the wording from the Revised Standard Version New Testament published in 1946.

2. As stated in the 1943 Basis of Union between the Congregational Christian Churches and the Evangelical and Reformed Church, "This name expresses a fact:

it stands for the accomplished union of two church bodies each of which has arisen from a similar union of two church bodies. It also expresses a hope: that in time soon to come, by further union between this Church and other bodies, there shall arise a more inclusive United Church." Joint Committee, Union Affirmed: "The Basis of Union—Without Interpretations" (1947), *The Living Theological Heritage of the United Church of Christ*, ed. Barbara Brown Zikmund, vol. 6 *Growing Toward Unity*, ed. Elsabeth Hilke (Cleveland: Pilgrim Press, 2000), part 5, document 77, 583, or go to http://www.ucc.org/beliefs/basis-of-union.html.

3. Mary Sue Brookshire, "That We May All Be One."

4. Reuben Sheares states that our "Constitution and Bylaws is itself a covenant within the covenant. It is the covenantal document of a people who have been drawn to one another because they have found a unity in Christ Jesus and who would now order their lives and their ways 'to express more fully [their] oneness in Christ . . . to make more effective their common witness . . . and to serve His kingdom in the world.'" See "A Covenant Polity," in *Theology and Identity*, ed. Daniel L. Johnson and Charles Hambrick-Stowe (Cleveland: United Church Press, 2007), 74.

5. Preamble, UCC Constitution and Bylaws, http://www.ucc.org/ucc_constitution_and_bylaws, par. 1.

6. General Synod of the UCC, "Union in Christ, 'Message to the Churches from the Uniting General Synod,'" (1957), in *Living Theological Heritage*, vol. 6 (Cleveland: Pilgrim Press, 2001), part 5, doc. 94, 749; or see http://www.ucc.org /education/polity/pdf-folder/message-to-the-churches-from-uniting-synod.pdf.

7. Susan E. Davies, "The Authority of the Church in the World: A United Church of Christ Perspective" (New York: Faith and Order Commission, National Council of Churches, 2007), https://wayback.archive-it.org/4735 /2014081920 3738/http:/www.ncccusa.org/faithandorder/authority.davies.htm. Used by permission of the National Council of Churches of Christ in the USA. All rights reserved worldwide, 2015.

8. Walter Brueggemann, "Introduction," 8.

9. Douglas Horton, "Theology: 'The Head of the Church'" (1962), in *Living Theological Heritage*, vol. 7, *United and Uniting*, "ed. Frederick R. Trost and Barbara Brown Zikmund (Cleveland: Pilgrim Press, 2005), part 1, doc. 9, 44–45.

In 1871, as the National Council of the Congregational Churches was forming, Congregational pastor William I. Buddington spoke of working "in friendly cooperation with all who love and serve our common Lord," [not making] "a pretension to be the only churches of Christ." See "Bound Together in Unity: 'The Oberlin Declaration on the Unity of the Church'" (1871), in Living Theological Heritage, vol. 6, part 1, doc. 2, 25.

10. UCC historian Randi Walker explains that "all of the UCC traditions held the Bible and some also the creeds to be authoritative, but all of them at the same time respected a critical approach to their interpretation based in a high regard for human reason. . . . A deep seated suspicion of the nature of creeds lies behind most of the traditions in the UCC." Randi Jones Walker, *The Evolution of a UCC Style* (United Church Press, 2005), 55–56.

11. Roger Shinn described his role in drafting the 1959 Statement of Faith: "The Statement came out of a group process. No one, working alone, would have produced anything resembling it. . . . But at one point somebody, for better or worse, had to become the voice of the group. It was given to me to be that." From Roger Shinn, "Historical Reflections on the Statement of Faith," lecture, UCC Historical Council, July 4, 1997, 9; see http://d3n8a8pro7vhmx.cloudfront.net/unitedchurch ofchrist/legacy_url/197/shinn-ucc-statement-of-faith.pdf?1418423560.

12. Shinn, "Historical Reflections," 3.

13. Roger Lincoln Shinn and Daniel Day Williams, *We Believe: An Interpretation of the United Church of Christ Statement of Faith* (Philadelphia: United Church Press, 1966), 16.

14. Cyril of Alexandria, "The Church as the Body of Christ," from *Commentary on John 17:20–21* (c. 430), in *Living Theological Heritage,* vol. 1, *Ancient and Medieval Legacies,* ed. Reinhard Ulrich (Cleveland: Pilgrim Press, 1995), part 1, doc. 15, 135.

15. "Statement of Faith of the United Church of Christ," http://www.ucc.org /beliefs/statement-of-faith.html.

Chapter Two

1. Augustine of Hippo, "The Church as the Company of the Elect," from *On Baptism V* (c. 400), in *Living Theological Heritage,* vol. 1, part 1, doc. 16, 143–44.

2. "What We Believe: Testimonies of Faith," posted at http://www.ucc.org /about-us/what-we-believe.html and used with permission.

3. Oliver Powell, "A Word Picture: 'The UCC: A Beautiful, Heady, Exasperating Mix,'" (1975), in *Living Theological Heritage,* vol. 7, part 4, Doc. 53, 301–305.

4. Daniel Hazard, "A heady exasperating mix? Don't forget 'beautiful,' 'hopeful,' too," June 30, 2007, http://www.ucc.org/ucnews/june-july-2007/a-heady-exasperating-mix.html.

5. Brookshire, "That We May All Be One."

6. Steering Committee of Confessing Christ, "Statement on Hospitality," May 2005, see http://www.ucc.org/god-is-still-speaking/church-resources/hospitality.html.

7. T. V. Philip, "The Holy Trinity (John 3:11–18)" http://www.religion-online.org/showarticle.asp?title=1543, accessed January 2016. Originally in T. V. Philip, *The Kingdom of God Is Like This* (Delhi, India: Indian Society for Promoting Christian Knowledge and Christava Sahitya Samithy, 2000).

With regard to the expectation of "sameness" of practice, David McMahill has remarked, "There is a tendency among those who aren't really up on our polity to turn 'common practices' into hard regulations."

8. Toni Dunbar, Conference staff conversation on diversity, 1997, quoted with permission.

9. Brookshire, "That We May All Be One," drawing from Walter Brueggemann's 2009 lecture, "Unity, Purity, and Miracle."

10. The Free Dictionary, www.thefreedictionary.com.

11. Marc Lesser, "Creative Tension" New World Library Unshelved, September 1, 2011, http://www.newworldlibrary.com/NewWorldLibraryUnshelved/tabid/767/articleType/CategoryView/CategoryID/7/CurrentPage/2/Default.aspx#.VwNHH_krIdU.

12. Rosemary McCombs Maxey, "Who Can Sit at the Lord's Table? The Experience of Indigenous Peoples," in Johnson and Hambrick-Stowe, *Theology and Identity*, 61.

13. Bill Hulteen, "A New Old Framework: 'Covenantal Relationships,'" (1987, 1997) Living Theological Heritage, vol. 7, part 8, doc. 140, 772, also at http://www.ucc.org/education/polity/pdf-folder/covenantal-relationships-lth-140.pdf.

Chapter Three

1. Louis H. Gunnemann, *The Shaping of the United Church of Christ* (New York: United Church Press, 1977).

2. The Sage English Dictionary, http://www.sequencepublishing.com/thesageonline.php?lemma=Governance.

3. Clyde J. Steckel, *New Ecclesiology and Polity*, (Cleveland: Pilgrim Press, 2009), 11.

4. Ibid., 12. See also Rollin O. Russell's 2003 paper "Covenant Theology, Covenantal Church Life," which explores the meaning of covenant in the Reformed tradition, and "why it is important," http://uccfiles.com/pdf/Russell-on-Covenant-Theology.pdf. Note also that Congregational churches in colonial times were "in covenant with one another for mutual support and guidance," Introduction to "Doctrine and Polity: 'The Cambridge Platform,'" (1648), *Living Theological Heritage*, vol. 3, *Colonial and National Beginnings,* ed. Charles Hambrick-Stowe (Cleveland: Pilgrim Press, 1998), part 1, doc. 6, 85.

5. Hoffman, *Covenant,* 31.

6. Ibid.

7. Ibid., 35. See Statement of Faith as doxology at http://www.ucc.org /beliefs_statement-of-faith#DOX.

8. Hoffman, *Covenant*, 38.

9. Brueggemann, "Introduction," 8.

10. Steckel, *New Ecclesiology*, 125.

11. Brueggemann, "The Risk of Heaven," 124–25.

Chapter Four

1. See Anthony B. Robinson, "Renewed Life," *Christian Century* 117/32 (15 November 2000).

2. Archbishop Desmond Tutu has said that we as the church are put here to be God's transfiguration. Through us God intends to transfigure hate into love, injustice into justice, privation into abundance, grief into joy, death into life.

3. UCC Constitution, par. 9.

4. Henry Jacob, cited by Louis Gunnemann, *The Shaping of the United Church of Christ* (New York: United Church Press, 1977), 141. Leaping forward 350 or so years, Vatican II brought forth "new" concepts of church, including the "teaching that the church is the whole *People of God*. In other words, the church is not only the hierarchy, the clergy, and/or members of religious communities. It is the whole community of the baptized." Richard McBrien, "Vatican II themes: The people of God," *National Catholic Reporter*, 7/25/11, http://ncronline.org/blogs /essays-theology/vatican-ii-themes-people-god.

5. UCC Constitution, par. 18.

6. John Thomas, "To Find the Proper Words," lecture, Craigville Colloquy, July 12–16, 2004, http://www.ucc.org/beliefs/theology/part-i-to-find-the-proper .html.

7. Henry Jacob, "Principles and Foundations of Christian Religion," 1604 or 1605, *Living Theological Heritage*, vol. 2, *Reformation Roots*, ed. John Payne (Cleveland: Pilgrim Press, 1997), art 3, doc. 29, 486–87.

8. Rollin Russell goes into detail about the application of covenant theology to congregational relationships. He refers to the statement by Henry Jacob just cited: "Here, a theological understanding of covenant which had formerly been used to elucidate Reformed perspective on salvation is used to describe the gathering of and basic pattern of relationships in a congregation. The writing and teaching of William Perkins made that critical connection. Perkins was considered a sound and orthodox Calvinist in his theology. But in describing the covenant of grace he stretched that garment into what other Calvinists would view as a distortion. His intentions were evangelical. . . . Perkins taught that the smallest element of hope and longing for regeneration in the soul was to be understood as

the work of God's spirit, and that it beckoned such a person toward the covenant of grace. . . . Thus, the grace of God was not a cataclysmic experience, nor an apparently arbitrary gift bestowed by a capricious Sovereign God. It was available by God's grace, it was understandable, it inspired the individual to actively cultivate the seed, and it was nurtured and brought to fruition in the covenant community." Russell, "Covenant Theology," 37.

9. William Ames, "The Marrow of Theology," (1629) *Living Theological Heritage,* vol. 2, part 3, doc. 31, 531.

10. That "re" before "ligio" means what you might expect based on such familiar words as return or re-do. "Religio" can be understood as "binding again" or "binding over and over" or "binding anew." Or you can juggle all those meanings.

11. Lillian Daniel, "Spiritual but Not Religious? Please Stop Boring Me," August 30, 2011, http://www.ucc.org/feed-your-spirit/daily-devotional/spiritual-but-not-religious.html.

12. Philip, "The Holy Trinity."

Chapter Five

1. There were two ads that launched on cable networks in December 2004, after being refused by the broadcast networks on the grounds of all that inclusivity being too controversial. The Bouncer ad featured [per a posting on ucc.org] "two muscle-bound 'bouncers' standing guard outside a symbolic, picturesque church and selecting which persons are permitted to attend Sunday services. This represents the alienation felt by some persons toward church and religion. Written text interrupts the scene, announcing, 'Jesus didn't turn people away. Neither do we.' A narrator then proclaims the United Church of Christ's commitment to Jesus' extravagant welcome: 'No matter who you are, or where you are on life's journey, you are welcome here.'" The second ad was a simple embodiment of the multifaceted, multifaced beloved community, with two children going through the familiar verse and hand gestures to "Here's the church; here's the steeple; open the doors and see all the people." They do this with a freshness and genuineness that made me feel like I was hearing it for the very first time. "*All* the people" was repeated by an array of diverse people.

G. Jeffrey MacDonald critiques these ads as a betrayal of "the UCC principle of ecumenism" in his book *Thieves in the Temple* (New York: Basic Books, 2010), 102.

2. See the article "Playing Catch With God," by Ron Buford and Randy Varco, in *New Conversations,* ed. Wilson Yates (Winter 2004), 63–67, for the story of the genuine during-sleep dream that generated "God Is Still Speaking," http://rescarta.ucc.org/jsp/RcWebImageViewer.jsp?doc_id=New+Conversations%2Fucoc0000%2FUD000001%2F00000109. See also this article, written about Ron

Buford, but encapsulating the Still Speaking initiative: "Buford, architect of UCC's 'Stillspeaking' campaign, to assume new role," by June 6, 2006, http://www.ucc.org /ucnews/augsep2006/buford-architect-of.html.

3. Confessing Christ, Statement on Hospitality, accessed at http://www.ucc .org/god-is-still-speaking/church-resources/hospitality.html.

4. From conversations on being church, quoted with permission.

5. Patricia De Jong, e-mail of March 4, 2013. Quoted with permission.

6. We used Martha Grace Reese's *Unbinding the Gospel*, as suggested by church growth consultant Paul Nickerson; find information about the book and program at http://www.gracenet.info/unbinding_the_gospel.aspx.

7. From a conversation on church growth, quoted with permission.

8. From a report to NCNC Annual Gathering. Quoted with permission.

9. John Dorhauer, *Beyond Resistance* (Chicago: Exploration Press, 2015), 29.

10. Ibid., 150.

11. The Center for Progressive Renewal puts forward guidance, direction, and online teaching for those who feel called to lead in church renewal or the founding of new churches: "The mission of The Center for Progressive Renewal is to renew Christianity by training new entrepreneurial leaders, supporting the birth of new congregations, and by renewing and strengthening existing churches," http://www .progressiverenewal.org/.

See also the New Beginnings assessment document at http://www.ucc.org /new-beginnings/:

> If your congregation can answer "yes" to three or more of the follow-ing, it may be time for a New Beginning:

- Less than seventy in worship, or more than seventy in worship but significant decline for a decade
- Wrestling with future vision for the church
- Significant building issues
- Aging membership
- Changing neighborhood
- Trouble paying bills and/or paying off a loan
- Currently in interim time of transition

Jonathan New has undertaken to describe and analyze the elements of min-isterial leadership that lead to increased congregational vitality in UCC churches. See *Stepping into the Fire: Ministerial Leadership for Congregational Vitality* (New-ton Centre, MA: Andover Newton Theological Seminary, 2011), https://books .google.com/books/about/Stepping_Into_the_Fire.html?id=LWlKywAACAAJ.

12. A phrase from William Sloan Coffin's sermon "Our Resurrection, Too," *The Collected Sermons of William Sloane Coffin: The Riverside Years, Volume 1* (Louisville: Westminster John Knox Press, 2008), 67.

13. "All persons who are or shall become members of a Local Church of the United Church of Christ are thereby members of the United Church of Christ." UCC Constitution, par. 12.

14. Randi Jones Walker, "Radical and Prophetic Hospitality," NCNC Annual Gathering 2005. Used by permission.

15. UCC minister Deborah Streeter succinctly voiced this distinction between welcome and hospitality in a conversation in 2014.

16. Walker, "Radical . . . Hospitality."

17. "Using scriptural wisdom, social research and extensive experience, Kyros Ministry develops leadership within the religious community to create healthy power relationships within congregations, prevent misuse of power, and protect those at risk of abuse," kyros.org.

18. Ames, "Marrow of Theology."

19. *Book of Worship,* United Church of Christ Office for Church Life and Leadership, (Cleveland: UCC Press, 1986), 161.

20. UCC Constitution, par. 10.

21. The specific question here is whether a person can retain their identity and practice as Hindu, Jewish, Muslim, etc., as a member of the UCC. See the paper "Multiple Religious Belonging" by Karen Georgia Thompson, UCC Minister for Ecumenical and Interfaith Relations, in the book *Many Yet One?* ed. Peniel Jesudson, Refus Rajkumar, and Joseph Prabhakar Dayam (Geneva, Switzerland: World Council of Churches, 2016).

22. Robin R. Meyers, *Saving Jesus from the Church* (New York: HarperOne, 2009), 218–19.

23. Clyde Steckel, *New Ecclesiology and Polity* (Cleveland: Pilgrim Press, 2009), 84.

24. Ibid., 119.

25. UCC Constitution, par. 10.

26. UCC Constitution, par. 11. See also UCC Leaders Box, "Membership," Parish Life and Leadership, Local Church Ministries, 2005, http://www.ucc.org /ministers/leaders-box/a8.pdf.

27. UCC Constitution, par. 11.

28. Meyers, *Saving Jesus*, 37.

29. Steckel, *New Ecclesiology*, 74.

30. Ibid., 71. UCC historian David Greenhaw has stated, "In the UCC, there is no central location of teaching, but there is an accidental location called the

General Synod, but the problem is that it has lacked the capacity to connect with the people in the pew. It has shallow roots of support in the life of the church." Quoted in J. Bennett Guess, "Who are you calling liberal," *United Church News*, September 30, 2004, http://www.ucc.org/ucnews/oct04/who-are-you-calling-liberal.html.

31. Confessing Christ, Statement on Hospitality, May 2005, http://d3n8a8 pro7vhmx.cloudfront.net/unitedchurchofchrist/legacy_url/19848/Confess-X-Statement-on-Christian-Hospitality-2005.pdf?1418446454.

32. Walker, *Evolution of a UCC Style*, 90.

33. Preamble, UCC Constitution, par. 2.

34. Walker, *Evolution of a UCC Style*, 136.

35. Steckel, *New Ecclesiology*, 125.

Chapter Six

1. Leaders Box, "Constitution and Bylaws of Your Church," http://www.ucc.org /ministers/leaders-box/a3.pdf.

2. "When starting a nonprofit corporation, the organization must file articles of incorporation with the state in which it resides or decides will be its jurisdiction for legal purposes. . . . Each state has various rules and regulations, but most require officers of the corporation, a board of directors, by-laws and annual meetings." (Nonprofit.pro, "What is a Nonprofit Organization?" http://www.nonprofit .pro/nonprofit_organization.htm).

The UCC Leaders Box lists the basics to be included in your church's governing statement: Name, affiliation with the Association and Conference of the United Church of Christ, purpose or mission, membership qualifications, officers, pastoral selection procedures and tenure, meetings of the membership, etc.: "Organization and Structure of Your Church," http:// www.ucc.org/ministers/leaders-box/a12.pdf; "Constitution and Bylaws of Your Church," http://www.ucc.org /ministers/leaders-box/a3.pdf; and "Local Church," http://www.ucc.org/ministers/leaders-box/a7.pdf.

For minutes, see "Minute Keeping" on the Leaders Box page or "How to Write Church Meeting Minutes," http://www.ehow.com/way_5150080_legal-requirements-church-meeting-minutes.html.

Legal issues regarding the validity of the church as corporation are addressed in a paper by UCC Conference Attorney Mike McKee. Although the paper "When A Church Leaves the UCC" refers specifically to churches that are closing or leaving the denomination, it is informative for all churches: http://www.ucc .org/ministers/pdfs/whenachurchleaves.pdf.

3. The study by the Pew Research Center on changes in religious affiliations between people surveyed in 2007 and those surveyed in 2014 offers more substantiated data: http://www.pewforum.org/2015/05/12/americas-changing-religious-landscape/.

4. Alan C. and Sharon D. Klaas, *Flexible, Missional Constitution/Bylaws—In One Day, Not Two Years* (N.p.: Mission Growth Publishing, 2000, 2003), 3, 5.

5. See the UCC Leaders Box, "Organization and Structure of Your Church," http://www.ucc.org/ministers/leaders-box/a12.pdf.

6. Brueggemann, "The Risk of Heaven," 124–25.

7. Ibid., 127.

8. Ibid., 126.

9. "*Vox populi, vox dei*" is a Latin phrase meaning "The voice of the people is the voice of God."

10. See Anthony B. Robinson, *Transforming Congregational Culture* (Grand Rapids, MI: Eerdmans, 2003), chap. 5.

11. Julianne Pirtle, e-mail of November 21, 2012, quoted with permission.

12. Steckel, *New Ecclesiology*, 94.

13. Most churches, like other organizations, "adopt language in their bylaws stating that they will follow a particular parliamentary procedure book. Such language has the effect of law because organization members who act contrary to the rules they adopted may be liable for actions that go against the rules" (Jim Slaughter, "Matching Parliamentary Procedure to Needs," http://www.jimslaughter.com /Matching-Parliamentary-Procedure-to-Needs.cfm). This means that, yes, if your bylaws state that you will abide by, say, Robert's Rules of Order and a disappointed church member challenges the church council's decision to sell a piece of property, based on there not having been a quorum, as defined by Robert's Rules, present for the vote, your church may be at legal risk. Search for Robert's at Church Law and Tax for updated commentary (http://www.churchlawandtax.com/?aid=153).

If your church chooses to use Robert's Rules of Order for the business portion of the Annual Meeting of the corporation, you will want to note recent changes to Robert's Rules, with regard to churches. This article noted seventeen areas of concern to churches in the 2011 revision of Robert's Rules: http://www.christianity today.org/mediaroom/news/2012/keychangesforchurches.html.

Go to Church Law and Tax for updates on tax law for churches. This site also posted an article on changes in Robert's Rules that affect churches: http://www .churchlawandtax.com/blog/2012/september/3-key-changes-for-churches-in-lat-est-emroberts-rules-em.html.

You can go to http://www.christianitytoday.org/search/?query=robert %27s+rules&x=0&y=0 for additional articles and updates, including reference to electronic meetings.

14. See Shelly Berman, "Comparison of Dialogue and Debate" 1993, http: //www.odec.umd.edu/CD/ACTIVITI/BERMAN.pdf.

Chapter Seven

1. *Book of Worship*, 154.

2. Tom Tupper, ed., "How Organizations Function," *Church Planning*, UCC Office for Church Life and Leadership, 1986.

3. Ibid., C-4.

4. Ibid. p. C-7.

5. Roger Fisher and William Ury, *Getting to Yes: Negotiating Agreement without Giving In,* (New York: Random House, 2012). Note that many Conferences and Associations offer conflict resolution services or can connect churches with local resources. In addition, the Center for Progressive Renewal offers a course and coaching titled "Conflict: How to Turn the Inevitable into an Opportunity," http://progressiverenewal.org/event/conflict-how-to-turn-the-inevitable-into-an-opportunity/.

6. Leaders Box, "Pastoral Relations Committee Member, http://www.ucc.org /ministers/leaders-box/b12.pdf.

7. Ibid.

8. For information on the Volga Germans, see William G. Chrystal, "German Congregationalism," *Hidden Histories in the United Church of Christ*, ed. Barbara Brown Zikmund (Cleveland: Pilgrim Press, 1984, 1987), 66–69, available also at http://www.ucc.org/about-us_hidden-histories_german-congregationalism-on.

Part III

1. Reuben A. Sheares, "A Covenant Polity," in Johnson and Hambrick-Stowe, *Theology and Identity,* 69.

Chapter Eight

1. UCC Constitution, par. 10.

2. Sheares, "A Covenant Polity," 69.

3. Ibid., 75.

4. Sociologist H. B. Calvacanti observes of UCC churches in the Shenandoah Valley, "An important trait of United Church of Christ identity in the valley is the sense of outside-ness that still pervades the older congregations. . . . It is not

necessarily that they do not feel like they belong to the United Church of Christ, but rather that the national church is not a natural, organic extension of their local religious life. . . . In that sense, the national structure exists as an autonomous actor with its own separate agenda." *The United Church of Christ in the Shenandoah Valley: Liberal Church, Traditional Congregations* (Lanham, MD: Lexington Books, 2010), 127.

5. The posture of hospitality to the new united church was not, of course, universally held throughout the membership. See, for example, Legal Arguments: "Decisions of the Courts in Regard to the Proposed Union," (1953), *Living Theological Heritage*, vol. 6, part 5, doc. 91, 717.

6. Introduction to Union in Christ: "Message to the Churches from the Uniting General Synod," (1957), *Living Theological Heritage*, vol. 6, part 5, doc. 94, 749, or see http://www.ucc.org/education/polity/pdf-folder/message-to-the-churches-from-uniting-synod.pdf.

7. Ibid.

8. Gunnemann, *Shaping of the United Church of Christ*, 33.

9. Louis H. Gunnemann, "Order and Identity in the United Church of Christ," *New Conversations* vol. 4, no. 2 (Fall 1979), 9.

10. Brueggemann, "Introduction,"7–8.

11. Scott Libbey, "Structures, Issues, and The Theological Task," *New Conversations Polity and Practice* vol. 4, no. 2 (Fall 1979), 35, http://rescarta.ucc.org/jsp/RcWebImageViewer.jsp?doc_id=New+Conversations%2Fucoc0000%2FUD000001%2F00000060&page_name=00350035&view_width=20&rotation=0&collection_filter=false&query1=&query1_field=0&search_doc=.

12. Preamble, UCC Constitution, par. 3.

Chapter Nine

1. Randi Walker observes that, in the Eastern United States, Associations, originally formed for the purpose of ordaining candidates for the ministry, predate Conferences. In the West churches were started through the home missionary movement, guided by a superintendent who "took on the role of oversight of the new congregations. Only when a number of self-supporting congregations were established did an Association develop. . . . To this day, in the West . . . the Associations are relatively weak and the Conferences strong, whereas in New England, the Associations are generally strong and the Conferences are weak." Walker, *Evolution of a UCC Style*, 168.

2. UCC Constitution, par. 37.

3. The Association of Hawaiian Evangelical Churches was established within the Hawai'i Conference in 1994 as an affirmation of the native Hawaiian biblical roots of its members and to "express our Christian faith through Hawaiian cultural forms, including Hawaiian values, traditions, language and spirituality," http://www.hcucc.org/#!after-ahec—-purpose/c1et8.

The Calvin Synod began as the Hungarian *Classes* of the Reformed Church in the United States in 1921. Members of the Hungarian Reformed Church immigrated to the United States and sought affiliation with a Reformed denomination that would preserve their language and unique traditions. After the merger of the Reformed Church in the United States with the Evangelical Synod of North America in 1934, the Hungarian *Classes* became the Magyar Synod of the Evangelical and Reformed Church. "Under the name of the Calvin Synod, as an acting conference, the Hungarian churches continued as an exception to the geographically defined conferences in the rest of the United Church of Christ. They argued then, and continue to argue, that the Basis of Union gave them the right to 'unite in the United Church of Christ without break in their respective historic continuities and traditions.'"—John Butosi, "The Calvin Synod: Hungarians in the United Church of Christ," in *Hidden Histories in the United Church of Christ*, ed. Barbara Brown Zikmund, (Cleveland: Pilgrim Press, 1984), 139.

In contrast, the nongeographic Convention of the South, made up of Afro-Christian and Black Congregational churches, was part of the Congregational Christian Churches when the United Church of Christ came into being and dispersed into the geographically formed Conferences. This "fragmented the Convention of the South," which had been, since it originated in 1950, "a mechanism for the inclusion of Afro-Christians in denominational life and work."—Percel O. Alston, "The Afro-Christian Connection," in Hidden Histories, 33, 34, http://www.ucc.org/about-us_hidden-histories_the-afro-christian-connection. Yet there was the recognition that the Convention of the South had been created "because of racism. . . . The conferences that were aligned at that time before the United Church of Christ did not want to fully integrate, and therefore [racism] created one huge conference for Black folks."—Yvonne Delk, "Between a Rock and Hard Places by Any Other Name," in Pamelajune Anderson, *Between a Rock and Hard Places* (N.p.: Create Space Independent Publishing Platform, 2015), 19. The dispersion of the Convention of the South was an act of commitment to racial justice and to a new church that would not organize in segregated patterns.

4. "A middle judicatory is an administrative structure or organization found in religious denominations between the local congregation and the widest or highest national or international level. . . . Depending on the polity, the middle judicatory can have decisive authority over a local church, can offer standing for clergy

members but little or no control over congregations, can offer counsel and services but no authority, or can serve as an informal vehicle for fellowship and communication," https://en.wikipedia.org/wiki/Middle_judicatory.

5. UCC Constitution, par. 168.

6. Ibid., par. 174.

7. Ibid., par. 175.

8. Ibid., par. 176–78.

9. For the meaning of terms like authorized ministry, you can refer to the glossary, chapter 17.

10. UCC Constitution, par. 162.

11. Ibid., par. 163.

12. Ibid., par. 164.

13. Ibid., par. 169.

14. Rollin Russell, as quoted by Walker, *Evolution of a UCC Style*, 169. See also two articles in *Prism* vol. 9, no. 2 (Fall 1994): Donald J. Sevetson's "The Idea of a Conference" and Rollin Russell's "UCC Conferences and the Council of Conference Ministers," http://d3n8a8pro7vhmx.cloudfront.net/united churchofchrist /legacy_url/232/prism-articles-on-conferences-1994.pdf.

15. UCC Consitution, par. 180.

16. See Steckel, *New Ecclesiology*, 117.

17. See Randi Walker on collegial episcopé, in Ministry: "Episcopé or Oversight," (1998), *Living Theological Heritage*, vol. 7, part 3, doc. 46, 256–57.

18. From e-mail correspondence of June 18, 2013. Used with permission.

19. From e-mail correspondence of September 16, 2013. Used with permission

20. From e-mail correspondence of August 23, 2013. Used with permission.

21. Composite from conversations 2001–2011. Used with permission.

22. Walker, *Evolution of a UCC Style*, 169.

23. Steckel, *New Ecclesiology*, 129.

24. From e-mail correspondence with Steve Gray, June 1, 2012, quoted with permission.

25. Bylaw 291 is part of Article VI, "Other Bodies," and includes Councils and Self-Created Groups, from the Council for American Indian Ministry through the United Church of Christ Coalition for Lesbian, Gay, Bisexual, and Transgender Concerns.

In 2009 the Council of Conference Ministers finalized a covenant with the intent of clarifying the Council's sense of identity, vocation, and relationship to the whole church while realigning, reconfiguring, and repurposing the Council so that it might be something more than what has been termed in Conference Minister parlance, "the periodic meeting of the CEOs of thirty-eight different corporations," http://uccfiles.com/pdf/CCM-Covenant.pdf.

Chapter Ten

1. This from Wikipedia. The Wikipedia article also states, "The word 'synod' comes from the Greek 'σύνοδος' (synodos) meaning 'assembly' or 'meeting,' and it is synonymous with the Latin word 'concilium,' meaning 'council,' http://en.wikipedia.org/wiki/Synod.

2. *The Constitution and Bylaws: United Church of Christ*, 2005 ed., par. 53, http://rescarta.ucc.org/jsp/RcWebImageViewer.jsp?doc_id=869eeea5-f451-445c-aecb-a7a9126334e8/ucoc0000/UD000001/00000049.

3. UCC Constitution [2013 ed, http://www.ucc.org/ucc_constitution_and _bylaws], par. 53.

4. Preamble, UCC Constitution, par. 3.

5. Gray, e-mail correspondence, June 1, 2012.

6. Susan E. Davies, "The Authority of the Church in the World: A United Church of Christ Perspective." Used by permission of the National Council of Churches of Christ in the USA. All rights reserved worldwide. 2015, https://wayback.archive-it.org/4735/20140819203738/http:/www.ncccusa.org/faithandorder/authority.davies.htm.

7. James W. Crawford, "Introduction," *The New Century Hymnal* (Cleveland: Pilgrim Press, 1995), viii. See Minutes of the Eleventh General Synod, 1977, 92, http://rescarta.ucc.org/jsp/RcWebImageViewer.jsp?doc_id=8abee2f6-352d-48f9-958b-49a311bc4489/ucoc0000/UD000001/00000012.

8. Inclusive language for God uses female as well as male and gender neutral pronouns and metaphors. Inclusive language for human beings acknowledges the varieties of gender, age, racial and ethnic identity, etc., that characterize the human race.

9. Ansley Coe Throckmorton, "Preface," *New Century Hymnal*, viii.

10. The UCC Constitution and Bylaws, United Church of Christ, 1992 ed., http://rescarta.ucc.org/jsp/RcWebImageViewer.jsp?doc_id=869eeea5-f451-445c-aecb-a7a9126334e8/ucoc0000/UD000001/00000044.

11. Ibid., par. 49.

12. Crawford, "Introduction," ix.

13. Thomas E. Dipko, "Foreword," New Century Hymnal, vii.

14. Minutes of the Nineteenth General Synod, 1993, 50–51, http://rescarta.ucc .org/jsp/RcWebImageViewer.jsp?doc_id=8abee2f6-352d-48f9-958b-49a311bc4489/ucoc0000/UD000001/00000020.

15. Minutes of the Nineteenth General Synod, 51.

16. Ibid., 57.

17. Ibid.

18. Minutes of the Nineteenth General Synod, 67.

19. "Autonomy in a Covenantal Polity," Lancaster Theological Seminary, January 1998, p. 1, http://d3n8a8pro7vhmx.cloudfront.net/unitedchurchofchrist /legacy_url/226/Autonomy-in-a-Covenantal-Polity-Freeman.pdf?1418423590. Several polity mavens still cite the configuration of the resolution followed by Thomas Dipko's statement and the Executive Council's apology as "an example of our polity at its most dysfunctional and in its strength," as Steve Gray put it in an e-mail correspondence.

20. This was a comparison Thomas Dipko used in discussions regarding the *New Century Hymnal.*

21. From a conversation with William Imes in the late 1990s. Recounted with his permission.

22. Preamble, UCC Constitution, par. 3.

23. See Article IX, UCC Constitution, par. 53, 54.

24. See Articles IX (The General Synod), X (United Church of Christ Board), XI (Covenanted Ministries), XII (Affiliated and Associated Ministries), and IV (Officers), UCC Constitution.

25. UCC Constitution, par. 227(b).

26. James Moos, conversation of February 14, 2014, used with permission.

27. See UCC Constitution, par. 57, 65, 66, and 67.

28. Ibid., par. 54(e), 56(a), 57, 59(c), 59(j), 61(a), 61(b), 62, and 63.

29. Paragraph 7, "Proposed Amendments to the Constitution" http://uccfiles .com/pdf/Red-Lined-Constition(2013-Ed)_no_GS_changes.pdf.

30. UCC Constitution, par. 68, 69.

31. Ibid., par. 180.

32. Ibid., 54 (i).

33. Karen Georgia Thompson, conversation of February 27, 2014. Used with permission.

34. General Synod Committee on Structure, "Introduction" draft, 1992, 3, UCC archives.

35. Article III, UCC Constitution.

36. "Report of the General Synod Committee on Structure" to General Synod 19, 1993, 3, UCC archives.

Chapter Eleven

1. "In 1989 the United Church of Christ and the Christian Church (Disciples of Christ) approved a historic partnership of full communion. The two churches proclaimed mutual recognition of their sacraments and ordained ministry. Though remaining two distinct denominations, the UCC and Disciples have committed through their partnership to seek opportunities for common

ministry, especially where work together will enhance the mission of the church." "UCC-Disciples Ecumenical Partnership," http://www.ucc.org/ecumenical/ucc-disciples-ecumenical.html.

2. UCC Constitution, par. 266; see also http://globalministries.org/about-us/.

3. There have been many partnership undertakings among congregations and between Regions and Conferences. "Welcome to Partnership Ministries!" was the salutation that greeted you when you Googled the Montana-Northern Wyoming Conference UCC in 2014. Conference and Regional Ministry was re-cast in Montana and Northern Wyoming in 2010 with a vision of "A community of growing, vital UCC and DOC congregations in Montana and Northern Wyoming committed and equipped to effectively carry out Christ's transforming ministry in the world" and a mission "to equip transformational leaders, to encourage the sharing of resources and congregational stories and to call DOC/UCC churches in Montana and Northern Wyoming to grow spiritually, to live as trustworthy communities and to participate in God's reconciling mission of healing, love, and justice." "The partnership calls for both churches to retain autonomy and separate denominational identity," and cost reduction for administrative functions was anticipated. Stephanie Ortiz, "UCC, Disciples form new partnership in Montana-Northern Wyoming region" November 3, 2010, http://www.ucc.org/news/ucc-disciples-form-new.html.

By 2015, however, Partnership Ministries were no longer prominent on the Conference website.

How have you seen the UCC/DOC Partnership working among Local Churches, in Conferences/Associations, or in the national and global settings of our two denominations? What has been learned through efforts deemed successful, and through those that didn't come out as expected?

4. In 1969 the Theological Commission of the United Church of Christ published the paper "Toward an Understanding of Local Autonomy," which included the following commentary on the "inescapable tension" between the responsibilities we might carry as a member of a Local Church who is also a representative of his Local Church to his Association or Conference, or, we might suppose, a representative of her Conference to General Synod:

> In these groups the members are more than liaison persons. . . .
> Representatives to Association or Conference have responsibilities both to the Local Church which they represent and to the groups where they represent them. Representatives to General Synod have responsibilities both to the Conference they represent and to the Synod.
> The delegate who represents his local church [or her Conference] is not to refuse to listen to others but rather to be open to their insights

and views. It is therefore bad churchmanship for a local church to "instruct" its representatives to vote according to a certain pattern at any meetings of the representative groups—as it would be equally bad churchmanship for any of these groups to refuse to hear any message sent to it by any of the local churches [or Conference]—since either of these procedures would violate the liaison. The representative members are related to the groups themselves just as the members of a local church are related to the totality of that church. The Theological Commission of the United Church of Christ, "Toward an Understanding of Local Autonomy," 1969, 3, http://www.ucc.org/education/polity/pdf-folder/toward-an-understanding-of-local-autonomy.pdf.

5. Article III, UCC Constitution.

6. Thomas, "To Find the Proper Words," http://www.ucc.org/beliefs/theology/part-i-to-find-the-proper.html.

7. Conference Minister Davida Foy Crabtree has remarked, "Our UCC bumper sticker is, in reality, 'Question Authority.'" Used with permission.

8. Steckel, *New Ecclesiology*, 63.

9. Iowa Conference Minister Rich Pleva, in an e-mail of January 27, 2012. His comment ended disarmingly with, "And I don't exempt myself from this indictment." Used with permission.

10. Gunnemann, "Order and Identity in the United Church of Christ," 15.

11. Excerpted from Communion Meditation, appendix 7a, *Minutes of the Adjourned Meeting of the Second General Synod of the United Church of Christ*, July 6–8, 1960, 95–97, http://rescarta.ucc.org/jsp/RcWebImageViewer.jsp?doc_id=General+Synod+Minutes%2Fucoc0000%2FUD000001%2F00000003&page_name=00780076&view_width=20&rotation=0&collection_filter=false&query1=&query1_field=0&search_doc=. (This excerpt is presented without ellipses for ease of reading and does not compromise the message as it was delivered.)

12. Statement of Co-President Hoskins, appendix 3, Minutes of the Adjourned Meeting of the Second General Synod, 75–76.

Chapter Twelve

1. *Ubuntu* is a Zulu word that means the quality of humanity, of being human. *Ubuntu* embraces past, future, and community. It presumes interdependence.

2. Theological Commission of the United Church of Christ, "Toward an Understanding of Local Church Autonomy" (1969), 3, http://d3n8a8pro7vhmx.cloudfront.net/unitedchurchofchrist/legacy_url/215/toward-an-understanding-of-local-autonomy.pdf?1418423579. The passage continues, "Within each congregation the majority of the adult members determine the corporate life of the

group, always with due consideration of the will of any minority. When there are differences of opinion which threaten the unity of the local church, it is the responsibility of all to seek for a consensus of the Spirit and through study and consultation to seek the wisdom of the wider church. Groups with conflicting views may separate; but that is an extreme step to be taken with sorrow and pain only when no hope for consensus or co-operation seems possible; and even then never without the continuing hope and genuine prayer that the separated may again be united by the Spirit of Christ. The United Church of Christ believes that this is the best way to translate Christian love into the framework of government." Although this paper was written with reference to the Local Church, at a time when the nature and organization of Local Churches was being envisioned and re-visioned, the principles and procedures can well be applied to all expressions of our church. As the paper notes, "These intra-congregational relationships become a paradigm for relationships intercongregational."

3. Theological Commission, "Toward an Understanding," 3.

4. Robinson, *Transforming Congregational Culture*, 93.

5. Leaders Box, "Covenant," http://www.ucc.org/ministers/leaders-box/a4.pdf.

6. Minutes of the Twenty-Seventh General Synod, 2009, 39 (pdf page41), http://rescarta.ucc.org/jsp/RcWebImageViewer.jsp?doc_id=General+Synod+Minutes%2FOhClUCC0%2F00000001%2F00000003&collection_filter=false.

7. Ibid., 38.

8. Ibid., 39.

9. Ibid.

10. Ibid.

11. Ibid.

12. Ibid.

13. Ibid.

14. Berman, "A Comparison of Dialogue and Debate."

15. Joseph Alonzo, "Introducing Dialogue Into The Workplace," June 19, 2012, Great Place to Work, http://www.greatplacetowork.com/publications-and-events/blogs-and-news/1064.

16. Walter Brueggemann, *Mandate to Difference* (Louisville: Westminster John Knox Press, 2007), 73.

17. Eleazar Fernandez, seminar of October 25, 2012, Alameda, California.

18. Thomas, "To Find the Proper Words."

Part IV

1. UCC Constitution, par. 20.

2. Ibid., par. 21.

Chapter Thirteen

1. In his lecture of March 14, 1996, at Andover Newton Theological School,, "Authorizing Ministry in the United Church of Christ: Slouching Towards Order," Clyde Steckel supplies historical context for the impact of *Manual on Ministry* (1986). He comments that the manual boldly spoke of "authorizing and authority at a time when those words were in disfavor" (p. 2). He notes that in the 1960s "more and more candidates for ordination were passing through college and seminary with a strong personal, or inner, or secret call, expecting association committees to embrace them, support them, and find them jobs in non-traditional ministries. . . . In the phrase 'authorizing ministry' the United Church of Christ tried to respond to this situation by reminding us that the ministry is finally the church's ministry, not the individual's, and that however profound a person's sense of call may be, the church has both the right and responsibility to examine candidates for the gifts and graces of ministry leadership, and for adequate scholarly and professional preparation" (pp. 1–2), http://d3n8a8pro7vhmx.cloudfront .net/unitedchurchofchrist/legacy_url/1389/authmin.pdf?1418424862.

2. An authorized minister is one who has been ordained, licensed, or commissioned by an Association or Conference of the United Church of Christ. The term "Representational Ministry" is used in ecumenical discussions, and might more fully convey what we are trying to say with our term "Authorized Ministry," that is, here is a ministry that, yes, has been authorized, but more significantly, the minister who has been authorized serves as a representative of the church who has authorized him or her.

3. Thomas, "To Find the Proper Words."

4. "The 1983–84 amendments to the Constitution and Bylaws of the United Church of Christ introduced for the first time provision for the review and discipline of the authorizations for ministry and the persons authorized for ministry in the United Church of Christ." This statement is from the section "Review and Discipline of Persons Authorized for Ministry" in the 1986 *Manual on Ministry*, 184, which was replaced in 2002 by "The Oversight of Ministries Authorized by the United Church of Christ."

5. Preface to the "The Oversight of Ministries Authorized by the United Church of Christ," (section 8 of 10) United Church of Christ *Manual on Ministry*, 2002, Parish Life and Leadership, 1 (pdf page 6), http://www.ucc.org/ministers /manual/mom-2008-20oversight-1.pdf.

6. Randi Jones Walker, Ministry: "Episcopé or Oversight," (1998), Living Theological Heritage, vol. 7, part 3, doc. 46, 255.

7. John Dorhauer while Conference Minister for the Southwest Conference, used with permission.

Chapter Fourteen

1. UCC Constitution, par. 9.

2. "What is a 'call' to ministry?" Questions & Answers, http://www.ucc.org/ask-the-question/q-a.html.

3. "Covenant of Discernment and Formation," brochure, http://www.ucc.org /seminarians/Covenant-of-Discernment-and-Formation-brochure.pdf.

4. "Ministry in the United Church of Christ: A Background Document," 2010, Ministry Issues Project, 5, http://www.ucc.org/ministers/ministry-issues /Ministry-in-the-United-Church-of-Christ-A-Background-Document.pdf.

5. Ibid., 7.

6. Ibid., 8.

7. The Ministry Issues pronouncement, approved by General Synod 25 in Atlanta in 2005, is not-to-be-missed reading, a focused theological document for our church, "Ministry Issues: Forming and Preparing Pastoral Leaders for God's Church," http://www.ucc.org/ministers/ministry-issues/mip.pdf.

8. "Understanding and Practicing Discernment with Individuals, A Resource for Committees on the Ministry," http://www.ucc.org/ministers/ministry-issues /discernment.html.

9. Ministry Issues pronouncement, 6.

10. Ibid.

11. See "The Marks of Faithful and Effective Authorized Ministers of the United Church of Christ," revised April 2009, http://uccfiles.com/pdf/THE-MARKS-OF-FAITHFUL-AND-EFFECTIVE-MINISTERS.pdf.

12. "Ministry in the United Church of Christ," 5.

13. Barbara Brown Zikmund, "Empowerment and Embodiment: Ministry in the UCC," in Johnson and Hambrick-Stowe, *Theology and Identity*, 88.

Lillian Daniel's and Martin Copenhaver's book *This Odd and Wondrous Calling* (Grand Rapids, MI: Eerdmans, 2009) gives substance to the interweaving of the ordinary and the extraordinary in the lives of pastors.

14. See "The Marks Rubric," which is "an assessment tool for Members in Discernment, their mentors, and Committees on Ministry using the Marks of Faithful & Effective Authorized Ministers. The Rubric is an invitation for discernment in reflecting on formation for ministry and identifying areas for further growth. The Marks Rubric is also a useful tool for authorized ministers in any season of ministry," http://www.uccresources.com/products/the-marks-rubric.

15. "Journaling the Journey" is a resource to support local churches, Members in Discernment (MIDs), authorized ministers, and Committees on Ministry (COMs) in unpacking and utilizing the Marks. It provides reflective space and

directed questions based on the four categories of the Marks, http://uccfiles.com /pdf/Journaling-the-Journey-preview.pdf.

16. "Journaling the Journey," 3.

17. Ibid.

18. Kathryn Clark , Minister for Members in Discernment, MESA, from a discussion at the 2015 gathering of the teachers of UCC history and polity, quoted with permission.

19. Zikmund, "Empowerment and Embodiment," 86.

20. UCC Constitution, par. 23.

21. Ibid., par. 29.

22. Ibid., par. 27.

23. Most Conferences require that their Conference Ministers be Ordained Ministers of the United Church of Christ. In 2013 the Kansas-Oklahoma Conference called as Conference Minister Edith Guffey, a Commissioned Minister for Church Administration. This call necessitated a change in the Conference's bylaws.

24. See the Ministry Issues pronouncement's description of ordained, licensed, and commissioned ministry, pages 4–8, and the proposals for action by Associations and Conferences, pages 9–10.

25. "Ministry in the United Church of Christ," 9.

26. Ibid., 7.

27. Ibid., 13.

28. See "Procedures for Transfer of Good Ministerial Standing between Associations of the United Church of Christ," a resource from the MESA Ministry Team, 3/1/2015, www.uccfiles.com/docs/Transfer-of-Ministerial-Standing.doc.

29. "An ordained minister of another denomination other than the Christian Church (Disciples of Christ) who wishes to retain ordained ministerial standing in that denomination and who has become pastor of a Local Church of the United Church of Christ, or serves in a Covenanted, Affiliated or Associated Ministry of the United Church of Christ, or has become pastor of a yoked charge or a federated church one part of which is affiliated with the United Church of Christ, or has been called to an ecumenical ministry one constituent of which is the United Church of Christ, may apply to the Association for dual ordained ministerial standing which is limited to duration of that pastorate or that responsibility, and during that period may have all the rights and privileges of such membership." UCC Constitution, par.133.

30. "Ordained ministerial partner standing is authorization granted to an Ordained Minister with ordained ministerial standing in the Christian Church (Disci-

ples of Christ) who has a call to perform the duties and exercise the prerogatives of ordained ministry in the United Church of Christ." UCC Constitution, par. 36.

"A person has ordained ministerial partner standing in the United Church of Christ only when serving a United Church of Christ calling body. Upon demonstrating knowledge of, and appreciation for, the history, polity, and practices of the United Church of Christ to the Association in which the person resides, an Ordained Ministerial Partner may seek a call in the United Church of Christ." UCC Constitution, par. 116–17.

31. "An ordained minister of another denomination who desires to enter the ordained ministry of the United Church of Christ applies for Privilege of Call to the Association within whose bounds he or she resides. The Committee on Ministry of the Association examines the applicant as to his or her abilities, reasons for desiring to enter the ordained ministry of the United Church of Christ, educational and theological attainments, knowledge of the history, polity, and practices of the United Church of Christ, and Christian faith and experience. If the applicant is found to be qualified, the Association grants Privilege of Call, thereby commending said applicant for placement in the United Church of Christ. Privilege of Call shall be granted for a period of one year and may be renewed. After accepting a call, the Ordained Minister applies for Ordained Ministerial Standing in the United Church of Christ to the Association of which the Local Church extending the call is a part." UCC Constitution, par.130–31.

32. Walker, "Radical and Prophetic Hospitality."

33. "Ministry Issues pronouncement," 1.

34. "Ministry in the United Church of Christ," 13.

35. Tony Stoik, retired Associate Conference Minister, Iowa Conference.

36. "Ministry Issues pronouncement," 10.

37. Adapted from Frank Rogers, Jr., "Discernment," *Practicing Our Faith,* ed. Dorothy Bass (San Francisco: Jossey-Bass, 1997), as stated in part V of "Understanding and Practicing Discernment with Individuals," http://www.ucc.org/ministers/ministry-issues/discernment.html.

Chapter Fifteen

1. Granted, the full-blown definitive declaration of ministerial standing appears in our constitution only with respect to ordained ministry: "Ordained ministerial standing is an ongoing covenant of mutual accountability . . ." (UCC Constitution, par. 24), but if we go into the bylaws, we find that paragraph 157 under the heading Ministerial Accountability declares, "All authorized ministers of the United Church of Christ are active partners in a covenant of mutual ac-

countability with their Association of standing, their Local Church, and, in the case of those serving in settings other than a local church, with their calling body." "Ministry in the United Church of Christ, A Background Document," page 10, states that "Authorized ministers (Ordained, Commissioned, Licensed) are persons charged to minister in the name of Jesus Christ on behalf of the whole United Church of Christ. *'Ministerial Standing'* is the term used to describe the continuing relationship of an authorized minister to the United Church of Christ."

2. "Ministry in the United Church of Christ" 10–11.

3. "Understanding and Practicing Discernment with Individuals—A Resource for Committees on the Ministry," http://www.ucc.org/ministers/ministry-issues/discernment.html.

4. "The Marks of Faithful and Effective Authorized Ministers."

5. The term "calling body" was introduced in the 1983–84 amendments to the UCC Constitution and Bylaws. For a description of "calling body" see "Partners in Authorizing Ministry, *Manual on Ministry*, section 1, 4-5, http://d3n8a8 pro7vhmx.cloudfront.net/unitedchurchofchrist/legacy_url/1298/mom-2001-20partners-1.pdf?1418424767.

6. Authorized ministers serving a church of another denomination or a non-denominational church are considered to be members of the church they are serving. Authorized ministers who are retired or on leave of absence might not live near a UCC congregation.

7. From "The Oversight of Ministries Authorized," 27 (pdf p. 33, http://www.ucc.org/ministers/manual/mom-2008-20oversight-1.pdf.):

"To be recognized as valid, calling bodies typically embody the following characteristics:

- The organization is a legitimate body with an identifiable organizational structure, governance, and leadership. This organization may or may not be an ecclesiastical body but it must meet the criteria listed below.

- The organization must be willing to recognize and confirm the individual's personal sense of call to ministry.

- The organization must be willing and able to provide support and oversight for the particular individual's call to ministry.

- The organization must be willing and committed to participate as a full covenantal partner in the four-way covenant with the individual, the Association, and the local church where the individual is a member."

8. See "Information Review" in "The Oversight of Ministries Authorized,"26–30 (pdf pp. 31–35).

9. See "Periodic Support Consultation" in "The Oversight of Ministries Authorized," 19–23 (pdf pp. 24–28).

10. Boundary Training helps authorized ministers be aware of the power dynamics in pastoral relationships, provides a safe situation in which to raise questions about appropriateness, heightens awareness of boundary issues in congregations, and educates about safety practices. Boundary issues encompass not only sexual ethics but also such things as holding of power of attorney for an elderly parishioner or the relationship between a former pastor and the congregation. Boundary training helps clarify the minister's role and evokes self-awareness.

11. Events of the late 1970s and early 1980s, such as the Jonestown mass suicides instigated by the Rev. Jim Jones and the public allegations of child sexual abuse by Roman Catholic priests gave impetus to the scrutiny of ministerial conduct by all religious bodies.

12. UCC ministers Marie Fortune (Faith Trust Institute, http://www.faithtrust institute.org/) and Kibbie Ruth (Kyros Ministry, http://kyros.org/) are two who have done pioneering work in this field.

13. "The Oversight of Ministries Authorized by the United Church of Christ," published in 2002, is section 8 of ten sections of the *Manual on Ministry*. It replaces the section "Review and Discipline of Persons Authorized for Ministry," which was published in 1986 as part of the *Manual on Ministry.*

14. "The Oversight of Ministries Authorized," 23. The full description of a Situational Support Consultation is found on pages 23–26 (pdf pp. 28–31).

15. "Disciplinary actions include: conditional affirmation of fitness with prescribed program of growth, censure, suspension, and termination [of authorization for ministry]." See "The Oversight of Ministries Authorized," 53 (pdf p. 58).

16. "The Oversight of Ministries Authorized," 30. The full description of a Fitness Review is found on pages 30–63 (pdf pp. 35–68).

17. Ibid., 35 (pdf p. 40).

18. The UCC Constitution and Bylaws, paragraph 113, refers to a retired minister holding standing "in the Association of his or her choice."

19. See the Ordained Minister's Code, 14–15; Commissioned Minister's Code, 16–17; and Licensed Minister's Code, 18–19; in "Partners in Authorizing Ministry," *Manual on Ministry*, section 1.

20. See UCC Constitution, par. 22.

21. "The Oversight of Ministries Authorized," 49–50 (pdf pp. 54–55).

22. Sheares, preface to *Manual on Ministry.*

23. Introduction to *Manual on Ministry,* 4–5.

24. Rachel Hackenberg on behalf of the Ministerial Excellence, Support & Authorization Team (MESA), in the Local Church, Ministries Announcement of

March 1, 2014. Prior to the announcement MESA Team Leader Holly Miller-Shank mentioned that it will "not be a 'manual' because of the legally binding nature of that term."

Chapter Sixteen

1. The search and call resources from MESA are an integral part of the process. In addition to those resources that are named in this chapter, you might want to look at "Vocabulary: Local Search and Call in the United Church of Christ." This document identifies "a common vocabulary of ministerial positions within the United Church of Christ. . . . The vocabulary is organized into four categories of ministerial positions: Settled, Intentional Interim, Designated-Term, and Supply." Each category gives a general definition and examples, www.uccfiles.com/docs/Vocabulary-for-Pastoral-Positions.doc.

2. UCC Constitution, par. 179.

3. Brueggemann, "The Risk of Heaven," 124, http://rescarta.ucc.org/jsp/RcWebImageViewer.jsp?doc_id=General+Synod+Minutes%2Fucoc0000%2FUD000001%2F00000013&collection_filter=true.

4. Parish Life and Leadership Ministry Team, Local Church Ministries, "Biblical Resources for Search Committees," 2002, http://www.ucc.org/ministers/pdfs/brsc.pdf.

5. Often a Local Church search committee and a candidate will agree to worship together in a "neutral" congregation, that is, one that is not seeking a minister. Arrangements are made with a "neutral" church in the area for the candidate to preach and the search committee to visit. See "The Search and Call Process in the United Church of Christ," in the resource "Search and Call—A Pilgrimage through Transitions and New Beginnings," section 3, 17 (pdf p. 18), http://d3n8a8pro7vhmx.cloudfront.net/unitedchurchofchrist/legacy_url/11308/section-3-the-search-and-call-process-in-the-ucc.pdf?1418437267.

6. See resource #2, "Covenanting Around the Pastoral Search Process," in "The Search and Call Process," 2-1 (pdf p. 29).

7. "The UCC Local Church Profile," in "Search and Call—A Pilgrimage," section 4, http://www.ucc.org/ministers/search-and-call/section-4-the-ucc-local-church-profile.pdf.

8. "The Ministerial Profile," http://www.ucc.org/ministers/profile/.

9. See the Sample Call Agreement suggestion that "Service to the wider church (such as summer camp leadership, mission trips, and National/Conference/Association meetings) is not construed as vacation time," "Sample Call Agreement," 6, http://uccfiles.com/docs/Sample-Call-Agreement-02-2014.doc.

10. "Sample Call Agreement," http://uccfiles.com/docs/Sample-Call-Agreement-02-2014.doc.

11. For notes on the candidating weekend see "The Search and Call Process in the United Church of Christ," in "Search and Call—A Pilgrimage," section 3, 18–21 (pdf p. 19–22).

12. The candidating sermon is preached during the candidating weekend, when the candidate is presented to the congregation. Note that in our search and call process only the final candidate is presented to the congregation, not a series of candidates to be considered. The vote of the congregation to call the candidate is also a vote of affirmation of the work of the Search Committee.

13. See a sample "Three-Way Ministry Covenant" and "Four-Way Ministry Covenant," www.uccfiles.com/docs/Sample-Covenants.doc.

14. See online resources available at http://www.ucc.org/ministers/pilgrimage .html.

15. See Resource #3, "Decision-Making," 3-8 (pdf p. 39), and Resource #12, "What Are We Doing Here—The Challenging Work of Group Discernment," 12-1 (pdf p. 39) in "The Search and Call Process," in "Search and Call—A Pilgrimage," section 3.

16. Brueggemann, "Introduction," 7–8.

17. Robin R. Meyers, *Saving Jesus from the Church* (New York: HarperOne, 2009), dedication.

18. Reinhold Niebuhr, "Leaves from the Notebook of a Tamed Cynic" (1929), *Living Theological Heritage*, vol. 4, *Consolidation and Expansion*, ed. Elizabeth Nordbeck and Lowell Zuck (Cleveland: Pilgrim Press, 1999, part 2, doc. 65, 393.

19. G. Jeffrey MacDonald, *Thieves in the Temple* (New York: Basic Books, 2010), 33.

20. "Ministry in the United Church of Christ," 9. Those making that commitment to be with authorized ministers may be the members of Committees on Ministry or individual mentors or ministerial groups of support and challenge. Ministers' groups of support and challenge may, of course, be informally drawn together or part of something like the Pastoral Excellence Program that was begun in the Massachusetts Conference and has been taken up by other Conferences. See "The Pastoral Excellence Program," http://www.macucc.org/pep, for more information.

Chapter Eighteen

1. Scott Libbey, "Structures, Issues, and the Theological Task," *New Conversations: Polity and Practice* vol. 4, no. 2 (Fall 1979), 37, http://rescarta.ucc.org/jsp /RcWebImageViewer.jsp?doc_id=642fcd35-55c4-4f9c-9c31-0888ea1dfe0f /ucoc0000/UD000001/00000060.

2. Ibid..

3. Leaders Box, "Theology in the UCC," 1, http://d3n8a8pro7vhmx.cloud-front.net/unitedchurchofchrist/legacy_url/1326/a18.pdf?1418424795 (this quote is cited without ellipses for ease of reading, without changing the meaning).

4. "What theological issues stir your interest?" http://www.ucc.org/beliefs_theology.

5. Leaders Box, "Theology in the UCC," 2.

6. Libbey, "Structures, Issues," 38. In that same article, Scott Libbey talks about major theological contributions that have been made at General Synod then "capriciously exploited, or, at worst, ignored." In stating this, he says, he is "not commenting on the quality of what each Synod-planning group creates," but holds that "a quasi-randomly chosen, democratically representative, not particularly prepared group of persons who have no clear accountability lines, programmatically or theologically" and "without the benefit of guidelines in our common life" cannot help but imprint a "remarkably ad hoc—uncoordinated—quality on our theological work. . . ." (37).

7. Libbey, "Structures, Issues," 38. "Covenant style" would refer to "a way of being committed to each other as God is committed to us" (Brueggemann, "The Risk of Heaven," 124); "a way of being defined by, accountable to, and responsible for each other . . . pledged to solidarity across ideological lines and prepared to live in sustained engagement with one another in ways that impinge on and eventually transform all parties to the transaction" (Brueggemann, "Introduction," 8).

8. "Minutes, Third General Synod of the United Church of Christ," Philadelphia, July 3–7, 1961, 12–13, http://rescarta.ucc.org/jsp/RcWebImageViewer.jsp?doc_id=8abee2f6-352d-48f9-958b-49a311bc4489/ucoc0000/UD000001/00000004.

9. Minutes, Theological Commission of the United Church of Christ, February 8–9, 1962, 1.

10. Ibid., 3–4. There was excitement about our statement of faith in 1962. The second meeting of the Theological Commission began with a report on the reflections of the "various commission heads . . . regarding the use of the statement of faith in their commissions. "This was followed by conversation on the use of the statement of faith in congregations—of the UCC and beyond the UCC—"liturgically, for study, as a theme for retreats." (Minutes, Theological Commission of the United Church of Christ, March 7–8, 1963, 1).

11. This may have been attributable to the historical reality that the uniting denominations' "dominant heritage called for a church committed to God's mission in the world . . . [and was] bent naturally toward a concern for the transformation of society and less toward the evangelistic effort to 'win souls for Christ.'" Gunnemann, *Shaping of the United Church of Christ*, 107.

12. David Greenhaw, quoted in Guess, "Who are you calling liberal?" http://www.ucc.org/ucnews/oct04/who-are-you-calling-liberal.html.

13. From Barbara Brown Zikmund, interviewed by Stephanie Ortiz, "UCC's founding built on church unity, not doctrinal purity," *United Church News*, May 31, 2004, http://www.ucc.org/uccs-founding-built-on-church: "Louis Gunnemann (1910–1989) wrote that the founders of the UCC believed that that church union was 'Christ's will.' Out of that conviction, they subordinated 'doctrinal differences to the goal of Christian unity.' In fact, Gunnemann argued, the UCC neglected and even avoided formal theological or ecclesiological questions about its identity as a church for many years. Furthermore, in its commitment to unity the UCC embraced social activism, sometimes without taking adequate 'time and energy for sustained theological reflection,' he wrote."

14. From the Seminar Report "Toward the Task of Sound Teaching in the United Church of Christ," Office for Church Life and Leadership, 1978, as cited by John Thomas, "To Find the Proper Words," 2004, http://www.ucc.org/beliefs /theology/part-i-to-find-the-proper.html.

15. From the introduction to Theological Ferment: "A Letter from Thirty-nine . . ." (1984) *Living Theological Heritage*, vol. 7, part IV, doc. 59, 324.

16. Lee Barrett, "Theological Worlds in the United Church of Christ," *Prism*, vol. 21, no. 2 (Winter 2007) p. 96 (pdf p. 13), http://www.ucc.org/education /polity/pdf-folder/Barrett-Theological-Worlds-in-the-UCC.pdf.

17. From the inside front cover of *Prism*, vol. 15, no. 2 (Fall 2000).

18. Minutes, General Synod 28, 49–50 (pdf pp. 53–54), http://rescarta.ucc.org /jsp/RcWebImageViewer.jsp?doc_id=8abee2f6-352d-48f9-958b-49a311bc4489 /OhClUCC0/20150519/00000001.

19. The Report to General Synod 29 (2013) on the Theological Forum stated that thus far the Theological Forum Table had "determined that its mission was to facilitate theological dialogue within and across the spectrum of theological perspectives in the United Church of Christ. In so doing, the Forum would not do theology. However, it would support and promote the theological work that is ongoing. . . .

"Engaged in an ongoing review of basic UCC theological documents. . . .

"Gathered a listing of United Church of Christ professional theologians and a catalogue of entities within the UCC where theological work is being done . . .

"Engaged in extensive dialogue in an effort to arrive at consensus regarding how it might best respond to the third goal in the Strategic Vision Plan: Engaged Discipleship—Every UCC person is well equipped to be growing in Faith, be theologically conversant and active in the global mission of the church. . . .

"Envision[ed] that the next step . . . will be the creation and initiation of a theological theme reflection loop. This would be a process that will ask for general feedback on a theme—then share the gathered responses with audiences in place of theological conversation in the UCC . . . who would then be invited to engage in critical reflection . . . beginning with the question, Where did I see God today?" http://uccfiles.com/pdf/gs29-Report-On-To-Form-Theological-Forum.pdf.

Prior to General Synod 30 (2015), these examples of theologically related materials were noted by staff members who have been working with the Theological Forum: Sermon Seeds provides theological reflection, but not conversation space, http://www.ucc.org/worship_samuel. There is the opportunity on Facebook to engage in conversation on sermon preparation using the Sermon Seeds resources: https://www.facebook.com/SermonSeeds. Feed Your Spirit is the location for daily and weekly devotionals, as well as other opportunities for theological reflection: http://www.ucc.org/feed_your_spirit. As of 2016, there is a UCC blog, "New Sacred" at http://newsacred.org/.

20. UCC Constitution, par. 212 b, http://www.ucc.org/ucc_constitution_and _bylaws. (This recognition was first made in the 2013 revision of the bylaws.)

21. Libbey, "Structures, Issues," 36.

22. Inclusive language for God uses female as well as male and gender neutral pronouns and metaphors. Inclusive language for human beings acknowledges the varieties of gender, age, racial and ethnic identity, etc., that characterize the human race. Go to http://www.ucc.org/worship/inclusive-language/ for more extensive definition of inclusive language. See "Expansive Language with Reference to God, Inclusive Language with Reference to the People of God," brochure, http://d3n8 a8pro7vhmx.cloudfront.net/unitedchurchofchrist/legacy_url/3574/ucc-inclusive-expansive-language-brochure.pdf?1418427375.

23. "Two diverse resolutions came to the 17th General Synod (1989). One affirmed inclusive language; the other opposed it. A compromise was brought to the floor endorsed by Marilyn Breitling, Executive Director of the Coordinating Center for Women, and Barbara Weller of the Biblical Witness Fellowship. This resolution (85 GS 92) affirmed 'the importance of continuing study of inclusive language and updating of the Inclusive Language Guidelines, marked with careful scholarship, theological vitality, and an openness to Biblical interpretation and faith language that may include new and renewed understandings of ancient texts' . . . It addressed the use of scripture and asked instrumentalities to continue to identify the version or source of rewritten or paraphrased material. The resolution stated:

Be it further resolved, the 17th General Synod recognizes that the responsibility for the use of inclusive language in worship, in the writing of material for publication or other public use of the Bible continues to rest with the person in leadership," http://www.ucc.org/worship/inclusive-language/general-synod-inclusive.html.

24. "Stillspeaking Daily Devotional," http://www.ucc.org/daily_devotional.

25. General Minister and President John Dorhauer introduced the podcast "Into the Mystic" in 2015, http://www.ucc.org/into_the_mystic.

26. Barrett, "Theological Worlds," 75 (pdf p. 2).

27. Ibid.

28. Gunnemann, *Shaping of the United Church of Christ*, 105.

29. Barrett, "Theological Worlds," 75– 76 (pdf pp. 2–3).

30. Mineo Katagiri, quoted in "Re-Conceptualizing the Ministries of the Northern California Nevada Conference," 1999.

31. Minutes, Third General Synod, 13.

32. Maxey, "Who Can Sit?" in Johnson and Hambrick-Stowe, *Theology and Identity*, 61.

33. Barrett, "Theological Worlds," 94–95. He adds, on page 96, "The launching of the seven volume *Living Theological Heritage* in 1989 also drew attention to the sheer variety of theological voices in the UCC."

34. Barbara Essex, Black Theology: "The Unfinished Agenda" (1989), *Living Theological Heritage*, vol. 7, part 7, doc. 116, 659.

35. Leslie Carole Taylor, African American Faithfulness: "The Power of the Faith Community" (1997), ibid., part 7, doc. 117, 662.

36. McCombs Maxey, Preaching: "Servanthood" (1993), ibid., part 7, doc. 121, 677.

37. Norman W. Jackson, Theology: "An Indian Perspective on the United Church of Christ" (2000), ibid., part 7, doc. 124, 690.

38. Teruo Kawata, Preaching: "On Being Troublemakers" (1981), ibid., part 7, doc. 127, 705.

39. David Hirano, "Theology: Asian American" (1986), ibid., part 7, doc. 129, 713.

40. Donald G. Bloesch, United Church People for Biblical Witness: "Scriptural Primacy" (1979) and "The Dubuque Declaration" (1983), *Living Theological Heritage*, ibid., part 4, doc. 63, 342.

41. United Church People for Biblical Witness, "Apostasy: The Dayton Declaration" (1991), ibid., doc. 70, 381.

42. Aaron Elek, The Calvin Synod: "Holy Communion" (1967), ibid., doc. 66, 363.

43. UCC Charismatic Fellowship: "Purpose and Theology" (1977, 1978), ibid., doc. 62, 340.

44. Confessing Christ: "Renewal" (1993), ibid., doc. 72, 389.

45. East Petersburg and Craigville: "A Declaration" (1979) and "A Letter" (1984), ibid., doc. 61, 332.

46. Alfonso A. Roman, The Latino/a Summit: "Our Response to Christ is Different" (1997), *Living Theological Heritage*, vol. 7, part 7, doc. 135, 735 and Enrique Armijo, Immigrant Theology: "Theology in Context" (2000), ibid., part 7, doc. 137, 744.

47. John Shetler, Mercersburg Theology: "What Does Mercersburg Have to Offer?" (1993) and "The Order of Corpus Christi" (1993), *Living Theological Heritage*, vol. 7, part 4, doc. 68, 342.

48. Liliuokalani, Hawaiian Traditions: Music and Metaphor, "The Queen's Prayer" (1893) and Abraham Akaka, "Four Strings on the Ukulele" (1961) *Living Theological Heritage*, vol. 7, part 7, doc. 125, 697.

49. Rose W. Lee and David Tuioasosopo, Assimilation: "The Asian American and Pacific Islander Experience" (1998), ibid., doc. 130, 719.

50. Sharon H. Ringe, "Feminist Theology" (1985), *Living Theological Heritage*, vol. 7, part 4, doc. 65, 355.

51. Mary Sue Gast, "Attentive to the Word" (1994), ibid., doc. 74, 396.

52. Barrett, "Theological Worlds," 97.

53. Walker, *Evolution of a UCC Style*, 91.

54. Leaders Box, "Theology in the UCC," 2.

55. Barrett, "Theological Worlds," 94.

56. Walker, *Evolution of a UCC Style*, 91.

Chapter Nineteen

1. Zikmund, in Oritz interview, "UCC's founding built on church unity, not doctrinal purity."

2. "Equal Marriage Rights for All," http://uccfiles.com/pdf/2005-EQUAL-MARRIAGE-RIGHTS-FOR-ALL.pdf.

3. "About Faithful and Welcoming," http://www.faithfulandwelcoming.org /about.htm.

4. Ibid.

5. Bob Thompson, "'Faithful and Welcoming' president: 'We will be constructive with criticism, dissent,'" *United Church News*, August 31, 2006, http:// www.ucc.org/ucnews/augsep2006/commentary-we-will-be.html, used with permission. Along with his permission Bob Thompson noted that much progress has been made since 2006, and that he still prays the Holy Spirit will lead us deeper into the Christ-centered unity that is our church's founding vision.

6. Nancy S. Taylor, "Denomination is 'work in progress,'" *United Church News*, August 31, 2006, http://www.ucc.org/ucnews/augsep2006/denomination-is-work-in.html. Used with permission.

7. Tupper, "How Organizations Function," C-4.

8. Ibid., C-7.

9. UCC Constitution, par. 17, http://www.ucc.org/about-us/constitution-of-the-ucc.html.

10. Jane Fisler Hoffman, "The Problem of the Prayer: Can the UCC be 'One' While Divided Over Issues of Sexuality?" D. Min. paper, 31, used by permission.

11. James D. G. Dunn writes that the New Testament canon "is important not just because it canonizes the unity of Christianity, but also because it canonizes the diversity of Christianity. . . . 'Conservatives' who want to draw firm lines of doctrine and practice out from the centre in accordance with their particular tradition's interpretation of the NT, and 'liberals' who want to sit loose to all but the central core must both learn to accept the other as equally 'in Christ', must learn to respect the other's faith and life as valid expressions of Christianity, must learn to welcome the other's attitude and style as maintaining the living diversity of the faith." *Unity and Diversity in the New Testament: An Inquiry into the Character of Earliest Christianity*, 2nd ed. (Norwich, UK: SCM Press, 1990), 378. This was cited by Jane Fisler Hoffman, "The Problem of the Prayer," 51.

12. "In 1986 Reuben Sheares argued that the UCC was based neither on mere toleration nor on compromise of two very different traditions, but on a willingness to argue in love." Barrett, "Theological Worlds," 96 (pdf p. 13).

13. "United and Uniting Churches," World Council of Churches, http://www.oikoumene.org/en/church-families/united-and-uniting-churches.

14. "How Organizations Function," C-4.

15. David Greenhaw has pointed out that "the UCC, founded in 1957 by the union of the Congregational Christian Churches and the Evangelical and Reformed Church, was a much more difficult enterprise than most realize. The tenuous 30-year effort that led up to the merger grew out of a deep ecumenical spirit that pervaded a generation of church leaders—many of whom either retired or died not long after the union occurred.

"'By the time the merger actually happened,' Greenhaw says, '[the succeeding generation] didn't share their same sense of ecumenical emergency.' This only made the differences between the two churches seem more prominent." Guess, "Who are you calling liberal?"

16. From a note passed to me by UCC pastor David Bahr during the 2014 gathering of teachers of UCC polity, used with permission.

17. Walker, *Evolution of a UCC Style*, 175.

18. "A Church for All People," http://www.ucc.org/justice/multiracial-multi cultural/all-people.html.

19. "Multi-Racial Multi-Cultural Church," http://www.ucc.org/justice/multi racial-multicultural/.

20. "A Church for All People." See also "Additional Reflection" on Mark 9:2–9 and twenty-first century racism by Elizabeth Leung, UCC Minister for Racial Justice, describing racism as disfiguration of the divine image, http://www.ucc .org/worship_samuel_february_15_2015#Additional.

21. "Another World Is Possible: A Peace with Justice Movement in the United Church of Christ," http://uccfiles.com/synod/resolutions/ANOTHER-WORLD-IS-POSSIBLE.pdf.

22. *Shine, God's People*, 2006, http://d3n8a8pro7vhmx.cloudfront.net/united churchofchrist/legacy_url/7822/studyguide50.pdf?1418432574, is a thoughtfully written and beautifully designed piece, well worth examining.

23. The phrasing of this question comes from sociologist H. B. Cavalcanti in his book *The United Church of Christ in the Shenandoah Valley: Liberal Church, Traditional Congregations* (Lanham, MD: Lexington Books, 2010), 2.

24. Reinhold Niebuhr, *Moral Man and Immoral Society* (Louisville: Westminster John Knox Press, 2013), 6. Walter Brueggemann, similarly, has warned us against the "shrill voice of certitude" and the "inevitable slippage between God's will and our perception of that will" and the coercive silencing of divergent viewpoints. See *Mandate to Difference*, 74. Brueggemann continues, "Such monologic practice seeks to silence. . . . I report to you that in my own church, the United Church of Christ, the same silencing is done . . . so that there is no room remaining in our national church [staff] for those who dissent from the dominant voice."

25. Cavalcanti, *United Church of Christ in the Shenandoah Valley*, 127.

26. Kurt Katzmar, "A Heady Exasperating Mix," sermon of September 22, 2013, quoted with permission, http://www.medforducc.org/september-22-2013/.

27. "Stewards of God's Extravagant Welcome: An MM, ONA, A2A, Just Peace Church," from "Stewards in the Household of God," October 2007, http://d3n8a 8pro7vhmx.cloudfront.net/unitedchurchofchrist/legacy_url/7839/october.pdf? 1418432704.

28. Tyler Connoley "United Church . . . of Christ," January 20, 2016, quoted with permission, http://www.southwestconferenceblog.org/2016/01/20/united-church-of-christ/.

29. Avery Post, "An Address to the Seventeenth General Synod," Minutes, Seventeenth General Synod, June 30, 1989, 131, http://rescarta.ucc.org/jsp/RcWeb ImageViewer.jsp?doc_id=8abee2f6-352d-48f9-958b-49a311bc4489%2fucoc 0000%2fUD000001%2f00000018.

Chapter Twenty

1. This is a great word. If you're not familiar with "cosmogonic," let me introduce you. "Cosmogonic" pertains to the branch of astronomy dealing with the origin and history, structure, and dynamics of the universe.

2. Mary Magoulick, "What Is Myth?" https://faculty.gcsu.edu/custom-website/mary-magoulick/defmyth.htm, used with permission.

3. Tom Tupper, e-mail correspondence of July 7, 2014, used with permission.

4. Tom Tupper, "Ideas on UCC Myth," October 2013, used with permission.

5. Elizabeth Wheeler, "Freedom's Church," introduction to 2009–10 UCC Polity and Practice Course for New York and Union Theological Seminaries in cooperation with the Metro Suffolk Association, New York Conference; used by permission.

6. Conversation of March 4, 2015.

7. See Barbara Brown Zikmund and Amos Yong, eds., *Remembering Jamestown: Hard Questions about Christian Mission* (Eugene, OR: Pickwick Publication, 2010). This is a collection of essays from writers of diverse backgrounds who gathered in 2008 for a conference on missiology. Tink Tinker's essay in this collection focuses on how European Americans view American history as romance, while Native Americans view it as tragedy. A reviewer states, "He asks a tantalizing question: 'How would it change our understanding of the past to tell the narrative of American colonial history as tragedy rather than romance?' (p. 16). He reflects on the genre of tragedy—a genre that laments and repents. Only when Euroamericans consider their history through this genre, notes Tinker, 'is salvation a real possibility' (p. 27)." Kathryn J. Smith, review in *Journal of Postcolonial Theory and Theology* vol. 1 (November 2010), http://www.postcolonialjournal.com/Resources /Review%20Remembering%20Jamestown.pdf.

8. In *The Evolution of a UCC Style* Randi Walker differentiates between particular forms of Christian belief that are characterized as "liberal" and apply to "theological position, approach to ethics and social mores, or political commitments" and what she calls a liberal style. She maintains that "what can be termed liberal in the United Church of Christ traditions is primarily a style or a way of thinking theologically, a theological culture whose essential element is a willingness to entertain doubt," 90.

9. Guess, "Who are you calling liberal?"

10. In the late nineteenth century there was a theological movement called liberalism, characterized by "openness to theological diversity, optimism about history and human ability, . . . skepticism about the absolute nature of various traditional Christian beliefs . . . profound social concern and a conviction that the churches must confront public as well as private, systemic as well as specific

sinfulness." Elizabeth Nordbeck, "Theological Tradition of Congregationalism," in Johnson and Hambrick-Stowe, *Theology and Identity,* 14.

As an example of liberal theology see Washington Gladden, Social Christianity: "The Church and the Social Crisis" (1907), *Living Theological Heritage,* vol. 5, *Outreach and Diversity,* ed. Margaret Bendroth, Lawrence Jones, and Robert Schneider, part 2, doc. 50, 406.

11. Elizabeth Nordbeck, quoted in Guess, "Who are you calling liberal?"

Chapter Twenty-one

1. Brueggemann, "The Risk of Heaven," 130.

2. Sheares, "A Covenant Polity," 75.

3. This is a lament often voiced by UCC pastor K. Ray Hill in the context of teaching polity.

4. Clyde J. Steckel, *New Ecclesiology,* 114.

5. Roger Shinn, quoted in Walker, *Evolution of a UCC Style,* 45.

6. Leaders Box, "Covenant," http://d3n8a8pro7vhmx.cloudfront.net/united churchofchrist/legacy_url/1312/a4.pdf.

The article continues, "Rather than being in covenant we come close to having contracts. 'If you pay your pledge we will pay for a Christian education program for your children.' 'If you provide us with help when we are looking for a pastor, we will take your counsel about Our Church's Wider Mission.' Contracts, however stated, are agreements that one party will receive a form of payment for services rendered or goods received. People may be tired of dealing with others on a contractual basis."

7. "Since 2007 we have received more than three hundred new congregations. . . . The number of churches voluntarily leaving has shrunk to the lowest since 2007 . . . and we are in the national setting living out covenant [in a time of] institutional and organizational change." J. Bennett Guess, Executive Minister for Local Church Ministries, conversation of May 29, 2014.

8. Geoffrey Black, General Minister and President, conversation, May 14, 2014, quoted with permission.

9. Ben Guess, conversation of May 29, 2014, quoted with permission.

10. "FAQ Sheet Regarding the Amendments to the Constitution and Bylaws," http://uccfiles.com/pdf/FAQ-sheet-regarding-the-Amendments-to-the-Constitution -and-By-Laws.pdf. See also "Notice of Proposed Amendments . . . ," http://ucc files.com/pdf/Notice-of-Amendments-3-25-15.pdf, "Proposed Amendments to the Constitution," http://uccfiles.com/pdf/Red-Lined-Constition(2013-Ed)_no _GS_changes.pdf, and "Proposed Amendments to the Bylaws," http://uccfiles .com/pdf/Red-Lined-Bylaws-re-formatted(2013-Ed)_no_GS_changes.pdf.

OCWM stands for Our Church's Wider Mission. "This is the name we give to congregational gifts that support wider UCC ministry in Conference and national settings." See OCWM Leader's Guide, http://www.uccfiles.com/pdf /OCWM%20Leader's%20Guide.pdf.

11. Donald Freeman, "Autonomy in a Covenantal Polity," 1, http://d3n8a8 pro7vhmx.cloudfront.net/unitedchurchofchrist/legacy_url/226/Autonomy-in-a-Covenantal-Polity-Freeman.pdf?1418423590.

12. Steckel, *New Ecclesiology*, 116.

13. Randi Walker, in an e-mail correspondence of July 18, 2012, wondered if "our fixation for getting governance right to protect a wide range (or diversity) of participation in decision making and the freedom of the congregations, both values of the polis, might restrict and conflict with our oikos values of covenant, which are more organic and relational—less dependent on a set of constitutional requirements and limits." Quoted with permission.

(As an aside, let me mention that if I were teaching a class based on this chapter and Oikos brand yogurt were still on the market, I would offer extra credit to anyone who pursued the theological connections between household and probiotics.)

14. Eleazar Fernandez, seminar of October 25, 2012, Alameda, California.

15. This is the actual wording of the statement from the Theological Commission of the United Church of Christ, "Toward an Understanding of Local Autonomy" (1969). Our local autonomy is completely misunderstood when it is regarded as a means to isolate a congregation from the rest of the church. Only the free know the fullness of love; and the local congregation has its freedom in the United Church of Christ in order that there may be no shadow of outer coercion, but only the inner compulsion of love, in its relationship to the church of the ages, the whole ministering church of this age, and the needs of humanity ministered to.

Specifically, "the local church is a school in the life of the Spirit." If it closes its mind to the rest of the church, it is comparable to a university that in an insane moment should shut itself off from the findings of scholars in other universities. http://www.ucc.org/education/polity/pdf-folder/toward-an-understanding-of-local-autonomy.pdf.

16. Paul Sherry related this incident at a meeting of the Council of Instrumentality Executives. It is retold with his permission.

17. Maxey, "Who Can Sit?" 61.

18. Reversing the direction from movement to denomination and heading back toward movement was suggested by UCC polity scholar Martha Baumer in a conversation of July 29, 2014.

19. Introduction to the Interim Report of the General Synod Committee on Structure to the Nineteenth General Synod, 3.

20. Tupper, July 7, 2014.

21. National Council of Churches, "Marks of Faithfulness," in "Interfaith Relations and the Churches, A Policy Statement of the National Council of Churches of Christ in the USA," par. 47–51, http://nationalcouncilofchurches.us/common-witness/1999/interfaith.php. Used by permission of the National Council of Churches of Christ in the USA (2009). All rights reserved worldwide. 2015.

22. Tupper, July 7, 2014.

23. In 2008, the Collegium urged that "Sacred Conversations on Race" take place throughout our church, trusting that "Our conversations will be sacred if we trust in the Spirit of the living God to do a new thing in our midst. . . . Our conversations will be sacred if we pray for the grace and courage to speak the truth in love and to hear one another all the way through," Sacred Conversations: A Pastoral Letter on Racism," http://d3n8a8pro7vhmx.cloudfront.net/unitedchurch ofchrist/legacy_url/1998/pastltrracism.pdf?1418425519.

24. David Greenhaw notes that General Synod has become our church's "primary teaching 'office' on important, complex social issues. . . . Unfortunately, he says, as the General Synod has grown more liberal, disaffected more-conservative members increasingly have stayed away . . . [and General Synod] has lacked the capacity to connect with the people in the pew. It has shallow roots of support in the life of the church.." Quoted in Guess, "Who are you calling liberal?"

25. Yvonne Delk, "The Unfinished Agenda: Racism," *New Conversations: The Amistad Event*, vol. 11, numbers 2 and 3 (Winter/Spring 1989), 40, http://rescarta .ucc.org/jsp/RcWebImageViewer.jsp?doc_id=642fcd35-55c4-4f9c-9c31-0888 ea1dfe0f/ucoc0000/UD000001/00000080.

26. Ibid., 40–41. For a faith-framed statement on justice, see number 2 in Section 2, "Marks of Faithful and Effective Ministers" where one of the marks of a faithful and effective authorized minister is "a passion for the oneness of the body of Christ as expressed through commitment to . . . justice, and the full embrace of all persons in the radical hospitality of God." Section 2, "Marks of Faithful and Effective Ministers," http://uccfiles.com/pdf/THE-MARKS-OF-FAITHFUL-AND-EFFECTIVE-MINISTERS.pdf, and Elizabeth Leung on racism as the disfiguration of the divine image, http://www.ucc.org/worship_samuel_february_15 _2015#Additional.

27. Louis H. Gunnemann, *Shaping of the United Church of Christ*, 123. This statement comes within the context of his writing of our forebears' Reformation heritage that "the New Creation is never a private estate for the self-satisfied . . . the transformation of the society [is] the church's responsibility and goal. . . . The hinge upon which all of this turns is the sovereignty of God" (122–23).

28. Deborah Streeter, "We Want to Come and See You," *Northern California Nevada Conference News*, November 3, 2015, https://ncncucc.org/we-want-to-come-and-see-you/.

29. Walker, "Ministry: Episcopé or Oversight," 256.

30. Ibid.

31. Arthur Cribbs, quoted in Guess, "Who are you calling liberal?"

32. Brookshire, "That We May All Be One."

Index